FRENCH

PHRASE BOOK

■ HarperCollins*Publishers*

first published in this edition 1995

© HarperCollins Publishers 1995

ISBN 0 00 470864-4

A catalogue record for this book is available from the British Library

Typeset by Morton Word Processing Ltd, Scarborough
Printed in Great Britain by
HarperCollins Manufacturing, Glasgow

Introduction

Your **Collins Phrase Book** is designed to give you instant access to all the words and phrases you will want while travelling abroad on business or for pleasure.

Unlike other phrase books it is arranged in A-Z order to take you straight to the word you want without having to search through different topics. And its simple, easy-to-use pronunciation guide to every word and phrase will ensure you communicate with confidence.

At the bottom of each page there is a list of *ABSOLUTE ESSENTIALS* – the key phrases and expressions you will need in any situation. And between the two sides of your **Phrase Book** you will find further explanations of pronunciation, charts showing how to convert from metric to imperial measures and easy reference lists of *Car Parts, Colours, Countries, Drinks, Fish and Seafood, Fruit and Nuts, Meats, Shops,* and *Vegetables*. These pages have a grey border to help you find them easily and to show you where one side of the **Phrase Book** ends and the other begins.

And finally, in the comprehensive glossary at the end of your **Phrase Book** you will find over 4,000 foreign-language words and phrases clearly translated. So in one complete package you have all the benefits of a dictionary with the simplicity of a phrase book. We hope you will enjoy using it.

Abbreviations used in the text

adj	adjective
adv	adverb
cm	centimetre(s)
conj	conjunction
equiv	equivalent
etc	etcetera
f	feminine noun
fpl	feminine plural noun
g	gram(s)
kg	kilogram(s)
km	kilometre(s)
m	masculine noun; metre(s)
m/f	masculine or feminine noun
mpl	masculine plural noun
n	noun
pl	plural noun
prep	preposition
®	registered trade mark
sing	singular
Switz	Switzerland
vb	verb

ENGLISH–FRENCH

a	un	"uñ"
	une	"oon"
▷ **a man**	un homme	"un om"
▷ **a woman**	une femme	"oon fam"
abbey	l'abbaye (f)	"abayee"
about:		
▷ **a book about Paris**	un livre sur Paris	"uñ leevr soor paree"
▷ **about 10 o'clock**	vers 10 heures	"vehr deez uhr"
above	au-dessus	"oh-duhsoo"
abseiling	la descente en rappel	"daysoñt oñ rapel"
access:		
▷ **is there access for the disabled?**	est-ce qu'il y a facilité d'accès pour les handicapés?	"es-keel ya faseeleetay dakseh poor lay oñdee-kapay"
accident	l'accident (m)	"akseedoñ"
▷ **I've had an accident**	j'ai eu un accident	"zhay oo un akseedoñ"
▷ **there's been an accident**	il y a eu un accident	"eel ya oo un akseedoñ"
accommodation	le logement	"lozhmoñ"
▷ **I need 3 nights' accommodation**	je voudrais une chambre pour 3 nuits	"zhuh voudray oon shoñbruh poor trwa nwee"
ache	la douleur	"doolur"
▷ **I've got a stomach ache**	j'ai des maux d'estomac	"zhay day moh destoma"
activities	les activités (fpl)	"akteeveetay"
▷ **do you have activities for children?**	est-ce que vous avez des activités pour les enfants?	"eskuh vooz avay dayz akteeveetay poor layz oñfoñ"
▷ **what indoor/outdoor activities are there?**	qu'est-ce qu'il y a comme activités en salle/en plein air?	"kes-keel ya kom akteeveetay oñ sal/oñ plen ehr"

adaptor (*electrical*)	la prise multiple	"preez moolteepl"
address	l'adresse (*f*)	"adress"
▷ my address is ...	j'habite ...	"zhabeet"
▷ take me to this address	à cette adresse	"a set adress"
▷ will you write down the address please?	pouvez-vous écrire l'adresse s'il vous plaît?	"poovay voo aykreer ladress seel voo pleh"
adhesive tape	le ruban adhésif	"rooboñ adayzeef"
▷ I need some adhesive tape	j'ai besoin de ruban adhésif	"zhay buhzwañ duh rooboñ adayzeef"
admission charge	l'entrée	"oñtray"
adult	l'adulte (*m/f*)	"adoolt"
advance:		
▷ in advance	à l'avance	"a lavoñs"
▷ do I pay in advance?	est-ce que c'est payable d'avance?	"es-kuh say payyabl davoñs"
▷ do I need to book in advance?	est-ce que je dois réserver à l'avance?	"es-kuh zhuh dwa rayzehr-vay a lavoñs"
aerobics	l'aérobic (*m*)	"a-ayrobeek"
after	après	"apray"
afternoon	l'après-midi (*m*)	"apraymeedee"
aftershave	la lotion après-rasage	"lohsyoñ apray-razazh"
again	de nouveau	"duh noovo"
▷ can you try again?	pouvez-vous essayer encore une fois?	"poovay-voo essayay oñkor oon fwa"
agent	l'agent (*m*)	"azhoñ"
ago:		
▷ a week ago	il y a une semaine	"eel ya oon smen"
Aids	le sida	"seeda"

air conditioning	la climatisation	"kleemateezasyoñ"
▷ **the air conditioning is not working**	la climatisation ne marche pas	"la kleemateezasyoñ nuh marsh pa"
air hostess	l'hôtesse (f) de l'air	"otess duh lehr"
airline	la compagnie aérienne	"koñpanyee a-ayree-añ"
air mail:		
▷ **by air mail**	par avion	"par avyoñ"
air mattress	le matelas pneumatique	"matla pnuhmateek"
airport	l'aéroport (m)	"a-ayropor"
▷ **to the airport, please**	a l'aéroport, s'il vous plaît	"a la-ayropor seel voo pleh"
aisle	le couloir	"koolwahr"
▷ **I'd like an aisle seat**	je voudrais une place couloir	"zhuh voodray oon plas koolwahr"
alarm call	l'appel (m) du service réveil	"apel doo sehrvees rayvay"
▷ **an alarm call at 7 am, please**	réveillez-moi à 7 heures s'il vous plaît	"rayvayay-mwa a set uhr seel voo pleh"
alarm clock	le réveil	"rayvay"
alcohol	l'alcool (m)	"alkol"
alcoholic	alcoolique	"alkoleek"
all	tout	"too"
allergic to	allergique à	"alehrzheek a"
▷ **I'm allergic to penicillin**	je suis allergique à la pénicilline	"zhuh sweez alehrzheek a la payneeseeleen"
all right	d'accord	"dakor"
▷ **are you all right?**	ça va?	"sa va"
almond	l'amande (f)	"amoñd"
almost	presque	"presk"

the **Alps**	les Alpes	"layz alp"
also	aussi	"ohsee"
always	toujours	"too-zhoor"
am:		
▷ **I am**	je suis	"zhuh swee"
ambulance	l'ambulance (f)	"oñbooloñs"
▷ **call an ambulance**	appelez une ambulance	"aplay oon oñbooloñs"
America	l'Amérique (f)	"amayreek"
American	américain (m)	"amayreekañ"
	américaine (f)	"amayreekenn"
amusement park	le parc d'attractions	"park datraksjoñ"
anaesthetic	l'anesthésique (m)	"anaystayzeek"
anchovy	l'anchois (m)	"oñshwa"
and	et	"ay"
Andorra	l'Andorre (f)	"oñdor"
anorak	l'anorak (m)	"anorak"
another	un autre	"un ohtr"
▷ **another beer?**	encore une bière?	"oñkor oon byehr"
antibiotic	l'antibiotique (m)	"oñteebyoteek"
antifreeze	l'antigel (m)	"oñtee-zhel"
antihistamine	l'antihistaminique (m)	"oñtee-eestameeneek"
antiseptic	l'antiseptique (m)	"oñteesepteek"
any:		
▷ **I haven't any**	je n'en ai pas	"zhuh non ay pa"
▷ **have you any apples?**	avez-vous des pommes?	"avay-voo day pom"
apartment	l'appartement (m)	"apartmoñ"

ABSOLUTE ESSENTIALS

I would like ...	j'aimerais ...	"zhemray"
I need ...	j'ai besoin de ...	"zhay buhswañ duh"
where is ...?	où se trouve ...?	"oo suh troov"
I'm looking for ...	je cherche ...	"zhuh shersh"

▷ we've booked an apartment in the name of ...	nous avons réservé un appartement au nom de ...	"nooz avoñ rayzehr-vay un apartmoñ oh noñ duh"
aperitif	l'apéritif (m)	"apayreeteef"
▷ we'd like an aperitif	un apéritif, s'il vous plaît	"uñ apayreeteef seel voo pleh"
apple	la pomme	"pom"
appointment	le rendez-vous	"roñdayvoo"
▷ I'd like to make an appointment	je voudrais prendre un rendez-vous	"zhuh voodray proñdr uñ roñdayvoo"
▷ can I please have an appointment?	est-ce que je pourrais avoir un rendez-vous?	"es-kuh zhuh poorayz avwar uñ roñdayvoo"
▷ I have an appointment with ...	j'ai un rendez-vous avec ...	"zhay uñ roñdayvoo avek"
April	avril (m)	"avreel"
apricot	l'abricot (m)	"abreeko"
are:		
▷ you are	vous êtes	"vooz et"
▷ we are	nous sommes	"noo som"
▷ they are	ils/elles sont	"eel/el soñ"
arm	le bras	"bra"
armbands (for swimming)	les flotteurs (mpl) de natation	"flotuhr duh natasyoñ"
arrival	l'arrivée (f)	"areevay"
arrivals (at airport)	arrivées (fpl)	"areevay"
to arrive	arriver	"areevay"
▷ what time does the bus/train arrive?	à quelle heure arrive le bus/train?	"a kel uhr areev luh boos/trañ"
▷ we arrived early/late	nous sommes arrivés en avance/en retard	"noo somz areevay on avoñs/oñ ruhtar"
art gallery	le musée d'art	"moozay dar"

ABSOLUTE ESSENTIALS

do you have ...?	avez-vous ...?	"avay-voo"
is there ...?	y a-t-il ...?	"ya-teel"
are there ...?	y a-t-il ...?	"ya-teel"
how much is ...?	combien coûte ...?	"koñbyañ koot"

artichoke	l'artichaut (m)	"arteesho"
ascent:		
▷ when is the last ascent?	à quelle heure part la dernière benne?	"a kel ur par la dehrn-yehr ben"
ashore:		
▷ can we go ashore now?	est-ce que nous pouvons débarquer maintenant?	"es-kuh noo poovoñ daybarkay mañtnoñ"
ashtray	le cendrier	"soñdreeyay"
▷ may I have an ashtray?	un cendrier, s'il vous plaît?	"uñ soñdreeyay seel voo pleh"
asparagus	les asperges (fpl)	"asperzh"
aspirin	l'aspirine (f)	"aspeereen"
asthma	l'asthme (m)	"asmuh"
▷ I suffer from asthma	je suis asthmatique	"zhuh sweez asmateek"
Athens	Athènes	"atenn"
aubergine	l'aubergine (f)	"obehr-zheen"
August	août (m)	"oot"
Australia	l'Australie (f)	"ostralee"
Australian	australien (m) australienne (f)	"ostralyañ" "ostralyenn"
Austria	l'Autriche (f)	"otreesh"
Austrian	autrichien (m) autrichienne (f)	"otreeshyañ" "otreeshyenn"
automatic	automatique	"otomateek"
▷ is it an automatic (car)?	est-ce que c'est une voiture automatique?	"es-kuh set oon vwatoor otomateek"
autumn	l'automne (m)	"otonn"
avalanche	l'avalanche (f)	"avaloñsh"

▷ **is there a risk of avalanches?**	y a-t-il risque d'avalanche?	"ee ateel reesk davaloñsh"
avocado	l'avocat (m)	"avoka"
baby	le bébé	"baybay"
baby food	les petits pots (mpl)	"puhtee poh"
baby seat (in car)	le siège auto pour bébé	"see-ezh oto poor baybay"
baby-sitter	le/la babysitter	"baybeeseetehr"
baby-sitting:		
▷ **is there a baby-sitting service?**	est-ce qu'il y a un service de babysitting?	"es-keel ya uñ sehrvees duh baybeeseeting"
back¹ n (of body)	le dos	"doh"
▷ **I've got a bad back**	j'ai le dos en mauvais état	"zhay luh doh oñ movez ayta"
▷ **I've hurt my back**	je me suis fait mal au dos	"zhuh muh swee feh mal oh doh"
back² adv:		
▷ **we must be back at the hotel before 6 o'clock**	il faut être de retour à l'hôtel avant 6 heures	"eel foht etr duh ruhtoor a lotel avoñ seez uhr"
bacon	le bacon	"baykon"
bad (food)	gâté(e)	"gahtay"
(weather, news)	mauvais (m)	"moveh"
	mauvaise (f)	"movez"
badminton	le badminton	"badmeentonn"
bag	le sac	"sak"
baggage	les bagages (mpl)	"bagazh"
baggage reclaim	la livraison des bagages	"leevrayzoñ day bagazh"

ABSOLUTE ESSENTIALS

I don't understand	je ne comprends pas	"zhuh nuh koñproñ pa"
I don't speak French	je ne parle pas français	"zhuh nuh parl pa froñsay"
do you speak English?	parlez-vous anglais?	"parlay-voo oñglay"
could you help me?	pourriez-vous m'aider?	"pooreeay-voo mayday"

baggage allowance:

▷ what is the baggage allowance?	quelle est la franchise de baggages?	"kel eh la froñsheez duh bagazh"
baker's	la boulangerie	"booloñzh-ree"
balcony	le balcon	"balkoñ"
▷ do you have a room with a balcony?	vous avez une chambre avec balcon?	"vooz avay oon shoñbr avek balkoñ"
ball	la balle	"bal"
ball game	le jeu de ballon	"zhuh duh baloñ"
banana	la banane	"banann"
band (*musical*)	la fanfare	"foñfar"
bandage	le pansement	"poñsmoñ"
bank	la banque	"boñk"
▷ is there a bank nearby?	est-ce qu'il y a une banque à proximité?	"es-keel ya oon boñk a prokseemeetay"
bar	le bar	"bar"
barber	le coiffeur	"kwafur"
basket	la corbeille	"korbay"
bath	la baignoire	"baynwahr"
▷ to take a bath	prendre un bain	"proñdr uñ bañ"
bathing cap	le bonnet de bain	"bonay duh bañ"
bathroom	la salle de bains	"sal duh bañ"
battery (*for car*)	la batterie	"batree"
(*for appliance*)	la pile	"peel"

ABSOLUTE ESSENTIALS		
I would like ...	j'aimerais ...	"zhemray"
I need ...	j'ai besoin de ...	"zhay buhswañ duh"
where is ...?	où se trouve ...?	"oo suh troov"
I'm looking for ...	je cherche ...	"zhuh shersh"

to be	être	"etr"

I am	je suis	"zhuh swee"
you are	vous êtes	"vooz et"
he/she/it is	il/elle est	"eel/el eh"
we are	nous sommes	"noo som"
they are	ils/elles sont	"eel/el soñ"

beach	la plage	"plazh"
beach ball	le ballon de plage	"baloñ duh plazh"
beach umbrella	le parasol de plage	"parasol duh plazh"
bean	le haricot	"areekoh"
beautiful	beau (*m*)	"boh"
	belle (*f*)	"bel"
bed	le lit	"lee"
bedding	la literie	"leetree"
▷ **is there any spare bedding?**	est-ce qu'il y a des couvertures supplémentaires?	"es-keel ya day koovehrtoor sooplaymoñtehr"
bedroom	la chambre à coucher	"shoñbra kooshay"
beef	le bœuf	"buf"
beefburger	le hamburger	"oñboorgehr"
beer	la bière	"byehr"
▷ **a draught beer, please**	une pression, s'il vous plaît	"oon prehsyoñ seel voo pleh"
before	avant	"avoñ"
to begin	commencer	"komoñsay"
behind	derrière	"dehr-yehr"
Belgian	belge	"belzh"

ABSOLUTE ESSENTIALS

do you have ...?	avez-vous ...?	"avay-voo"
is there ...?	y a-t-il ...?	"ya-teel"
are there ...?	y a-t-il ...?	"ya-teel"
how much is ...?	combien coûte ...?	"koñbyañ koot"

Belgium	la Belgique	"bel-zheek"
below	sous	"soo"
belt	la ceinture	"sañtoor"
Berlin	Berlin	"behrlañ"
beside	à côté de	"a kohtay duh"
best	meilleur	"may-yur"
▷ **the best**	le meilleur	"luh may-yur"
better	mieux	"myuh"
between	entre	"oñtr"
bicycle	la bicyclette	"beeseeklett"
big	grand (m)	"groñ"
	grande (f)	"groñd"
▷ **it's too big**	c'est trop grand	"seh tro groñ"
bigger	plus grand	"ploo groñ"
▷ **do you have a bigger one?**	est-ce que vous en avez un plus grand?	"es-kuh vooz on avay uñ ploo groñ"
bikini	le bikini	"beekeenee"
bill	l'addition (f)	"adeesyoñ"
▷ **put it on my bill**	mettez-le sur ma note	"metay-luh soor ma not"
▷ **the bill, please**	l'addition, s'il vous plaît	"ladeesyoñ seel voo pleh"
▷ **can I have an itemized bill?**	est-ce que je pourrais avoir une addition détaillée?	"es-kuh zhuh poorayz avwar oon adeesyoñ daytye-yay"
bin	la poubelle	"poobell"
binoculars	les jumelles (fpl)	"zhoomell"
bird	l'oiseau (m)	"wazoh"
birthday	l'anniversaire (m)	"aneevehrsehr"
▷ **Happy Birthday!**	bon anniversaire!	"bon aneevehrsehr"

birthday card	la carte d'anniversaire	"kart daneevehrsehr"
bit (*piece*)	le morceau	"morsoh"
▷ **a bit (of)**	un peu (de)	"uñ puh (duh)"
bite[1] *n*	la morsure	"morsoor"
to bite[2] *vb*	mordre	"mordr"
bitten	mordu(e)	"mordoo"
(*by insect*)	piqué(e)	"pee-kay"
bitter	amer (*m*)	"amehr"
	amère (*f*)	"amehr"
black	noir(e)	"nwahr"
blackcurrants	les cassis (*mpl*)	"kasee"
blanket	la couverture	"koovehrtoor"
bleach	l'eau (*f*) de Javel	"oh duh zhavel"
blister	l'ampoule (*f*)	"oñpool"
blocked	bouché(e)	"booshay"
▷ **the drain is blocked**	les canalisations sont bouchées	"lay kanaleezasyoñ soñ booshay"
blood group	le groupe sanguin	"groop soñgañ"
▷ **my blood group is ...**	mon groupe sanguin est ...	"moñ groop soñgañ eh"
blouse	le chemisier	"shuhmeezyay"
blow-dry	le brushing	"bruhsheeng"
▷ **a cut and blow-dry, please**	coupe et brushing, s'il vous plaît	"koop ay bruhsheeng seel voo pleh"
blue	bleu(e)	"bluh"
boarding card	la carte d'embarquement	"kart doñbarkmoñ"
boarding house	la pension (de famille)	"poñsyoñ (duh fameey)"

ABSOLUTE ESSENTIALS

I don't understand	je ne comprends pas	"zhuh nuh koñproñ pa"
I don't speak French	je ne parle pas français	"zhuh nuh parl pa froñsay"
do you speak English?	parlez-vous anglais?	"parlay-voo oñglay"
could you help me?	pourriez-vous m'aider?	"pooreeay-voo mayday"

boat	le bateau	"batoh"
boat trip	l'excursion (*f*) en bateau	"ekskoorsyoñ oñ batoh"
▷ **are there any boat trips on the river/lake?**	y a-t-il des excursions en bateau sur la rivière/le lac?	"ee ateel dayz ekskoorsyoñ oñ batoh soor la reevyehr/luh lak"
boiled	bouilli(e)	"booyee"
Bonn	Bonn	"bonn"
book¹ *n*	le livre	"leevr"
▷ **book of tickets**	le carnet de tickets	"karneh duh teekeh"
to **book²** *vb*	réserver	"rayzehr-vay"
▷ **the table is booked for eight o'clock this evening**	on a réservé une table pour huit heures ce soir	"on a rayzehr-vay oon tabl poor weet ur suh swahr"
▷ **can you book me into a hotel?**	pouvez-vous me réserver une chambre dans un hôtel?	"poovayvoo muh rayzehr-vay oon shoñbr doñz un otel"
▷ **should I book in advance?**	est-ce que je devrais faire une réservation?	"es-kuh zhuh duhvray fehr oon rayzehr-vasyoñ"
booking	la réservation	"rayzehr-vasyoñ"
▷ **can I change my booking?**	est-ce que je peux changer ma réservation?	"es-kuh zhuh puh shoñzhay ma rayzehr-vasyoñ"
▷ **I confirmed my booking by letter**	j'ai confirmé ma réservation par lettre	"zhay koñfeermay ma rayzehr-vasyoñ par letr"
booking fee:		
▷ **is there a booking fee?**	est-ce qu'il y a des frais de réservation?	"es-keel ya day fray duh rayzehr-vasyoñ"
booking office	le bureau de location	"booroh duh lokasyoñ"
bookshop	la librairie	"leebrayree"
boot	le coffre	"kofr"
boots	les bottes (*fpl*)	"bott"

border	la frontière	"froñtyehr"
botanic gardens	le jardin botanique	"zhardañ botaneek"
both	les deux	"lay duh"
bottle	la bouteille	"bootay"
▷ **a bottle of mineral water, please**	une bouteille d'eau minérale, s'il vous plaît	"oon bootay doh meenayral seel voo pleh"
▷ **a bottle of gas**	une bouteille de gaz	"oon bootay duh gaz"
bottle opener	l'ouvre-bouteilles (m)	"oovr-bootay"
box	la boîte	"bwat"
box office	le bureau de location	"booroh duh lokasyoñ"
boy	le garçon	"garsoñ"
boyfriend	le petit ami	"puhteet amee"
bra	le soutien-gorge	"sootyañ-gorzh"
bracelet	le bracelet	"braslay"
brake fluid	le liquide pour freins	"leekeed poor frañ"
brakes	les freins (mpl)	"frañ"
brandy	le cognac	"konyak"
▷ **I'll have a brandy**	un cognac, s'il vous plaît	"uñ konyak seel voo pleh"
bread	le pain	"pañ"
▷ **could we have some more bread?**	encore du pain, s'il vous plaît	"oñkor du pañ seel voo pleh"
breakable	fragile	"fra-zheel"
breakdown	la panne	"pann"
breakdown van	la dépanneuse	"daypanuz"
▷ **can you send a breakdown van?**	est-ce que vous pouvez envoyer une dépanneuse?	"es-kuh voo poovay oñvwayay oon daypanuz"
breakfast	le petit déjeuner	"puhtee day-zhuhnay"

ABSOLUTE ESSENTIALS

do you have ...?	avez-vous ...?	"avay-voo"
is there ...?	y a-t-il ...?	"ya-teel"
are there ...?	y a-t-il ...?	"ya-teel"
how much is ...?	combien coûte ...?	"koñbyañ koot"

▷ what time is breakfast?	le petit déjeuner est à quelle heure?	"luh puhtee day-zhuhnay et a kel uhr"
▷ can we have breakfast in our room?	est-ce que vous pouvez nous servir le petit déjeuner dans la chambre?	"es-kuh voo poovay noo sehrveer luh puhtee day-zhuhnay doñ la shoñbr"
breast (of woman)	le sein	"sañ"
(chest)	la poitrine	"pwatreen"
(of chicken)	le blanc	"bloñ"
to **breast-feed**	allaiter	"alaytay"
to **breathe**	respirer	"rehspeeray"
▷ he can't breathe	il a de la difficulté à respirer	"eel a duh la deefeekooltay a rehspeeray"
briefcase	la serviette	"sehrvyet"
to **bring**	apporter	"aportay"
Britain	la Grande-Bretagne	"groñd bruhtanyuh"
▷ have you ever been to Britain?	est-ce que vous êtes déjà allé en Grande-Bretagne?	"es-kuh vooz et day-zha alay oñ groñd bruhtanyuh"
British	britannique	"breetaneek"
▷ I am British	je suis britannique	"zhuh swee breetaneek"
Brittany	la Bretagne	"bruhtanyuh"
broccoli	le brocoli	"brokolee"
brochure	la brochure	"broshoor"
broken	cassé(e)	"kassay"
▷ I have broken the window	j'ai cassé la fenêtre	"zhay kassay la fuhnetr"
▷ the lock is broken	la serrure est cassée	"la sehroor eh kassay"
broken down	en panne	"oñ pann"
▷ my car has broken down	ma voiture est en panne	"ma vwatoor et oñ pann"

broken into:

▷ my car has been broken into — ma voiture a été cambriolée — "ma vwatoor a aytay koñbreeyolay"

brooch — la broche — "brosh"

brother — le frère — "frehr"

brown — brun (m) — "bruñ"
brune (f) — "broon"

brush — la brosse — "bros"

Brussels — Bruxelles — "broosell"

Brussels sprouts — les choux (mpl) de Bruxelles — "shoo duh broosell"

bucket — le seau — "soh"

buffet — le buffet — "boofay"

buffet car — la voiture-buffet — "vwatoor-boofay"

bulb — l'ampoule (f) — "oñpool"

bum bag — la sacoche banane — "sakosh banann"

bun — le petit pain — "puhtee pañ"

bungee jumping:

▷ where can I go bungee jumping? — où est-ce que je peux faire du saut à l'élastique? — "oo es-kuh zhuh puh fehr doo soh a laylasteek"

bureau de change — le bureau de change — "booroh duh shoñzh"

burst — crevé(e) — "kruhvay"

▷ a burst tyre — un pneu crevé — "uñ pnuh kruhvay"

bus — le bus — "boos"

▷ where do I get the bus to town? — où est-ce que je prends le bus pour aller en ville? — "oo es-kuh zhuh proñ luh boos poor alay oñ veel"

ABSOLUTE ESSENTIALS

I don't understand	je ne comprends pas	"zhuh nuh koñproñ pa"
I don't speak French	je ne parle pas français	"zhuh nuh parl pa froñsay"
do you speak English?	parlez-vous anglais?	"parlay-voo oñglay"
could you help me?	pourriez-vous m'aider?	"pooreeay-voo mayday"

▷ does this bus go to ...?	est-ce que ce bus va à ...?	"es-kuh suh boos va a"
▷ where do I get a bus for the cathedral?	où est-ce que je peux prendre un bus pour aller à la cathédrale?	"oo es-kuh zhuh puh proñdr uñ boos poor alay a la kataydral"
▷ which bus do I take for the museum?	quel bus va au musée?	"kel boos va oh moozay"
▷ how frequent are the buses to town?	il y a des bus pour la ville tous les combien?	"eel ya day boos poor la veel too lay koñbyañ"
▷ what time is the last bus?	à quelle heure est le dernier bus?	"a kel uhr eh luh dehrnyay boos"
▷ what time does the bus leave?	le bus part à quelle heure?	"luh boos par a kel uhr"
▷ what time does the bus arrive?	le bus arrive à quelle heure?	"luh boos areev a kel uhr"
business	les affaires (fpl)	"afehr"
▷ I am here on business	je suis ici en voyages d'affaires	"zhuh sweez eesee oñ vwayazh dafehr"
▷ a business trip	un voyage d'affaires	"uñ vwayazh dafehr"
bus station	la gare routière	"gar rootyehr"
bus stop	l'arrêt (m) d'autobus	"areh dotoboos"
bus tour	l'excursion (f) en autobus	"eskoorsyoñ oñ otoboos"
busy	occupé(e)	"okoopay"
▷ the line is busy	la ligne est occupée	"la leen-yet okoopay"
but	mais	"meh"
butcher's	la boucherie	"booshree"
butter	le beurre	"buhr"
button	le bouton	"bootoñ"
to **buy**	acheter	"ashtay"
▷ where do we buy our tickets?	où est-ce qu'on achète les billets?	"oo es kon ashet lay beeyay"

ABSOLUTE ESSENTIALS

I would like ...	j'aimerais ...	"zhemray"
I need ...	j'ai besoin de ...	"zhay buhswañ duh"
where is ...?	où se trouve ...?	"oo suh troov"
I'm looking for ...	je cherche ...	"zhuh shersh"

▷ **where can I buy some postcards?**	où est-ce que je peux acheter des cartes postales?	"oo es-kuh zhuh puh ashtay day kart postall"
by (*via*)	via	"vya"
(*beside*)	à côté de	"a kotay duh"
bypass	la route de contournement	"root duh koñtoornmoñ"
cabaret	le cabaret	"kabaray"
▷ **where can we go to see a cabaret?**	où est-ce qu'on peut aller voir un spectacle de cabaret?	"oo es-koñ puh alay vwar uñ spektakl duh kabaray"
cabbage	le chou	"shoo"
cabin (*hut*)	la cabane	"kabann"
(*on ship*)	la cabine	"kabeen"
▷ **a first/second class cabin**	une cabine de première/deuxième classe	"oon kabeen duh pruhmyehr/duhzyem klass"
cable car	le téléphérique	"taylayfayreek"
cactus	le cactus	"kaktoos"
café	le café	"kafay"
cake	le gâteau	"gatoh"
calculator	la calculette	"kalkoolett"
call[1] *n* (*on telephone*)	l'appel (*m*)	"apell"
▷ **I'd like to make a call**	je voudrais téléphoner	"zhuh voodray taylayfonay"
▷ **long-distance call**	la communication interurbaine	"komooneekasyoñ añtehroorben"
▷ **an international call**	un appel international	"uñ apell añtehrnasyonal"
to **call**[2] *vb*	appeler	"aplay"
▷ **may I call you tomorrow?**	est-ce que je peux vous appeler demain?	"es-kuh zhuh puh vooz aplay duhmañ"

ABSOLUTE ESSENTIALS

do you have ...?	avez-vous ...?	"avay-voo"
is there ...?	y a-t-il ...?	"ya-teel"
are there ...?	y a-t-il ...?	"ya-teel"
how much is ...?	combien coûte ...?	"koñbyañ koot"

▷ please call me back	rappelez-moi s'il vous plaît	"raplay-mwa seel voo pleh"
call box	la cabine téléphonique	"kabeen taylayfoneek"
calm	calme	"kalm"
▷ keep calm!	ne paniquez pas!	"nuh paneekay pa"
camcorder	le camescope	"kamskop"
camera	l'appareil-photo (m)	"aparayfoto"
to camp	camper	"koñpay"
▷ may we camp here?	est-ce que nous pouvons camper ici?	"es-kuh noo poovoñ koñpay eesee"
camp bed	le lit de camp	"lee duh koñ"
camp site	le camping	"koñpeeng"
▷ we're looking for a camp site	nous cherchons un camping	"noo shershoñ uñ koñpeeng"
can¹ n	la boîte	"bwat"

can² vb:

I can	je peux	"zhuh puh"
you can	vous pouvez	"voo poovay"
he/she/it can	il/elle peut	"eel/el puh"
we can	nous pouvons	"noo poovoñ"
they can	ils/elles peuvent	"eel/el puhv"

▷ we can't come	nous ne pouvons pas venir	"noo nuh poovoñ pa vneer"
Canada	le Canada	"kanada"
Canadian	canadien (m) canadienne (f)	"kanadyañ" "kanadyenn"
canal	le canal	"kanal"

to **cancel**	annuler	"anoolay"
▷ **I want to cancel my booking**	je voudrais annuler ma réservation	"zhuh voodrayz anoolay ma rayzehr-vasyoñ"
cancellation	l'annulation (*f*)	"anoolasyoñ"
▷ **are there any cancellations?**	est-ce qu'il y a des annulations?	"es-keel ya dayz anoolasyoñ"
canoe	le canoë	"kanoeh"
canoeing	le canoë	"kanoeh"
▷ **where can we go canoeing?**	où est-ce que nous pouvons faire du canoë?	"oo es-kuh noo poovoñ fehr doo kanoeh"
can-opener	l'ouvre-boîtes (*m*)	"oovrbwat"
car	la voiture	"vwatoor"
▷ **I want to hire a car**	je voudrais louer une voiture	"zhuh voodray looay oon vwatoor"
▷ **my car has been broken into**	ma voiture a été cambriolée	"ma vwatoor a aytay koñbreeyolay"
▷ **my car has broken down**	ma voiture est en panne	"ma vwatoor et oñ pann"
carafe	la carafe	"karaf"
▷ **a carafe of house wine please**	une carafe de la réserve du patron s'il vous plaît	"oon karaf duh la rayzehrv doo patroñ seel voo pleh"
caramel	le caramel	"karamell"
caravan	la caravane	"karavann"
▷ **can we park our caravan here?**	pouvons-nous garer notre carvane ici?	"poovoñ-noo garay notr karavann eesee"
caravan site	le terrain de caravanes	"tehrañ duh karavann"
carburettor	le carburateur	"karbooratuhr"
card	la carte	"kart"
▷ **birthday card**	la carte d'anniversaire	"la kart daneevehr-sehr"

ABSOLUTE ESSENTIALS

I don't understand	je ne comprends pas	"zhuh nuh koñproñ pa"
I don't speak French	je ne parle pas français	"zhuh nuh parl pa froñsay"
do you speak English?	parlez-vous anglais?	"parlay-voo oñglay"
could you help me?	pourriez-vous m'aider?	"pooreeay-voo mayday"

cardigan

▷ **playing cards**	les cartes à jouer	"lay kart a zhooay"
cardigan	le gilet de laine	"zheelay duh len"
careful	soigneux (m)	"swanyuh"
	soigneuse (f)	"swanyuz"
▷ **be careful!**	faites attention!	"fets atoñsyoñ"
car ferry	le ferry	"feree"
car number	le numéro d'immatriculation	"noomayro deematreekoo-lasyoñ"
car park	le parking	"parkeeng"
▷ **is there a car park near here?**	y a-t-il un parking près d'ici?	"ya-teel uñ parkeeng preh deesee"
carpet	le tapis	"tapee"
carriage (railway)	la voiture	"vwatoor"
carrier bag	le sac en plastique	"sak oñ plasteek"
▷ **can I have a carrier bag please?**	puis-je avoir un sac en plastique?	"pweezh avwar uñ sak oñ plasteek"
carrot	la carotte	"karott"
to **carry**	porter	"portay"
car wash	le lave-auto	"lav-oto"
▷ **how do I use the car wash?**	comment marche le lave-auto?	"komoñ marsh luh lav-oto"
case (suitcase)	la valise	"valeez"
cash¹ n	l'argent (m) liquide	"ar-zhoñ leekeed"
▷ **I haven't any cash**	je n'ai pas d'argent liquide	"zhuh nay pa dar-zhoñ leekeed"
▷ **can I get cash with my credit card?**	est-ce que je peux obtenir de l'argent liquide avec ma carte de crédit?	"es-kuh zhuh puh optneer duh lar-zhoñ leekeed avek ma kart duh kraydee"

ABSOLUTE ESSENTIALS

I would like ...	j'aimerais ...	"zhemray"
I need ...	j'ai besoin de ...	"zhay buhswañ duh"
where is ...?	où se trouve ...?	"oo suh troov"
I'm looking for ...	je cherche ...	"zhuh shersh"

to **cash**[2] *vb*:

▷ can I cash a cheque?	est-ce que je peux encaisser un chèque?	"es-kuh zhuh puh oñkessay uñ shekk"
cash desk	la caisse	"kess"
cash dispenser	le distributeur automatique de billets	"deestreebootuhr otomateek duh beeyay"
cashier	le caissier (*m*)	"kehsyay"
	la caissière (*f*)	"kehsyehr"
casino	le casino	"kazeenoh"
cassette	la cassette	"kassett"
cassette player	le lecteur de cassettes	"lektuhr duh kassett"
castle	le château	"shatoh"
▷ is the castle open to the public?	est-ce que le château est ouvert au public?	"es-kuh luh shatoh et oovehr oh poobleek"
to **catch**	attraper	"atrapay"
▷ where do we catch the ferry to ...?	où est-ce que nous pouvons prendre le ferry pour aller à ...?	"oo es-kuh noo poovoñ proñdr luh feree poor alay a"
cathedral	la cathédrale	"kataydral"
▷ excuse me, how do I get to the cathedral?	pardon, pour la cathédrale s'il vous plaît?	"pardoñ poor la kataydral seel voo pleh"
Catholic	catholique	"katoleek"
cauliflower	le chou-fleur	"shoofluhr"
cave	la caverne	"kavehrn"
caviar	le caviar	"kavyar"
CD	le compact	"koñpakt"
cemetery	le cimetière	"seemtyehr"
centimetre	le centimètre	"soñteemetr"

ABSOLUTE ESSENTIALS

do you have ...?	avez-vous ...?	"avay-voo"
is there ...?	y a-t-il ...?	"ya-teel"
are there ...?	y a-t-il ...?	"ya-teel"
how much is ...?	combien coûte ...?	"koñbyañ koot"

central	central(e)	"soñtrall"
central station:		
▷ **where is the central station?**	où est la gare centrale?	"oo eh la gar soñtrall"
centre	le centre	"soñtr"
▷ **how far are we from the town centre?**	à quelle distance du centre-ville sommes-nous?	"a kel deestoñs doo soñtr-veel som noo"
cereal (for breakfast)	les céréales (fpl)	"sayrayal"
certain (sure)	certain (m)	"sehrtañ"
	certaine (f)	"sehrtenn"
certificate	le certificat	"sehrteefeeka"
▷ **an insurance certificate**	un certificat d'assurances	"sehrteefeeka dasooroñs"
chain	la chaîne	"shen"
▷ **do I need chains?**	est-ce que les chaînes sont nécessaires?	"es-kuh lay shen soñ naysaysehr"
chair	la chaise	"shez"
chairlift	le télésiège	"taylaysyezh"
chalet	le chalet	"shalay"
champagne	le champagne	"shoñpanyuh"
change[1] n (money)	la monnaie	"monay"
▷ **do you have change?**	est-ce que vous avez de la monnaie?	"es-kuh vooz avay duh la monay"
▷ **can you give me change for a 50 franc note?**	est-ce que vous avez la monnaie de 50 francs?	"es-kuh vooz avay la monay duh sañkoñt froñ"
▷ **sorry, I don't have any change**	désolé, je n'ai pas de monnaie	"dayzolay zhuh nay pa duh monay"
▷ **keep the change**	gardez la monnaie	"garday la monay"
to **change**[2] vb	changer	"shoñ-zhay"

ABSOLUTE ESSENTIALS

yes (please)	oui (merci)	"wee (mehrsee)"
no (thank you)	non (merci)	"noñ (mehrsee)"
hello	bonjour	"boñzhoor"
goodbye	au revoir	"o ruhvwar"

▷ **where can I change some money?** — où est-ce que je peux changer de l'argent? — "oo es-kuh zhuh puh shoñ-zhay duh lar-zhoñ"

▷ **I'd like to change these traveller's cheques** — je voudrais changer ces travellers — "zhuh voodray shoñ-zhay say travlurz"

▷ **I want to change some pounds into francs** — je voudrais changer des livres en francs — "zhuh voodray shoñ-zhay day leevr oñ froñ"

▷ **where can I change the baby?** — où est-ce que je peux changer le bébé? — "oo es-kuh zhuh puh shoñ-zhay luh baybay"

▷ **where do we change?** (*clothes*) — où est-ce qu'on se change? — "oo es-koñ suh shoñzh"

▷ **where do I change?** (*bus etc*) — où est-ce que je change? — "oo es-kuh zhuh shoñzh"

▷ **is the weather going to change?** — est-ce que le temps va changer? — "es-kuh luh toñ va shoñ-zhay"

▷ **can I change my booking?** — est-ce que je peux changer ma réservation? — "es-kuh zhuh puh shoñ-zhay ma rayzehr-vasyoñ"

changing room — le salon d'essayage — "saloñ dessay-yazh"

Channel tunnel — le tunnel sous la Manche — "toonell soo la moñsh"

chapel — la chapelle — "shapell"

charge¹ *n* — le prix — "pree"

▷ **is there a charge per kilometre?** — est-ce que le kilométrage est en plus? — "es-kuh luh keelomaytrazh eh oñ ploos"

▷ **I want to reverse the charges** — je voudrais téléphoner en PCV — "zhuh voodray taylayfonay oñ paysayvay"

▷ **is there a charge?** — est-ce qu'il y a quelque chose à payer? — "es-keel ya kelkuh shohz a pay-yay"

to charge² *vb*:

▷ **how much do you charge?** — combien est-ce que vous prenez? — "koñbyañ es-kuh voo pruhnay"

▷ **please charge it to my room** — portez l'addition sur mon compte s'il vous plaît — "portay ladeesyoñ soor moñ koñt seel voo pleh"

ABSOLUTE ESSENTIALS

I don't understand	je ne comprends pas	"zhuh nuh koñproñ pa"
I don't speak French	je ne parle pas français	"zhuh nuh parl pa froñsay"
do you speak English?	parlez-vous anglais?	"parlay-voo oñglay"
could you help me?	pourriez-vous m'aider?	"pooreeay-voo mayday"

cheap	bon marché	"boñ marshay"
cheaper	moins cher	"mwañ shehr"
▷ have you anything cheaper?	est-ce que vous avez quelque chose de moins cher?	"es-kuh vooz avay kelkuh shohz duh mwañ shehr"
to check	vérifier	"vayreefyay"
to check in	enregistrer	"oñruh-zheestray"
▷ I'd like to check in, please	j'aimerais faire enregistrer mes bagages s'il vous plaît	"zhemray fehr oñruh-zheestray may bagazh seel voo pleh"
▷ where do I check in for the flight to London?	où est-ce que je dois me présenter pour le vol en partance pour Londres?	"oo es-kuh zhuh dwah muh prayzoñtay poor luh vol oñ partoñs poor loñdr"
▷ where do I check in my luggage?	où est-ce que je fais enregistrer mes bagages?	"oo es-kuh zhuh fayz oñruh-zheestray may bagazh"
▷ when do I have to check in?	quand est-ce que je dois me présenter à l'enregistrement?	"koñt es-kuh zhuh dwa muh prayzoñtay a loñruh-zheestr-moñ"
check-in desk	l'enregistrement (m) des bagages	"oñruh-zheestr-moñ day bagazh"
cheerio	au revoir	"oh ruhvwar"
cheers!	à la vôtre!	"a la vohtr"
cheese	le fromage	"fromazh"
cheeseburger	le hamburger au fromage	"oñboorgehr oh fromazh"
cheesecake	le cheese-cake	"cheese-cake"
chemist's	la pharmacie	"farmasee"
cheque	le chèque	"shekk"
▷ can I pay by cheque?	est-ce qu'il est possible de payer par chèque?	"es-keel eh poseebl duh payyay par shekk"

▷ I want to cash a cheque, please	j'aimerais encaisser un chèque, s'il vous plaît	"zhemray oñkessay uñ shekk seel voo pleh"
cheque book	le carnet de chèques	"karneh duh shekk"
▷ I've lost my cheque book	j'ai perdu mon carnet de chèques	"zhay pehrdoo moñ karneh duh shekk"
cheque card	la carte d'identité bancaire	"kart deedoñteetay boñkehr"
cherry	la cerise	"sreez"
chest (of body)	la poitrine	"pwatreen"
▷ I have a pain in my chest	j'ai mal dans la poitrine	"zhay mal doñ la pwatreen"
chestnut	la châtaigne	"sha-tehnyuh"
chewing gum	le chewing-gum	"shooeeng gum"
chicken	le poulet	"pooleh"
chickenpox	la varicelle	"vareesell"
chicken soup	le potage au poulet	"potazh oh pooleh"
child	l'enfant (m)	"oñfoñ"
child minder	la nourrice	"nooreess"
children	les enfants (mpl)	"oñfoñ"
▷ do you have activities for children?	est-ce que vous avez des activités pour les enfants?	"eskuh vooz avay dayz akteeveetay poor layz oñfoñ"
▷ is there a children's pool?	y a-t-il une piscine pour enfants?	"ya-teel oon peeseen poor oñfoñ"
▷ is there a paddling pool for the children?	y a-t-il un petit bassin pour les enfants?	"ya-teel uñ puhtee basañ poor layz oñfoñ"
chilli	le piment rouge	"peemoñ roozh"
chips	les frites (fpl)	"freet"
chives	la ciboulette	"seeboolett"

do you have ...?	avez-vous ...?	"avay-voo"
is there ...?	y a-t-il ...?	"ya-teel"
are there ...?	y a-t-il ...?	"ya-teel"
how much is ...?	combien coûte ...?	"koñbyañ koot"

chocolate	le chocolat	"shokola"
▷ **a bar of chocolate, please**	une tablette de chocolat, s'il vous plaît	"oon tablett duh shokola seel voo pleh"
chocolates	les chocolats (*mpl*)	"shokola"
chop:		
▷ **a pork/lamb chop**	une côtelette de porc/ d'agneau	"oon kohtlett duh por/ danyoh"
Christmas	Noël	"noell"
▷ **Merry Christmas!**	joyeux Noël!	"zhwayuh noell"
church	l'église (*f*)	"aygleez"
▷ **where is the nearest church?**	où est l'église la plus proche?	"oo eh laygleez la ploo prosh"
▷ **where is there a Protestant/Catholic church?**	où est-ce qu'il y a une église protestante/ catholique?	"oo es-keel ya oon aygleez protestoñt/katoleek"
cider	le cidre	"seedr"
cigar	le cigare	"seegar"
cigarette	la cigarette	"seegarett"
▷ **a packet of cigarettes, please**	un paquet de cigarettes, s'il vous plaît	"uñ pakeh duh seegarett seel voo pleh"
cigarette papers	les papiers (*mpl*) à cigarettes	"papyay a seegarett"
cinema	le cinéma	"seenayma"
▷ **what's on at the cinema?**	qu'est-ce qui passe au cinéma?	"kes-kee pas oh seenayma"
circus	le cirque	"seerk"
city	la ville	"veel"
clean¹ *adj*	propre	"propr"

ABSOLUTE ESSENTIALS

yes (please)	oui (merci)	"wee (mehrsee)"
no (thank you)	non (merci)	"noñ (mehrsee)"
hello	bonjour	"boñzhoor"
goodbye	au revoir	"o ruhvwar"

▷ **could I have a clean spoon/fork please?**	est-ce que je pourrais avoir une cuillère/ fourchette propre s'il vous plaît?	"es-kuh zhuh poorayz avwar oon kweeyehr/ foorshett propr seel voo pleh"
▷ **the room isn't clean**	la chambre n'est pas propre	"la shoñbr neh pa propr"
to clean² vb	nettoyer	"netwa-yay"
▷ **where can I get this skirt cleaned?**	où est-ce que je peux faire nettoyer cette jupe?	"oo es-kuh zhuh puh fehr netwa-yay set zhoop"
cleaner	la femme de ménage	"fam duh maynazh"
▷ **when does the cleaner come?**	la femme de ménage vient quand?	"la fam duh maynazh vyañ koñ"
cleansing cream	la crème démaquillante	"krem daymakeeyoñt"
cleansing solution for contact lenses	la solution d'aseptisation pour lentilles de contact	"soloosyoñ dasepteezasyoñ poor loñteey duh koñtakt"
client	le client (*m*) la cliente (*f*)	"kleeoñ" "kleeoñt"
cliff	la falaise	"falehz"
climbing	l'escalade (*f*)	"eskalad"
climbing boots	les chaussures (*fpl*) d'escalade	"shohsoor deskalad"
cloakroom	le vestiaire	"vestyehr"
clock	l'horloge (*f*)	"orlozh"
close¹ adj (near)	proche	"prosh"
to close² vb	fermer	"fehrmay"
▷ **what time do you close?**	vous fermez à quelle heure?	"voo fehrmay a kel uhr"
▷ **the door will not close**	la porte ne ferme pas	"la port nuh fehrm pa"
closed	fermé(e)	"fehrmay"

ABSOLUTE ESSENTIALS

I don't understand	je ne comprends pas	"zhuh nuh koñproñ pa"
I don't speak French	je ne parle pas français	"zhuh nuh parl pa froñsay"
do you speak English?	parlez-vous anglais?	"parlay-voo oñglay"
could you help me?	pourriez-vous m'aider?	"pooreeay-voo mayday"

cloth	le chiffon	"sheefoñ"
clothes	les vêtements (*mpl*)	"vetmoñ"
clothes peg	le pince à linge	"pañs a lañzh"
cloudy	nuageux (*m*)	"nwa-zhuh"
	nuageuse (*f*)	"nwa-zhuz"
cloves	les clous (*mpl*) de girofle	"kloo duh zheerofl"
club	le club	"klub"
▷ **a night club**	une boîte de nuit	"oon bwat duh nwee"
▷ **a set of golf clubs**	un jeu de clubs de golf	"uñ zhuh duh klub duh golf"
coach (*bus*)	l'autobus (*m*)	"otoboos"
(*train*)	la voiture	"vwatoor"
▷ **when does the coach leave in the morning?**	le car part à quelle heure le matin?	"luh kar par a kel uhr luh matañ"
coach station	la gare routière	"gar rootyehr"
coach trip	l'excursion (*f*) en car	"ekskoorsyoñ oñ kar"
coast	la côte	"koht"
coastguard	le garde-côte	"gardkoht"
coat	le manteau	"moñtoh"
coat hanger	le cintre	"sañtr"
cockroaches	les cafards (*mpl*)	"kafar"
cocktail	le cocktail	"koktell"
cocoa	le cacao	"kaka-oh"
coconut	la noix de coco	"nwa duh kokoh"
cod	le cabillaud	"kabeeyoh"
coffee	le café	"kafay"
▷ **white coffee**	le café au lait	"kafay oh leh"
▷ **black coffee**	le café noir	"kafay nwar"

coin	la pièce de monnaie	"pyes duh monay"
▷ what coins do I need?	j'ai besoin de quelles pièces?	"zhay buhzwañ duh kel pyess"
Coke ®	le coca	"koka"
colander	la passoire	"paswar"
cold[1] *n*	le rhume	"room"
▷ I have a cold	je suis enrhumé	"zhuh sweez oñroomay"
cold[2] *adj*	froid (*m*)	"frwa"
	froide (*f*)	"frwad"
▷ I'm cold	j'ai froid	"zhay frwa"
▷ will it be cold tonight?	est-ce qu'il va faire froid cette nuit?	"es-keel va fehr frwa set nwee"
cold meat	la viande froide	"vyoñd frwad"
colour	la couleur	"kooluhr"
▷ I don't like the colour	je n'aime pas la couleur	"zhuh nem pa la kooluhr"
▷ I need a colour film for this camera	je voudrais un film couleur pour cet appareil	"zhuh voodrayz uñ feelm kooluhr poor set aparay"
▷ do you have it in another colour?	est-ce que vous l'avez dans une autre couleur?	"es-kuh voo lavay doñz oon ohtr kooluhr"
colour TV	la télévision en couleur	"taylayveezyoñ oñ kooluhr"
comb	le peigne	"pehnyuh"
to come	venir	"vneer"
▷ how much does that come to?	ça fait combien?	"sa feh koñbyañ"
to come back	revenir	"ruhvneer"
to come in	entrer	"oñtray"
▷ come in!	entrez!	"oñtray"
comfortable	confortable	"koñfortabl"
commission	la commission	"koñmeesyoñ"

ABSOLUTE ESSENTIALS

do you have ...?	avez-vous ...?	"avay-voo"
is there ...?	y a-t-il ...?	"ya-teel"
are there ...?	y a-t-il ...?	"ya-teel"
how much is ...?	combien coûte ...?	"koñbyañ koot"

▷ how much commission do you charge?	combien est-ce que vous prenez de commission?	"koñbyañ es-kuh voo pruhnay duh koñmeesyoñ"
compact disc	le disque compact	"deesk koñpakt"
compact disc player	le lecteur de disques compacts	"lektuhr duh deesk koñpakt"
company	la compagnie	"koñpanyee"
compartment	le compartiment	"koñparteemoñ"
▷ I would like to book a seat in a non-smoking compartment	je voudrais réserver une place dans un compartiment non-fumeur	"zhuh voodray rayzehr-vay oon plass doñz uñ koñparteemoñ noñ-foomuhr"
to complain	se plaindre	"suh plañdr"
▷ I want to complain about the service	je désire me plaindre du service	"zhuh dayseer muh plañdr doo sehrvees"
comprehensive insurance cover	l'assurance (f) tous-risques	"asooroñs too-reesk"
▷ how much extra is comprehensive insurance cover?	il y a un supplément de combien pour l'assurance tous-risques?	"eel ya uñ sooplaymoñ duh koñbyañ poor lasooroñs too-reesk"
compulsory	obligatoire	"obleegatwar"
computer	l'ordinateur (m)	"ordeenatuhr"
concert	le concert	"koñsehr"
condensed milk	le lait concentré	"leh koñsoñtray"
conditioner	l'après-shampooing (m)	"apray-shoñpwañ"
condom	le préservatif	"prayzehrvateef"
▷ a packet of condoms	un paquet de préservatifs	"uñ pakeh duh prayzehrvateef"
conductor (on train)	le chef de train	"shef duh trañ"
conference	la conférence	"koñfayroñs"

ABSOLUTE ESSENTIALS

yes (please)	oui (merci)	"wee (mehrsee)"
no (thank you)	non (merci)	"noñ (mehrsee)"
hello	bonjour	"boñzhoor"
goodbye	au revoir	"o ruhvwar"

confession	la confession	"koñfesyoñ"
▷ I want to go to confession	je voudrais aller me confesser	"zhuh voodray alay muh koñfessay"
to **confirm**	confirmer	"koñfeermay"
congratulations!	félicitations!	"fayleeseetasyoñ"
connection	la correspondance	"korespoñdoñs"
▷ I missed my connection	j'ai raté ma correspondance	"zhay ratay ma korespoñdoñs"
constipated	constipé(e)	"koñsteepay"
constipation	la constipation	"koñsteepasyoñ"
consulate	le consulat	"koñsoola"
▷ where is the British/ American consulate?	où est le consulat britannique/américain?	"oo eh luh koñsoola breetaneek/amayreekañ"
to **contact**	contacter	"koñtaktay"
▷ where can I contact you?	où est-ce que je peux vous contacter?	"oo es-kuh zhuh puh voo koñtaktay"
contact lens cleaner	le produit pour nettoyer les lentilles de contact	"prodwee poor netwayay lay loñteey duh koñtakt"
contact lenses	les lentilles (fpl) de contact	"loñteey duh koñtakt"
▷ hard contact lenses	les lentilles dures	"loñteey door"
▷ soft contact lenses	les lentilles souples	"loñteey soopl"
continental breakfast	le petit déjeuner complet	"puhtee day-zhuhnay koñpleh"
contraceptive	le contraceptif	"koñtrasepteef"
controls	les commandes (fpl)	"komoñd"
▷ how do I operate the controls?	comment fonctionnent les commandes?	"komoñ foñksyonn lay komoñd"
cook	le cuisinier (m) la cuisinière (f)	"kweezeenyay" "kweezeenyehr"

ABSOLUTE ESSENTIALS

I don't understand	je ne comprends pas	"zhuh nuh koñproñ pa"
I don't speak French	je ne parle pas français	"zhuh nuh parl pa froñsay"
do you speak English?	parlez-vous anglais?	"parlay-voo oñglay"
could you help me?	pourriez-vous m'aider?	"pooreeay-voo mayday"

cooker	la cuisinière	"kweezeenyehr"
▷ **how does the cooker work?**	comment fonctionne la cuisinière?	"komoñ foñksyonn la kweezeenyehr"
cool	frais (m)	"freh"
	fraîche (f)	"fresh"
copy[1] n	un exemplaire	"egzoñplehr"
▷ **5 copies please**	5 exemplaires s'il vous plaît	"sañk egzoñplehr seel voo pleh"
to **copy**[2] vb	copier	"kopyay"
▷ **I want to copy this document**	je voudrais copier ce document	"zhuh voodray kopyay suh dokoomoñ"
corkscrew	le tire-bouchon	"teerbooshoñ"
corner	le coin	"kwañ"
▷ **it's on the corner**	c'est au coin de la rue	"set oh kwañ duh la roo"
cornflakes	les cornflakes (fpl)	"cornflakes"
Corsica	la Corse	"kors"
cortisone	la cortisone	"korteezonn"
cosmetics	les cosmétiques (mpl)	"kozmayteek"
cost[1] n	le coût	"koo"
to **cost**[2] vb	coûter	"kootay"
▷ **how much does it cost to get in?**	l'entrée coûte combien?	"loñtray koot koñbyañ"
▷ **how much does that cost?**	ça coûte combien?	"sa koot koñbyañ"
cot	le lit de bébé	"lee duh baybay"
▷ **do you have a cot for the baby?**	avez-vous un petit lit pour le bébé?	"avay-voo uñ puhtee lee poor luh baybay"
cotton	le coton	"kotoñ"
cotton wool	le coton hydrophile	"kotoñ eedrofeel"

ABSOLUTE ESSENTIALS

I would like ...	j'aimerais ...	"zhemray"
I need ...	j'ai besoin de ...	"zhay buhswañ duh"
where is ...?	où se trouve ...?	"oo suh troov"
I'm looking for ...	je cherche ...	"zhuh shersh"

couchette	la couchette	"kooshett"
▷ I want to reserve a couchette	je voudrais réserver une couchette	"zhuh voodray rayzehrvay oon kooshett"

cough	la toux	"too"
▷ I have a cough	je tousse	"zhuh tooss"
▷ do you have any cough mixture?	est-ce que vous avez un sirop pour la toux?	"es-kuh vooz avay uñ seeroh poor la too"

could:

I could	je pourrais	"zhuh pooray"
you could	vous pourriez	"voo pooreeay"
he/she/it could	il/elle pourrait	"eel/el pooray"
we could	nous pourrions	"noo pooreeoñ"
they could	ils/elles pourraient	"eel/el pooray"

country (not town)	la campagne	"koñpanyuh"
(nation)	le pays	"pay-ee"
couple (two people)	le couple	"koopl"
courgettes	les courgettes (fpl)	"koor-zhett"
courier (for tourists)	le guide	"geed"
(express delivery service)	le coursier	"koorsyay"
▷ I want to send this by courier	je voudrais envoyer cela par coursier	"zhuh voodray oñvwahyay sla par koorsyay"
course (of meal)	le plat	"pla"
cover charge	le couvert	"koovehr"
crab	le crabe	"krab"

cramp:

▷ I've got cramp (in my leg)	j'ai une crampe (dans la jambe)	"zhay oon kroñp (doñ la zhoñb)"

ABSOLUTE ESSENTIALS

do you have ...?	avez-vous ...?	"avay-voo"
is there ...?	y a-t-il ...?	"ya-teel"
are there ...?	y a-t-il ...?	"ya-teel"
how much is ...?	combien coûte ...?	"koñbyañ koot"

crash	l'accident (*m*)	"akseedoñ"
▷ **I've crashed my car**	j'ai eu un accident de voiture	"zhay oo un akseedoñ duh vwatoor"
▷ **there's been a crash**	il y a eu un accident	"eel ya oo un akseedoñ"
crash helmet	le casque protecteur	"kask protektuhr"
cream	la crème	"krem"
cream cheese	le fromage à tartiner	"fromazh a tarteenay"
credit card	la carte de crédit	"kart duh kraydee"
▷ **can I pay by credit card?**	est-ce qu'il est possible de payer avec une carte de crédit?	"es-keel eh poseebl duh payyay avek oon kart duh kraydee"
▷ **I've lost my credit card**	j'ai perdu ma carte de crédit	"zhay pehrdoo ma kart duh kraydee"
crisps	les chips (*mpl*)	"sheeps"
croissant	le croissant	"krwasoñ"
croquette	la croquette	"krokett"
to cross (*road*)	traverser	"travehrsay"
cross-country skiing:		
▷ **is it possible to go cross-country skiing?**	est-ce que l'on peut faire du ski de fond?	"es-kloñ puh fehr doo skee duh foñ"
crossing	la traversée	"travehrsay"
▷ **how long does the crossing take?**	la traversée dure combien de temps?	"la travehrsay door koñbyañ duh toñ"
crossroads	le carrefour	"karfoor"
crowded	bondé(e)	"boñday"
cruise	la croisière	"krwaz-yehr"
cucumber	le concombre	"koñkoñbr"
cup	la tasse	"tass"

▷ **could we have another cup of tea/coffee, please?**	encore une tasse de thé/café, s'il vous plaît	"oñkor oon tass duh tay/kafay seel voo pleh"
cupboard	le placard	"plakar"
currant	le raisin sec	"rayzañ sek"
current	le courant	"kooroñ"
▷ **are there strong currents?**	est-ce qu'il y a de forts courants?	"es-keel ya duh for kooroñ"
cushion	le coussin	"koossañ"
custard	la crème anglaise	"krem oñglez"
customs	la douane	"dwan"
cut¹ *n*	la coupure	"koopoor"
▷ **a cut and blow-dry, please**	coupe et brushing, s'il vous plaît	"koop ay bruhsheeing seel voo pleh"
to cut² *vb*	couper	"koopay"
▷ **he has cut himself**	il s'est coupé	"eel seh koopay"
▷ **I've been cut off**	nous avons été coupés	"nooz avoñ aytay koopay"
cutlery	les couverts (*mpl*)	"koovehr"
cycle	la bicyclette	"beeseeklett"
cycle helmet	le casque de cyclisme	"kask duh seekleezmuh"
cycle path	la piste cyclable	"peest seeklabl"
cycling	le cyclisme	"seekleezmuh"
▷ **we would like to go cycling**	nous voudrions faire du vélo	"nooz voodreeoñ fehr doo vayloh"
daily (*each day*)	tous les jours	"too lay zhoor"
dairy products	les produits (*mpl*) laitiers	"prodwee letyay"
damage	les dégâts (*mpl*)	"dayga"
damp	humide	"oomeed"

ABSOLUTE ESSENTIALS

I don't understand	je ne comprends pas	"zhuh nuh koñproñ pa"
I don't speak French	je ne parle pas français	"zhuh nuh parl pa froñsay"
do you speak English?	parlez-vous anglais?	"parlay-voo oñglay"
could you help me?	pourriez-vous m'aider?	"pooreeay-voo mayday"

▷ **my clothes are damp**	mes vêtements sont humides	"meh vetmoñ soñt oomeed"
dance¹ *n*	le bal	"bal"
to **dance²** *vb*	danser	"doñsay"
dangerous	dangereux (*m*)	"doñ-zhuruh"
	dangereuse (*f*)	"doñ-zhuruz"
dark	foncé(e)	"foñsay"
date (*calendar*)	la date	"dat"
(*appointment*)	le rendez-vous	"roñday-voo"
(*fruit*)	la datte	"dat"
▷ **what is the date today?**	quelle est la date aujourd'hui?	"kel eh la dat ohzhoordwee"
date of birth	la date de naissance	"dat duh nehsoñs"
daughter	la fille	"feey"
day	le jour	"zhoor"
day trip	l'excursion (*f*) pour la journée	"ekskoorsyoñ poor la zhoornay"
dear	cher (*m*)	"shehr"
	chère (*f*)	"shehr"
decaffeinated	décaféiné(e)	"daykafayeenay"
December	décembre (*m*)	"daysoñbr"
deck	le pont	"poñ"
▷ **can we go out on deck?**	est-ce qu'on peut sortir sur le pont?	"es-koñ puh sorteer soor luh poñ"
deck chair	la chaise longue	"shez loñg"
to **declare**	déclarer	"dayklaray"
▷ **I have nothing to declare**	je n'ai rien à déclarer	"zhuh nay ryañ a dayklaray"
▷ **I have a bottle of spirits to declare**	j'ai une bouteille d'alcool à déclarer	"zhay oon bootay dalkol a dayklaray"

deep	profond (*m*)	"profoñ"
	profonde (*f*)	"profoñd"
▷ **how deep is the water?**	quelle est la profondeur de l'eau?	"kel eh la profoñduhr duh loh"
deep freeze	le congélateur	"koñzhaylatuhr"
to **defrost**	dégivrer	"dayzheevray"
to **de-ice**	dégivrer	"dayzheevray"
delay	le retard	"ruhtar"
▷ **the flight has been delayed (by 6 hours)**	le vol a été retardé (de 6 heures)	"luh vol a aytay ruhtarday (duh seez uhr)"
delicious	délicieux (*m*)	"dayleesyuh"
	délicieuse (*f*)	"dayleesyuz"
dentist	le dentiste	"doñteest"
▷ **I need to see a dentist (urgently)**	je dois voir le dentiste (d'urgence)	"zhuh dwah vwar luh doñteest (doorzhoñs)"
dentures	le dentier	"doñtyay"
▷ **my dentures need repairing**	mon dentier a besoin d'être réparé	"moñ doñtyay a buhzwañ detr rayparay"
deodorant	le déodorant	"dayodoroñ"
department store	le grand magasin	"groñ magazañ"
departure	le départ	"daypar"
departure lounge	la salle de départ	"sal duh daypar"
deposit	les arrhes (*fpl*)	"ar"
▷ **what is the deposit?**	combien d'arrhes doit-on verser?	"koñbyañ dar dwa-toñ vehrsay"
dessert	le dessert	"dessehr"
▷ **we'd like a dessert**	nous aimerions un dessert	"nooz ehmryoñ uñ dessehr"
▷ **the dessert menu please**	la carte des desserts s'il vous plaît	"la kart deh dessehr seel voo pleh"

ABSOLUTE ESSENTIALS

do you have ...?	avez-vous ...?	"avay-voo"
is there ...?	y a-t-il ...?	"ya-teel"
are there ...?	y a-t-il ...?	"ya-teel"
how much is ...?	combien coûte ...?	"koñbyañ koot"

details	les détails (*mpl*)	"daytye"
detergent	le détergent	"daytehrzhoñ"
detour	la déviation	"dayvyasyoñ"
to **develop**	développer	"dayvlopay"
diabetic	diabétique	"dyabayteek"
▷ **I am diabetic**	je suis diabétique	"zhuh swee dyabayteek"
dialling code	l'indicatif (*m*)	"añdeeka-teef"
▷ **what is the dialling code for the UK?**	quel est l'indicatif pour le Royaume-Uni?	"kel eh lañdeeka-teef poor luh rwayohm-oonee"
diamond	le diamant	"dyamoñ"
diarrhoea	la diarrhée	"dyaray"
▷ **I need something for diarrhoea**	il me faudrait quelque chose contre la diarrhée	"eel muh fodreh kelkuh shoz koñtruh la dyaray"
diary	l'agenda (*m*)	"azhañda"
dictionary	le dictionnaire	"deeksyonehr"
diesel	le gas-oil	"gazol"
diet	le régime	"rayzheem"
different	différent (*m*)	"deefayroñ"
	différente (*f*)	"deefayroñt"
▷ **I would like something different**	j'aimerais quelque chose de différent	"zhemray kelkuh shoz duh deefayroñ"
difficult	difficile	"deefeeseel"
dinghy	le youyou	"yooyoo"
dining car	le wagon-restaurant	"vagoñ restoroñ"
dining room	la salle à manger	"sal a moñzhay"
dinner	le dîner	"deenay"
direct (*train etc*)	direct(e)	"deerekt"

directory	l'annuaire (m)	"anooehr"
directory enquiries	les renseignements (mpl)	"roñsehnyuh-moñ"
▷ what is the number for directory enquiries?	quel est le numéro des renseignements?	"kel eh luh noomayro day roñsehnyuh-moñ"
dirty	sale	"sal"
▷ the washbasin is dirty	le lavabo est sale	"luh lavabo eh sal"
disabled	handicapé(e)	"oñdee-kapay"
▷ is there a toilet for the disabled?	est-ce qu'il y a des toilettes pour handicapés?	"es-keel ya day twalet poor oñdee-kapay"
▷ do you have facilities for the disabled?	est-ce qu'il y a des aménagements prévus pour les handicapés?	"es-keel ya dayz amay-nazh-moñ prayvoo poor lay oñdee-kapay"
▷ is there access for the disabled?	est-ce qu'il y a une facilité d'accès pour les handicapés?	"es-keel ya faseeleetay dakseh poor lay oñdee-kapay"
disco	la discothèque	"deeskotek"
discount	la remise	"ruhmeez"
▷ do you offer a discount for cash?	offrez-vous une remise pour paiement au comptant?	"ofray-voo oon ruhmeez poor paymoñ oh koñtoñ"
▷ are there discounts for students/children/senior citizens?	y a-t-il des remises pour les étudiants/enfants/personnes du troisième âge	"ee yateel day ruhmeez poor layz aytoodyoñ/oñfoñ/pehrsonn doo trwazyem azh"
dish	le plat	"pla"
▷ how is this dish cooked?	comment est-ce que ce plat est accommodé?	"komoñ es-kuh suh pla et akomoday"
▷ how is this dish served?	ce plat est servi comment?	"suh pla eh sehrvee komoñ"
▷ what is in this dish?	ce plat est préparé avec quoi?	"suh pla eh prayparay avek kwa"
dishtowel	le torchon	"torshoñ"

dishwasher	le lave-vaisselle	"lav-vehsell"
disinfectant	le désinfectant	"dayzañfektoñ"
distilled water	l'eau (f) distillée	"oh deesteelay"
to **dive**	plonger	"ploñzhay"
▷ where is the best place to dive?	quel est le meilleur endroit pour faire de la plongée?	"kel eh luh mayuhr oñdrwa poor fehr duh la ploñzhay"
diversion	la déviation	"dayvyasyoñ"
▷ is there a diversion?	est-ce qu'il y a une déviation?	"es-keel ya oon dayvyasyoñ"
diving	la plongée	"ploñzhay"
▷ I'd like to go diving	j'aimerais faire de la plongée	"zhemray fehr duh la ploñzhay"
divorced	divorcé(e)	"deevorsay"
dizzy	pris de vertige (m) prise de vertige (f)	"pree duh vehrtizh" "preez duh vehrtizh"
▷ I feel dizzy	j'ai la tête qui tourne	"zhay la tet kee toorn"
to **do**	faire	"fehr"

I do	je fais	"zhuh feh"
you do	vous faites	"voo fet"
he/she/it does	il/elle fait	"eel/el feh"
we do	nous faisons	"noo fzoñ"
they do	ils/elles font	"eel/el foñ"

dock	le dock	"dok"
doctor	le médecin	"maytsañ"
▷ call a doctor	appelez un médecin	"aplay uñ maytsañ"
▷ I need a doctor	j'ai besoin d'un médecin	"zhay buhzwañ duñ maytsañ"

ABSOLUTE ESSENTIALS		
I would like ...	j'aimerais ...	"zhemray"
I need ...	j'ai besoin de ...	"zhay buhzwañ duh"
where is ...?	où se trouve ...?	"oo suh troov"
I'm looking for ...	je cherche ...	"zhuh shersh"

▷ **can I please have an
  appointment with the
  doctor?**
est-ce que je pourrais
avoir un rendez-vous
avec le médecin s'il
vous plaît?
"es-kuh zhuh pooreh
avwar uñ roñdayvoo
avec luh maytsañ seel
voo pleh"

doll   la poupée   "poopay"

dollar   le dollar   "dolar"

door   la porte   "port"

double   double   "doobl"

double bed   le grand lit   "groñ lee"

double room   la chambre pour deux   "shoñbr poor duh
                              personnes   pehrsonn"

▷ **I want to reserve a
  double room**
je voudrais réserver une
chambre pour deux
personnes
"zhuh voodray rayzehrvay
oon shoñbr poor duh
pehrsonn"

doughnut   le beignet   "baynyay"

down:

▷ **to go down** (*stairs, hill*) descendre   "dehsoñdr"

downstairs   en bas   "oñ ba"

drain:

▷ **the drain is blocked**   les canalisations sont   "lay kanaleezasyoñ soñ
                              bouchées   booshay"

draught   le courant d'air   "kooroñ dehr"

draught beer   la bière à la pression   "byehr a la presyoñ"

▷ **a draught beer please**   une pression s'il vous   "oon presyoñ seel voo
                              plaît   pleh"

dress¹ *n*   la robe   "rob"

to dress² *vb*:

▷ **to get dressed**   s'habiller   "sabee-yay"

dressing (*for food*)   la vinaigrette   "veenaygrett"

ABSOLUTE ESSENTIALS

do you have ...?	avez-vous ...?	"avay-voo"
is there ...?	y a-t-il ...?	"ya-teel"
are there ...?	y a-t-il ...?	"ya-teel"
how much is ...?	combien coûte ...?	"koñbyañ koot"

drink

drink[1] *n*	la boisson	"bwasoñ"
▷ **would you like a drink?**	est-ce que je peux vous offrir quelque chose à boire?	"es-kuh zhuh puh vooz ofreer kelkuh shohz a bwar"
▷ **a cold/hot drink**	une boisson froide/chaude	"oon bwasoñ frwad/shohd"
to **drink**[2] *vb*	boire	"bwar"
▷ **what would you like to drink?**	qu'est-ce que vous désirez boire?	"kes-kuh voo dayzeeray bwar"
drinking chocolate	le chocolat chaud	"shokola shoh"
drinking water	l'eau (*f*) potable	"oh potabl"
to **drive**	conduire	"koñdweer"
▷ **he was driving too fast**	il conduisait trop vite	"eel koñdweezeh troh veet"
driver (*of car*)	le conducteur	"koñdooktuhr"
driving licence	le permis de conduire	"pehrmee duh koñdweer"
▷ **my driving licence number is ...**	le numéro de mon permis de conduire est ...	"luh noomayro duh moñ pehrmee duh koñdweer eh"
▷ **I don't have my driving licence on me**	je n'ai pas mon permis de conduire sur moi	"zhuh nay pa moñ pehrmee duh koñdweer soor mwa"
to **drown**:		
▷ **someone is drowning!**	quelqu'un est en train de se noyer!	"kelkuñ et oñ trañ duh suh nwayay"
drunk	ivre	"eevr"
dry[1] *adj*	sec (*m*)	"sek"
	sèche (*f*)	"sesh"
to **dry**[2] *vb*	sécher	"sayshay"
▷ **where can I dry my clothes?**	où est-ce que je peux faire sécher mes vêtements?	"oo es-kuh zhuh puh fehr sayshay may vetmoñ"

ABSOLUTE ESSENTIALS

yes (please)	oui (merci)	"wee (mehrsee)"
no (thank you)	non (merci)	"noñ (mehrsee)"
hello	bonjour	"boñzhoor"
goodbye	au revoir	"o ruhvwar"

to dry-clean:

▷ **I need this dry-cleaned** | je voudrais faire nettoyer cela à sec | "zhuh voodreh fehr netwayay sla a sek"

dry-cleaner's | le pressing | "presseeng"

duck | le canard | "kanar"

due:

▷ **when is it due to be paid?** | quand doit-on payer cela? | "koñ dwa-toñ pehyay sla"

dummy | la sucette | "soosett"

dune | la dune | "doon"

during | pendant | "poñdoñ"

duty-free | exempté(e) de douane | "exoñtay duh dwan"

duty-free shop | la boutique hors taxe | "booteek or tax"

duvet | la couette | "kwett"

dynamo | la dynamo | "deenamoh"

each | chacun (m) | "shakuñ"
 | chacune (f) | "shakoon"

ear | l'oreille (f) | "oray"

earache:

▷ **I have earache** | j'ai mal aux oreilles | "zhay mal ohz oray"

earlier | plus tôt | "ploo toh"

▷ **I would prefer an earlier flight** | je préférerais un vol plus tôt | "zhuh prayfayruhray uñ vol ploo toh"

early | tôt | "toh"

earrings | les boucles (fpl) d'oreille | "bookl doray"

east | l'est (m) | "est"

Easter | Pâques (m or fpl) | "pak"

ABSOLUTE ESSENTIALS

I don't understand	je ne comprends pas	"zhuh nuh koñproñ pa"
I don't speak French	je ne parle pas français	"zhuh nuh parl pa froñsay"
do you speak English?	parlez-vous anglais?	"parlay-voo oñglay"
could you help me?	pourriez-vous m'aider?	"pooreeay-voo mayday"

easy	facile	"faseel"
to eat	manger	"moñzhay"
▷ I don't eat meat	je ne mange pas de viande	"zhuh nuh moñzh pa duh vyoñd"
▷ would you like something to eat?	est-ce que vous aimeriez manger quelque chose?	"es-kuh vooz emuh-ryay moñzhay kelkuh shohz"
▷ have you eaten?	est-ce que vous avez mangé?	"es-kuh vooz avay moñzhay"
EC	la CE	"say-uh"
egg	l'œuf (m)	"luf"
▷ eggs	les œufs	"layzuh"
▷ fried egg	l'œuf frit	"luf free"
▷ hard-boiled egg	l'œuf dur	"luf door"
▷ scrambled eggs	les œufs brouillés	"layzuh brooyay"
eight	huit	"weet"
eighteen	dix-huit	"deez-weet"
eighty	quatre-vingts	"katr-vañ"
either:		
▷ either one	l'un ou l'autre	"luñ oo lohtr"
elastic	l'élastique (m)	"aylasteek"
elastic band	l'élastique (m)	"aylasteek"
electric	électrique	"aylektreek"
electrician	l'électricien (m)	"aylektreesyañ"
electricity	l'électricité (f)	"aylektreeseetay"
▷ is the cost of electricity included in the rental?	est-ce que l'électricité est comprise dans la location?	"es-kuh laylektreeseetay eh koñpreez doñ la lokasyoñ"
electricity meter	le compteur d'électricité	"koñtuhr daylektreeseetay"

ABSOLUTE ESSENTIALS

I would like ...	j'aimerais ...	"zhemray"
I need ...	j'ai besoin de ...	"zhay buhswañ duh"
where is ...?	où se trouve ...?	"oo suh troov"
I'm looking for ...	je cherche ...	"zhuh shersh"

electric razor	le rasoir électrique	"razwar aylektreek"
eleven	onze	"oñz"
to embark:		
▷ **when do we embark?**	quand est-ce que nous embarquons?	"koñt es-kuh nooz oñbarkoñ"
embassy	l'ambassade (f)	"oñbasad"
emergency:		
▷ **it's an emergency**	c'est très urgent	"seh trayz oorzhoñ"
empty	vide	"veed"
end	la fin	"fañ"
engaged (*to be married*)	fiancé(e)	"fyoñsay"
(*toilet, phone*)	occupé(e)	"okoopay"
▷ **the line's engaged**	la ligne est occupée	"la leenyuh et okoopay"
engine	le moteur	"motuhr"
England	l'Angleterre (f)	"oñgl-tehr"
English	anglais (m)	"oñglay"
	anglaise (f)	"oñglez"
▷ **do you speak English?**	parlez-vous anglais?	"parlay-voo oñglay"
▷ **I'm English**	je suis anglais/anglaise	"zhuh sweez oñglay/ oñglez"
▷ **do you have any English books/ newpapers?**	est-ce que vous avez des livres/journaux en anglais?	"es-kuh vooz avay deh leevr/zhoornoh on oñglay"
to enjoy:		
▷ **I enjoyed the tour**	j'ai aimé l'excursion	"zheh ehmay lekskoorsyoñ"
▷ **I enjoy swimming**	j'aime nager	"zhem nazhay"
▷ **enjoy your meal**	bon appétit!	"boñ apaytee"
enough	assez	"assay"
enquiry desk	les renseignements (mpl)	"roñsaynyuh-moñ"

ABSOLUTE ESSENTIALS

do you have ...?	avez-vous ...?	"avay-voo"
is there ...?	y a-t-il ...?	"ya-teel"
are there ...?	y a-t-il ...?	"ya-teel"
how much is ...?	combien coûte ...?	"koñbyañ koot"

entertainment:

▷ what entertainment is there?	qu'est-ce qu'il y a comme distractions?	"kes-keel ya kom deestraksyoñ"
entrance	l'entrée (f)	"oñtray"
entrance fee	le prix d'entrée	"pree doñtray"
entry visa	le visa	"veeza"
▷ I have an entry visa	j'ai un visa	"zhay uñ veeza"
envelope	l'enveloppe (f)	"oñvlop"
epileptic	épileptique	"aypee-lepteek"
equipment	l'équipement (m)	"aykeepmoñ"
▷ can we rent the equipment?	est-ce qu'on peut louer l'équipement?	"es-koñ puh looay laykeepmoñ"
escalator	l'escalier (m) roulant	"eskalay rooloñ"
especially	surtout	"soortoo"
essential	indispensable	"añdeespoñsabl"
Eurocheque	l'eurochèque (m)	"uhroshekk"
▷ do you take Eurocheques?	est-ce que vous prenez les eurochèques?	"es-kuh voo pruhnay layz uhroshekk"
Europe	l'Europe (f)	"uhrop"
European	européen (m)	"uhropayañ"
	européenne (f)	"uhropayenn"
European Community	la Communauté européenne	"komoonotay uhropayenn"
evening	le soir	"swar"
▷ in the evening	le soir	"luh swar"
▷ what is there to do in the evenings?	qu'est-ce qu'il y a à faire le soir?	"kes-keel ya a fehr luh swar"
▷ what are you doing this evening?	qu'est-ce que vous faites ce soir?	"kes-kuh voo fet suh swar"
▷ an evening meal	un dîner	"uñ deenay"

ABSOLUTE ESSENTIALS		
yes (please)	oui (merci)	"wee (mehrsee)"
no (thank you)	non (merci)	"noñ (mehrsee)"
hello	bonjour	"boñzhoor"
goodbye	au revoir	"o ruhvwar"

every	chaque	"shak"
everyone	tout le monde	"too luh moñd"
everything	tout	"too"
excellent	excellent (*m*)	"ekseloñ"
	excellente (*f*)	"ekseloñt"
▷ **the meal was excellent**	le repas était excellent	"luh ruhpah ayteh ekseloñ"
except	sauf	"sohf"
excess luggage	l'excédent (*m*) de bagages	"eksaydoñ duh bagazh"
exchange¹ *n*	l'échange (*m*)	"ayshoñzh"
to exchange² *vb*	échanger	"ayshoñ-zhay"
▷ **could I exchange this please?**	est-ce que je pourrais échanger ceci s'il vous plaît?	"es-kuh zhuh pooray ayshoñ-zhay suhsee seel voo pleh"
exchange rate	le taux de change	"toh duh shoñzh"
▷ **what is the exchange rate?**	quel est le taux de change?	"kel eh luh toh duh shoñzh"
excursion	l'excursion (*f*)	"ekskoorsyoñ"
▷ **what excursions are there?**	qu'est-ce qu'il y a comme excursions?	"kes-keel ya kom ekskoorsyoñ"
to excuse:		
▷ **excuse me!** (*sorry*)	excusez-moi	"ekskoozay-mwa"
exhaust pipe	le pot d'échappement	"poh dayshapmoñ"
exhibition	l'exposition (*f*)	"ekspozeesyoñ"
exit	la sortie	"sortee"
▷ **where is the exit?**	où est la sortie?	"ooh eh la sortee"
expensive	cher (*m*)	"shehr"
	chère (*f*)	"shehr"

▷ I want something more expensive	je voudrais quelque chose de plus cher	"zhuh voodray kelkuh shohz duh ploo shehr"
▷ it's too expensive	c'est trop cher	"seh troh shehr"
expert	l'expert (m)	"ekspehr"
to expire (ticket, passport)	expirer	"ekspeeray"
express¹ n (train)	le rapide	"rapeed"
express² adv:		
▷ to send a parcel express	envoyer un paquet par exprès	"oñvwayay uñ pakeh par ekspress"
extra:		
▷ extra money	plus d'argent	"ploo darzhoñ"
eye	l'œil (m)	"uhy"
▷ eyes	les yeux	"layz yuh"
▷ I have something in my eye	j'ai quelque chose dans l'œil	"zheh kelkuh shohz doñ luhy"
eye liner	l'eye-liner (m)	"eyeliner"
eye shadow	l'ombre (f) à paupières	"oñbra poh-pyehr"
face	le visage	"veezazh"
face cream	la crème pour le visage	"krem poor luh veezazh"
facilities	les installations (fpl)	"añstalasyoñ"
▷ do you have facilities for the disabled?	est-ce qu'il y a des aménagements prévus pour les handicapés?	"es-keel ya dayz amaynazhmoñ prayvoo poor lay oñdee-kapay"
▷ what facilities do you have here?	qu'est-ce que vous avez comme aménagements?	"kes-kuh vooz avay kom amaynazhmoñ"
▷ what facilities do you have for children?	qu'est-ce qui est prévu pour les enfants?	"kes-kee eh prayvoo poor layz onfoñ"

ABSOLUTE ESSENTIALS

I would like ...	j'aimerais ...	"zhemray"
I need ...	j'ai besoin de ...	"zhay buhswañ duh"
where is ...?	où se trouve ...?	"oo suh troov"
I'm looking for ...	je cherche ...	"zhuh shersh"

▷ **are there facilities for mothers with babies?**	y a-t-il quelque chose de prévu pour les mères accompagnées de bébés?	"ee ya-teel kelkuh shohz duh prayvoo poor lay mehr akoñpanyay duh baybay"
▷ **what sports facilities are there?**	qu'est-ce qu'il y a comme équipements sportifs?	"kes-keel ya kom aykeepmoñ sporteef"

factor:

▷ **factor 8/15 suntan lotion**	lotion solaire indice de protection 8/15	"losyoñ solehr añdees duh proteksyoñ weet/kañz"
factory	l'usine (f)	"oozeen"
▷ **I work in a factory**	je travaille dans une usine	"zhuh travye doñz oon oozeen"
to faint	s'évanouir	"sayvanweer"
▷ **she has fainted**	elle s'est évanouie	"el set ayvanwee"
fair (*fun fair*)	la fête foraine	"fet foren"
to fall	tomber	"toñbay"
family	la famille	"fameey"
famous	célèbre	"saylehbr"
fan (*electric*)	le ventilateur	"voñteelatuhr"
fan belt	la courroie de ventilateur	"koorwa duh voñteelatuhr"
far	loin	"lwañ"
▷ **how far is it to ...?**	à quelle distance se trouve ...?	"ah kel deestoñs suh troov"
▷ **is it far?**	est-ce que c'est loin?	"es-kuh seh lwañ"
fare	le prix du billet	"pree doo beeyeh"
▷ **what is the fare to the town centre?**	ça coûte combien pour aller au centre-ville?	"sa koot koñbyañ poor alay oh soñtr-veel"
farm	la ferme	"fehrm"
farmhouse	la maison de ferme	"mehzoñ duh fehrm"

ABSOLUTE ESSENTIALS

do you have ...?	avez-vous ...?	"avay-voo"
is there ...?	y a-t-il ...?	"ya-teel"
are there ...?	y a-t-il ...?	"ya-teel"
how much is ...?	combien coûte ...?	"koñbyañ koot"

fast	rapide	"rapeed"
▷ **he was driving too fast**	il conduisait trop vite	"eel koñdweezeh troh veet"
fast food	la restauration rapide	"restorasyoñ rapeed"
fat	gros (*m*)	"groh"
	grosse (*f*)	"grohs"
father	le père	"pehr"
fault:		
▷ **it's not my fault**	ce n'était pas de ma faute	"suh naytay pa duh ma foht"
favourite	préféré(e)	"prayfayray"
▷ **what's your favourite drink?**	quelle est votre boisson préférée?	"kel eh votr bwasoñ prayfayray"
fax	le fax	"faks"
▷ **can I send a fax from here?**	est-ce que je peux envoyer un fax d'ici?	"es-kuh zhuh puh oñvwayay uñ faks deesee"
▷ **what is the fax number?**	quel est le numéro de fax?	"kel eh luh noomayro duh faks"
February	février (*m*)	"fayvree-ay"
to feed:		
▷ **where can I feed the baby?**	où est-ce que je peux allaiter le bébé?	"oo es-kuh zhuh puh alaytay luh baybay"
to feel	tâter	"tahtay"
▷ **I don't feel well**	je ne me sens pas bien	"zhuh nuh muh soñ pa byañ"
▷ **I feel sick**	j'ai envie de vomir	"zhay oñvee duh vomeer"
ferry	le ferry	"fayree"
festival	le festival	"festeeval"
to fetch	aller chercher	"alay shehr-shay"

ABSOLUTE ESSENTIALS

yes (please)	oui (merci)	"wee (mehrsee)"
no (thank you)	non (merci)	"noñ (mehrsee)"
hello	bonjour	"boñzhoor"
goodbye	au revoir	"o ruhvwar"

fever	la fièvre	"fee-ehvr"
▷ he has a fever	il a de la fièvre	"eel a duh la fee-ehvr"
few:		
▷ a few	un peu (de ...)	"uñ puh (duh)"
fiancé(e)	le fiancé (m)	"fyoñsay"
	la fiancée (f)	"fyoñsay"
field	le champ	"shoñ"
fifteen	quinze	"kañz"
fifty	cinquante	"sañkoñt"
to fill	remplir	"roñpleer"
to fill up (container)	remplir	"roñpleer"
▷ fill it up, please	le plein, s'il vous plaît	"luh plañ seel voo pleh"
fillet	le filet	"fileh"
filling:		
▷ a filling has come out	un plombage est parti	"uñ ploñbazh eh partee"
▷ could you do a temporary filling?	est-ce que vous pourriez faire un plombage temporaire?	"es-kuh voo pooreeay fehr uñ ploñbazh toñporehr"
film[1] n (for camera)	la pellicule	"payleekool"
(movie)	le film	"feelm"
▷ can you develop this film?	pouvez-vous développer cette pellicule?	"poovay-voo dayvlopay set payleekool"
▷ the film has jammed	la pellicule est bloquée	"la payleekool eh blokay"
▷ I need a colour film for this camera	je voudrais une pellicule couleur pour cet appareil	"zhuh voodray oon payleekool kooluhr poor set aparay"
▷ which film is on at the cinema?	quel film passe actuellement au cinéma?	"kel feelm pass aktwelmoñ oh seenayma"

ABSOLUTE ESSENTIALS

I don't understand	je ne comprends pas	"zhuh nuh koñproñ pa"
I don't speak French	je ne parle pas français	"zhuh nuh parl pa froñsay"
do you speak English?	parlez-vous anglais?	"parlay-voo oñglay"
could you help me?	pourriez-vous m'aider?	"pooreeay-voo mayday"

film

to film² *vb*:		
▷ am I allowed to film here?	est-ce que j'ai le droit de filmer ici?	"es-kuh zhay luh drwa duh feelmay eesee"
filter	le filtre	"feeltr"
filter coffee	le café filtre	"kafay feeltr"
fine¹ *n*	l'amende (*f*)	"amoñd"
▷ how much is the fine?	l'amende est de combien?	"lamoñd eh duh koñbyañ"
fine² *adj*	beau (*m*)	"boh"
	belle (*f*)	"bel"
▷ is it going to be fine?	est-ce qu'il va faire beau?	"es-keel va fehr boh"
to finish	finir	"feeneer"
▷ when does the show finish?	quand finit le spectacle?	"koñ feenee luh spektakl"
▷ when will you have finished?	quand aurez-vous fini?	"koñt oray-voo feenee"
fire	le feu	"fuh"
fire brigade	les pompiers (*mpl*)	"poñpyay"
fire extinguisher	l'extincteur (*m*)	"ekstañktuhr"
firework display	les feux (*mpl*) d'artifice	"fuh darteefees"
fireworks	les feux (*mpl*) d'artifice	"fuh darteefees"
first	premier (*m*)	"pruhmyay"
	première (*f*)	"pruhmyehr"
first aid	les premiers soins (*mpl*)	"pruhmyay swañ"
first class	en première	"oñ pruhmyehr"
▷ a first class return to ...	un aller-retour en première pour ...	"un alay-ruhtoor oñ pruhmyehr poor"
first floor	le premier étage	"pruhmyehr aytazh"

first name	le prénom	"praynoñ"
fish[1] *n*	le poisson	"pwasoñ"
to fish[2] *vb*	pêcher	"pehshay"
▷ **can we fish here?**	est-ce qu'on peut pêcher ici?	"es-koñ puh pehshay eesee"
▷ **can we go fishing?**	est-ce qu'on peut aller à la pêche?	"es-koñ puh alay a la pesh"
▷ **where can I go fishing?**	où est-ce que je peux aller pêcher?	"oo es-kuh zhuh puh alay pehshay"
fishing rod	la canne à pêche	"kann a pesh"
fit[1] *n*	la crise	"kreez"
fit[2] *adj* (*healthy*)	en forme	"oñ form"
to fit[3] *vb*:		
▷ **it doesn't fit**	ça ne me va pas	"sa nuh muh va pa"
five	cinq	"sañk"
to fix (*mend*)	réparer	"rayparay"
▷ **where can I get this fixed?**	où est-ce que je peux faire réparer ceci?	"oo es-kuh zhuh puh fehr rayparay suhsee"
fizzy (*soft drink, water*)	gazeux (*m*)	"gazuh"
	gazeuse (*f*)	"gazuhz"
(*wine*)	pétillant (*m*)	"payteeyoñ"
	pétillante (*f*)	"payteeyoñt"
▷ **a fizzy drink**	une boisson gazeuse	"oon bwasoñ gazuhz"
flash	le flash	"flash"
▷ **the flash is not working**	le flash ne marche pas	"luh flash nuh marsh pa"
flask	la thermos	"tehrmos"
▷ **a flask of coffee**	une thermos de café	"oon tehrmos duh kafay"
flat (*apartment*)	l'appartement (*m*)	"apartuhmoñ"
flat tyre	la crevaison	"kruhvehzoñ"

flavour	le parfum	"parfañ"
▷ **what flavours do you have?**	quels parfums avez-vous?	"kel parfañ avay-voo"
flight	le vol	"vol"
▷ **I've missed my flight**	j'ai raté mon vol	"zhay ratay moñ vol"
▷ **my flight has been delayed**	mon vol a du retard	"moñ vol a doo ruhtar"
▷ **are there any cheap flights?**	est-ce qu'il y a des vols à prix réduits?	"es-keel ya day vol a pree raydwee"
flint	le silex	"seelex"
flippers	les palmes (fpl)	"palm"
flooded:		
▷ **the bathroom is flooded**	la salle de bain est inondée	"la sal duh bañ et inoñday"
floor (of building)	l'étage (m)	"aytazh"
(of room)	le plancher	"ploñshay"
▷ **what floor is it on?**	à quel étage est-ce que ça se trouve?	"a kel aytazh es-kuh sa suh troov"
▷ **on the top floor**	au dernier étage	"oh dehrnyehr aytazh"
flour	la farine	"fareen"
▷ **plain flour**	farine ordinaire	"fareen ordeenehr"
▷ **self-raising flour**	farine avec levure incorporée	"fareen avek lvoor añkorporay"
▷ **wholemeal flour**	farine complète	"fareen koñplett"
flower	la fleur	"fluhr"
▷ **a bunch/bouquet of flowers**	un bouquet de fleurs	"uñ bookeh duh fluhr"
flu	la grippe	"greep"
▷ **I've got flu**	j'ai la grippe	"zhay la greep"
to flush:		
▷ **the toilet won't flush**	la chasse d'eau ne marche pas	"la shas doh nuh marsh pa"

ABSOLUTE ESSENTIALS

yes (please)	oui (merci)	"wee (mehrsee)"
no (thank you)	non (merci)	"noñ (mehrsee)"
hello	bonjour	"boñzhoor"
goodbye	au revoir	"o ruhvwar"

fork

fly (*insect*)	la mouche	"moosh"
flying:		
▷ **I hate flying**	je déteste prendre l'avion	"zhuh daytest proñdr lavyoñ"
fly sheet	le double toit	"doobl twa"
fog	le brouillard	"brooyar"
foggy:		
▷ **it's foggy**	il y a du brouillard	"eel ya doo brooyar"
to follow	suivre	"sweevr"
▷ **follow me!**	suivez-moi	"sweevay-mwa"
food	la nourriture	"nooreetoor"
▷ **where is the food department?**	où est le rayon d'alimentation?	"oo eh luh rayoñ daleemoñtasyoñ"
food poisoning	l'intoxication (*f*) alimentaire	"añtokseekasyoñ aleemoñtehr"
foot (*part of body*) (*metric equiv = 0.30 m*)	le pied le pied	"pyay" "pyay"
football (*sport*) (*ball*)	le football le ballon de football	"footbal" "baloñ duh footbal"
▷ **to play football**	faire une partie de football	"fehr oon partee duh footbal"
for	pour	"poor"
foreign	étranger (*m*) étrangère (*f*)	"aytroñ-zhay" "aytroñ-zyehr"
forest	la forêt	"foray"
to forget	oublier	"oobl-yay"
▷ **I've forgotten my passport/the key**	j'ai oublié mon passeport/la clé	"zhay oobl-yay moñ passpor/la klay"
fork	la fourchette	"foorshett"
(*in road*)	l'embranchement (*m*)	"oñbroñshmoñ"

ABSOLUTE ESSENTIALS

I don't understand	je ne comprends pas	"zhuh nuh koñproñ pa"
I don't speak French	je ne parle pas français	"zhuh nuh parl pa froñsay"
do you speak English?	parlez-vous anglais?	"parlay-voo oñglay"
could you help me?	pourriez-vous m'aider?	"pooreeay-voo mayday"

fortnight

fortnight	la quinzaine	"kañzen"
forty	quarante	"karoñt"
fountain	la fontaine	"foñten"
four	quatre	"katr"
fourteen	quatorze	"katorz"
France	la France	"froñs"
free (*not occupied*)	libre	"leebr"
(*costing nothing*)	gratuit (*m*)	"gratwee"
	gratuite (*f*)	"gratweet"
▷ **I am free tomorrow morning/for lunch**	je suis libre demain matin/à l'heure du déjeuner	"zhuh swee libr duhmañ matañ/a luhr doo dayzhuhnay"
▷ **is this seat free?**	est-ce que cette place est libre?	"es-kuh set plas eh leebr"
freezer	le congélateur	"koñzhaylatuhr"
French	français (*m*)	"froñsay"
	française (*f*)	"froñsez"
▷ **I don't speak French**	je ne parle pas français	"zhuh nuh parl pa froñsay"
French beans	les haricots verts	"areekoh vehr"
frequent	fréquent (*m*)	"fraykoñ"
	fréquente (*f*)	"fraykoñt"
▷ **how frequent are the buses?**	les bus passent tous les combien de temps?	"lay boos pass too lay koñbyañ duh toñ"
fresh	frais (*m*)	"freh"
	fraîche (*f*)	"fresh"
▷ **are the vegetables fresh or frozen?**	les légumes sont-ils frais ou congelés?	"lay laygoom soñt-eel freh oo koñzh-lay"
fresh air	le grand air	"groñd ehr"
Friday	vendredi (*m*)	"voñdruhdee"

fridge	le frigo	"freego"
fried	frit (*m*)	"free"
	frite (*f*)	"freet"
friend	l'ami (*m*)	"amee"
	l'amie (*f*)	"amee"
from	de	"duh"
▷ **I want to stay three nights from ... till ...**	je désire rester trois nuits du ... au ...	"zhuh dayzeer restay trwa nwee doo ... oh"
front	le devant	"duhvoñ"
frozen (*food*)	surgelé(e)	"soor-zhuhlay"
fruit	le fruit	"frwee"
fruit juice	le jus de fruit	"zhoo duh frwee"
fruit salad	la salade de fruits	"salad duh frwee"
frying pan	la poêle	"pwal"
fuel	le combustible	"koñboosteebl"
fuel pump	la pompe d'alimentation	"poñp daleemoñtasyoñ"
full	plein (*m*)	"plañ"
	pleine (*f*)	"plenn"
▷ **I'm full (up)**	j'ai assez mangé	"zhay asay moñzhay"
full board	la pension complète	"poñsyoñ koñplett"
funny (*amusing*)	amusant (*m*)	"amoozoñ"
	amusante (*f*)	"amoozoñt"
fur	la fourrure	"fooroor"
fuse	le fusible	"foozeebl"
▷ **a fuse has blown**	un fusible a sauté	"uñ foozeebl a sotay"
▷ **can you mend a fuse?**	pouvez-vous changer un fusible?	"poovay-voo shoñzhay uñ foozeebl"
gallery	la galerie	"galree"

ABSOLUTE ESSENTIALS

do you have ...?	avez-vous ...?	"avay-voo"
is there ...?	y a-t-il ...?	"ya-teel"
are there ...?	y a-t-il ...?	"ya-teel"
how much is ...?	combien coûte ...?	"koñbyañ koot"

gallon	≈ 5 litres	"sañk leetr"
gambling	le jeu	"zhuh"
game	le jeu	"zhuh"
▷ a game of chess	une partie d'échecs	"oon partee dayshek"
garage	le garage	"garazh"
▷ can you tow me to a garage?	est-ce que vous pouvez me remorquer jusqu'à un garage?	"es-kuh voo poovay muh ruhmorkay zhooska uñ garazh"
garden	le jardin	"zhardañ"
▷ can we visit the gardens?	est-ce que nous pouvons visiter les jardins?	"es-kuh noo poovoñ veezeetay lay zhardañ"
garlic	l'ail (m)	"eye"
▷ is there any garlic in it?	est-ce que cela contient de l'ail?	"es-kuh sla koñtyañ duh lye"
gas	le gaz	"gaz"
▷ I can smell gas	ça sent le gaz	"sa soñ luh gaz"
gas cylinder	la bouteille de gaz	"bootay duh gaz"
gear	la vitesse	"veetess"
▷ first/third gear	première/troisième vitesse	"pruhmyehr/trwaz-yem veetess"
Geneva	Genève	"zhu-nehv"
gentleman	le monsieur	"muhsyuh"
gents	les toilettes (fpl)	"twalett"
▷ where is the gents?	où sont les toilettes pour hommes?	"oo soñ les twalett poor om"
genuine	authentique	"otoñteek"
German	allemand (m) allemande (f)	"almoñ" "almoñd"
German measles	la rubéole	"roobayol"

<u>ABSOLUTE ESSENTIALS</u>

yes (please)	oui (merci)	"wee (mehrsee)"
no (thank you)	non (merci)	"noñ (mehrsee)"
hello	bonjour	"boñzhoor"
goodbye	au revoir	"o ruhvwar"

Germany	l'Allemagne (f)	"almanyuh"
to **get** (obtain)	obtenir	"optneer"
▷ **please tell me when we get to ...**	dites-moi, s'il vous plaît, lorsque nous serons à ...	"deetmwa seel voo pleh lorskuh noo sroñ a"
▷ **I must get there by 8 o'clock**	je dois y être à 8 heures au plus tard	"zhuh dwaz ee etr a weet uhr oh ploo tar"
▷ **please get me a taxi**	commandez-moi un taxi s'il vous plaît	"komoñday-mwa uñ taxi seel voo pleh"
▷ **when do we get back?**	quand est-ce que nous serons de retour?	"koñt es-kuh noo sroñ duh ruhtoor"
to **get into** (vehicle)	monter dans	"moñtay doñ"
to **get off** (bus etc)	descendre de	"dessoñdr duh"
▷ **where do I get off?**	où est-ce que je descends?	"oo es-kuh zhuh dessoñ"
▷ **will you tell me where to get off?**	est-ce que vous pouvez me dire quand je dois descendre?	"es-kuh voo poovay muh deer koñ zhuh dwa dessoñdr"
gift	le cadeau	"kado"
gift shop	la boutique de souvenirs	"booteek duh soovneer"
to **giftwrap**:		
▷ **please giftwrap it**	faites-moi un emballage cadeau s'il vous plaît	"fet-mwa un oñbalazh kado seel voo pleh"
gin	le gin	"djeen"
▷ **I'll have a gin and tonic, please**	un gin-tonic, s'il vous plaît	"uñ djeen-toneek seel voo pleh"
girl	la fille	"feey"
girlfriend	la petite amie	"puhteet ami"
to **give**	donner	"donay"
to **give way**	laisser la priorité	"lessay la preeoreetay"

ABSOLUTE ESSENTIALS

I don't understand	je ne comprends pas	"zhuh nuh koñproñ pa"
I don't speak French	je ne parle pas français	"zhuh nuh parl pa froñsay"
do you speak English?	parlez-vous anglais?	"parlay-voo oñglay"
could you help me?	pourriez-vous m'aider?	"pooreeay-voo mayday"

▷ **he did not give way**	il n'a pas laissé la priorité	"eel na pa lessay la preeoreetay"
glass	le verre	"vehr"
▷ **a glass of lemonade, please**	un verre de limonade, s'il vous plaît	"uñ vehr duh leemonad seel voo pleh"
▷ **broken glass**	des verres brisés	"day vehr breezay"
glasses	les lunettes (fpl)	"loonett"
▷ **can you repair my glasses?**	est-ce que vous pouvez réparer mes lunettes?	"es-kuh vooz poovay rayparay may loonett"
gloves	les gants (mpl)	"goñ"
glue	la colle	"kol"
gluten	le gluten	"glootenn"
to go	aller	"alay"

I go	je vais	"zhuh vay"
you go	vous allez	"vooz alay"
he/she/it goes	il/elle va	"eel/el va"
we go	nous allons	"nooz aloñ"
they go	ils/elles vont	"eel/el voñ"

▷ **I'm going to the beach**	je vais à la plage	"zhuh vayz a la plazh"
▷ **you go on ahead**	allez donc en avant	"alay donk on avoñ"
to go back	retourner	"ruhtoornay"
▷ **I must go back now**	je dois retourner maintenant	"zhuh dwa ruhtoornay mañtnoñ"
to go down (downstairs etc)	descendre	"dessoñdr"
to go in	entrer	"oñtray"
to go out (leave)	sortir	"sorteer"
goggles	les lunettes (fpl) protectrices	"loonett protektrees"

ABSOLUTE ESSENTIALS		
I would like ...	j'aimerais ...	"zhemray"
I need ...	j'ai besoin de ...	"zhay buhswañ duh"
where is ...?	où se trouve ...?	"oo suh troov"
I'm looking for ...	je cherche ...	"zhuh shersh"

(for swimming)	les lunettes (fpl) de plongée	"loonett duh ploñzhay"
gold	l'or (m)	"or"
gold-plated	plaqué(e) or	"plakay or"
golf	le golf	"golf"
▷ where can we play golf?	où est-ce qu'on peut jouer au golf?	"oo es-koñ puh zhooay oh golf"
golf ball	la balle de golf	"bal duh golf"
golf club (stick, association)	le club de golf	"klub duh golf"
golf course	le terrain de golf	"tehrañ duh golf"
▷ is there a public golf course near here?	est-ce qu'il y a un terrain de golf public près d'ici?	"es-keel ya uñ tehrañ duh golf poobleek preh deesee"
good	bon (m)	"boñ"
	bonne (f)	"bonn"
good afternoon	bonjour	"boñzhoor"
goodbye	au revoir	"o ruhvwar"
good evening	bonsoir	"boñswar"
Good Friday	le Vendredi saint	"voñdruhdee sañ"
good-looking	beau (m)	"bo"
	belle (f)	"bel"
good morning	bonjour	"boñzhoor"
good night	bonne nuit	"bon nwee"
goose	l'oie (f)	"wah"
gram	le gramme	"gram"
▷ 500 grams of mince meat	500 grammes de viande hachée	"sañsoñ gram duh vyoñd ashay"
granddaughter	la petite-fille	"puhteetfeey"

ABSOLUTE ESSENTIALS

do you have ...?	avez-vous ...?	"avay-voo"
is there ...?	y a-t-il ...?	"ya-teel"
are there ...?	y a-t-il ...?	"ya-teel"
how much is ...?	combien coûte ...?	"koñbyañ koot"

grandfather	le grand-père	"groñpehr"
grandmother	la grand-mère	"groñmehr"
grandson	le petit-fils	puhteefees
grapefruit	le pamplemousse	"poñpluhmoos"
grapefruit juice	le jus de pamplemousse	"zhoo duh poñpluhmoos"
grapes	les raisins (*mpl*)	"rayzañ"
▷ **a bunch of grapes**	une grappe de raisins	"oon grap duh rayzañ"
▷ **seedless grapes**	des raisins sans pépins	"day rayzañ soñ paypañ"
grass	l'herbe (*f*)	"ehrb"
gravy	la sauce (au jus de viande)	"sohs (oh zhoo duh vyoñd)"
greasy	gras (*m*)	"gra"
	grasse (*f*)	"gras"
▷ **the food is very greasy**	la cuisine est très grasse	"la kweezeen eh treh grass"
▷ **shampoo for greasy hair**	du shampooing pour cheveux gras	"doo shoñpwañ poor shvuh gra"
Greece	la Grèce	"gres"
Greek	grec(que)	"grek"
green	vert (*m*)	"vehr"
	verte (*f*)	"vehrt"
green card	la carte verte	"kart vehrt"
green pepper	le poivron vert	"pwavroñ vehr"
grey	gris (*m*)	"gree"
	grise (*f*)	"greez"
grilled	grillé(e)	"greeyay"
grocer's	l'épicerie (*f*)	"aypeesree"
ground	la terre	"tehr"

ABSOLUTE ESSENTIALS

yes (please)	oui (merci)	"wee (mehrsee)"
no (thank you)	non (merci)	"noñ (mehrsee)"
hello	bonjour	"boñzhoor"
goodbye	au revoir	"o ruhvwar"

ground floor	le rez-de-chaussée	"ray-duh-shohsay"
▷ could I have a room on the ground floor?	est-ce que je pourrais avoir une chambre au rez-de-chaussée?	"es-kuh zhuh pooray avwar oon shoñbr oh ray-duh-shohsay"
groundsheet	le tapis de sol	"tapee duh sol"
group	le groupe	"groop"
▷ do you give discounts for groups?	est-ce que vous accordez des remises aux groupes?	"es-kuh vooz akorday day ruhmeez oh groop"
group passport	le passeport de groupe	"passpor duh groop"
guarantee	la garantie	"garoñtee"
▷ it's still under guarantee	c'est encore sous garantie	"set oñkor soo garoñtee"
▷ a five-year guarantee	une garantie de cinq ans	"oon garoñtee duh sañk oñ"
guard (*on train*)	le chef de train	"shef duh trañ"
▷ have you seen the guard?	est-ce que vous avez vu le chef de train?	"es-kuh vooz avay voo luh shef duh trañ"
guest (*house guest*)	l'invité (*m*) l'invitée (*f*)	"añveetay" "añveetay"
(*in hotel*)	le client (*m*) la cliente (*f*)	"klee-oñ" "klee-oñt"
guesthouse	la pension	"poñsyoñ"
guide	le guide	"geed"
▷ is there an English-speaking guide?	y a-t-il un guide qui parle anglais?	"ya-teel un geed kee parl oñglay"
guidebook	le guide	"geed"
▷ do you have a guidebook in English?	est-ce que vous avez un guide touristique en anglais?	"es-kuh vooz avay uñ geed tooreesteek on oñglay"

ABSOLUTE ESSENTIALS

I don't understand	je ne comprends pas	"zhuh nuh koñproñ pa"
I don't speak French	je ne parle pas français	"zhuh nuh parl pa froñsay"
do you speak English?	parlez-vous anglais?	"parlay-voo oñglay"
could you help me?	pourriez-vous m'aider?	"pooreeay-voo mayday"

▷ do you have a guidebook to the cathedral?	est-ce que vous avez un guide sur la cathédrale?	"es-kuh vooz avay uñ geed soor la kataydral"
guided tour	la visite guidée	"veezeet geeday"
▷ what time does the guided tour begin?	à quelle heure commence la visite guidée?	"a kel uhr komoñs la veezeet geeday"
gum	la gencive	"zhoñseev"
▷ my gums are bleeding/sore	mes gencives saignent/ me font mal	"may zhoñseev saynyuh/ muh foñ mal"
gym (place) (sport)	le gymnase la gymnastique	"zheemnaz" "zheemnasteek"
gym shoes	les chaussures (fpl) de tennis	"shohsoor duh tenees"
haddock	l'églefin (m)	"aygluhfañ"
haemorrhoids	les hémorroïdes (fpl)	"aymoro-eed"
▷ I need something for haemorrhoids	il me faut quelque chose pour les hémorroïdes	"eel muh foh kelkuh shohz poor layz aymoro-eed"
hair	les cheveux (mpl)	"shvuh"
▷ my hair is naturally curly	mes cheveux frisent naturellement	"may shvuh freez natoorelmoñ"
▷ I have greasy/dry hair	j'ai les cheveux gras/ secs	"zhay lay shvuh gra/sek"
hairbrush	la brosse à cheveux	"bros a shvuh"
haircut	la coupe de cheveux	"koop duh shvuh"
hairdresser	le coiffeur (m) la coiffeuse (f)	"kwafuhr" "kwafuz"
hair dryer	le sèche-cheveux	"sesh-shvuh"
hairgrip	la pince à cheveux	"pañs a shvuh"
hair spray	la laque	"lak"

hake	le colin	"kolañ"
halal	halal	"alall"
half	la moitié	"mwatyay"
▷ **half past two/three**	deux/trois heures et demie	"duh/trwaz uhr ay duhmee"
half board	la demi-pension	"duhmee-poñsyoñ"
half bottle	la demi-bouteille	"duhmee-bootay"
half fare	le demi-tarif	"duhmee-tareef"
half-price	à moitié prix	"a mwatyay pree"
ham	le jambon	"zhoñboñ"
hamburger	le hamburger	"oñboorgehr"
hand	la main	"mañ"
handbag	le sac à main	"sak a mañ"
▷ **my handbag's been stolen**	on m'a volé mon sac à main	"oñ ma volay moñ sak a mañ"
handbrake	le frein à main	"frañ a mañ"
handicap (*golf*):		
▷ **my handicap is ...**	je suis handicapé de ...	"zhuh swee oñdee-kapay duh"
▷ **what's your handicap?**	de quoi êtes-vous handicapé?	"duh kwa et voo oñdee-kapay"
handicapped	handicapé(e)	"oñdee-kapay"
handkerchief	le mouchoir	"mooshwar"
handle	la poignée	"pwanyay"
▷ **the handle has come off**	la poignée s'est détachée	"la pwanyay seh daytashay"
hand luggage	les bagages (*mpl*) à main	"bagazh a mañ"
handmade	fait main	"feh mañ"

▷ **is this handmade?**	c'est fait main?	"seh feh mañ"
hang-glider	le deltaplane	"deltaplan"
hang-gliding:		
▷ **I'd like to go hang-gliding**	j'aimerais faire du deltaplane	"zhemray fehr doo deltaplan"
hangover	la gueule de bois	"gul duh bwa"
to **happen**	arriver	"areevay"
▷ **what happened?**	qu'est-ce qui s'est passé?	"kes-kee seh passay"
▷ **when did it happen?**	quand est-ce que ça s'est passé?	"koñt es-kuh sa seh passay"
happy	heureux (m)	"uruh"
	heureuse (f)	"uruz"
▷ **I'm not happy with ...**	je ne suis pas satisfait de ...	"zhuh nuh swee pa sateesfay duh"
harbour	le port	"por"
hard	dur(e)	"door"
hat	le chapeau	"shapo"
to **have**	avoir	"avwar"

I have	j'ai	"zhay"
you have	vous avez	"vooz avay"
he/she/it has	il/elle a	"eel/el a"
we have	nous avons	"nooz avoñ"
they have	ils/elles ont	"eelz/elz oñ"

▷ **do you have ...?**	est-ce que vous avez ...?	"es-kuh vooz avay"
hay fever	le rhume des foins	"room day fwañ"
hazelnut	la noisette	"nwazett"
he	il	"eel"

ABSOLUTE ESSENTIALS

yes (please)	oui (merci)	"wee (mehrsee)"
no (thank you)	non (merci)	"noñ (mehrsee)"
hello	bonjour	"boñzhoor"
goodbye	au revoir	"o ruhvwar"

head	la tête	"tet"
headache	le mal de tête	"mal duh tet"
▷ **I have a headache**	j'ai mal à la tête	"zhay mal a la tet"
▷ **I want something for a headache**	je voudrais quelque chose pour les maux de tête	"zhuh voodray kelkuh shohz poor leh moh duh tet"
headlights	les phares (*mpl*)	"far"
head waiter	le maître d'hôtel	"mehtr dotell"
health food shop	le magasin de diététique	"magazañ duh deeay-tayteek"
to **hear**	entendre	"oñtoñdr"
heart	le cœur	"kuhr"
heart attack	la crise cardiaque	"kreez kardyak"
heart condition:		
▷ **I have a heart condition**	je suis malade du cœur	"zhuh swee malad doo kuhr"
heater	l'appareil (*m*) de chauffage	"aparay duh shofazh"
▷ **the heater isn't working**	le chauffage ne marche pas	"luh shofazh nuh marsh pa"
heating	le chauffage	"shofazh"
▷ **I can't turn the heating off/on**	je ne peux pas fermer/ ouvrir le chauffage	"zhuh nuh puh pa fehrmay/oovreer luh shofazh"
heavy	lourd (*m*)	"loor"
	lourde (*f*)	"loord"
▷ **this is too heavy**	c'est trop lourd	"seh troh loor"
hello	bonjour	"boñzhoor"
(*on telephone*)	allô	"alo"
help¹ *n*	l'aide (*f*)	"ed"

ABSOLUTE ESSENTIALS

I don't understand	je ne comprends pas	"zhuh nuh koñproñ pa"
I don't speak French	je ne parle pas français	"zhuh nuh parl pa froñsay"
do you speak English?	parlez-vous anglais?	"parlay-voo oñglay"
could you help me?	pourriez-vous m'aider?	"pooreeay-voo mayday"

▷ **help!**	au secours!	"oh skoor"
▷ **fetch help quickly!**	allez chercher de l'aide, vite!	"alay shershay duh led veet"
to help² *vb*	aider	"ayday"
▷ **can you help me?**	pouvez-vous m'aider?	"poovay-voo mayday"
▷ **help yourself!**	servez-vous!	"sehrvay-voo"
herb	l'herbe (f)	"ehrb"
her:		
▷ **her father**	son père	"soñ pehr"
▷ **her mother**	sa mère	"sa mehr"
▷ **her parents**	ses parents	"say paroñ"
here	ici	"eesee"
▷ **here you are!**	voilà!	"vwala"
herring	le hareng	"arañ"
hers	le sien	"syen"
high	haut (m)	"oh"
	haute (f)	"oht"
▷ **how high is it?**	quelle en est la hauteur?	"kel on eh la otuhr"
▷ **200 metres high**	200 mètres de hauteur	"duhsoñ metr duh otuhr"
high blood pressure	la tension	"toñsyoñ"
high chair	la chaise haute	"shez oht"
highlights (*in hair*)	les mèches (fpl)	"mesh"
high tide	la marée haute	"maray oht"
▷ **when is high tide?**	quand est-ce que la marée est haute?	"koñt es-kuh la maray eh oht"
hill	la colline	"koleen"
hill walking	la randonnée en montagne	"roñdonay oñ moñtanyuh"
to hire	louer	"looay"

ABSOLUTE ESSENTIALS		
I would like ...	j'aimerais ...	"zhemray"
I need ...	j'ai besoin de ...	"zhay buhswoñ duh"
where is ...?	où se trouve ...?	"oo suh troov"
I'm looking for ...	je cherche ...	"zhuh shersh"

| ▷ I want to hire a car | je voudrais louer une voiture | "zhuh voodray looay oon vwatoor" |
| ▷ is it possible to hire a deck chair/a boat? | est-ce qu'il est possible de louer une chaise longue/un bateau? | "es-keel eh poseebl duh looay oon shez loñg/uñ bato" |

his¹ *adj:*
▷ his father	son père	"soñ pehr"
▷ his mother	sa mère	"sa mehr"
▷ his parents	ses parents	"say paroñ"

his² *pron* | le sien | "syen" |

to hit | frapper | "frapay" |

to hitchhike | faire de l'auto-stop | "fehr duh lohtostop" |

HIV negative | séronégatif (*m*) | "sayro-naygateef" |
| | séronégative (*f*) | "sayro-naygateev" |

HIV positive | séropositif (*m*) | "sayro-pozeeteef" |
| | séropositive (*f*) | "sayro-pozeeteev" |

to hold | tenir | "tneer" |
| (*contain*) | contenir | "koñtneer" |
| ▷ could you hold this for me? | est-ce que vous pouvez tenir cela pour moi? | "es-kuh voo poovay tneer sla poor mwa" |

hold-up (*traffic jam*) | l'embouteillage (*m*) | "oñbootay-yazh" |
| ▷ what is causing the hold-up? | quelle est la cause du bouchon? | "kel eh la kohz doo booshoñ" |

hole | le trou | "troo" |

holiday | les vacances (*fpl*) | "vakoñs" |
| ▷ on holiday | en vacances | "oñ vakoñs" |
| ▷ I'm on holiday here | je suis en vacances ici | "zhuh sweez oñ vakoñs eesee" |

holiday resort | le centre de vacances | "soñtr duh vakoñs" |

holiday romance | l'aventure (*f*) de vacances | "avoñtoor duh vakoñs" |

ABSOLUTE ESSENTIALS

do you have ...?	avez-vous ...?	"avay-voo"
is there ...?	y a-t-il ...?	"ya-teel"
are there ...?	y a-t-il ...?	"ya-teel"
how much is ...?	combien coûte ...?	"koñbyañ koot"

home	la maison	"mehzoñ"
▷ **when do you go home?**	quand est-ce que vous rentrez?	"koñt es-kuh voo roñtray"
▷ **I'm going home tomorrow/on Tuesday**	je rentre demain/mardi	"zhuh roñtr duhmañ/ mardee"
▷ **I want to go home**	je veux rentrer chez moi	"zhuh vuh roñtray shay mwa"
homesick:		
▷ **to be homesick**	avoir le mal du pays	"avwar luh mal doo payee"
honey	le miel	"myel"
honeymoon	la lune de miel	"loon duh myel"
▷ **we are on our honeymoon**	c'est notre lune de miel	"seh notr loon duh myel"
to **hope**	espérer	"espayray"
▷ **I hope so/not**	j'espère que oui/que non	"zhehspehr kwee/kuh noñ"
hors d'œuvre	le hors d'œuvre	"or duhvr"
horse	le cheval	"shval"
horse riding	l'équitation (f)	"aykeetasyoñ"
▷ **to go horse riding**	faire de l'équitation	"fehr duh laykeetasyoñ"
hose	la durit	"dooreet"
hospital	l'hôpital (m)	"opeetal"
▷ **we must get him to hospital**	il faut le transporter à l'hôpital	"eel foh luh troñsportay a lopeetal"
▷ **where's the nearest hospital?**	où est l'hôpital le plus proche?	"oo eh lopeetal luh ploo prosh"
hot	chaud (m)	"shoh"
	chaude (f)	"shohd"
▷ **I'm hot**	j'ai chaud	"zhay shoh"
▷ **it's hot** (weather)	il fait chaud	"eel feh shoh"
▷ **a hot curry**	un curry très épicé	"uñ kooree trayz aypeesay"

hotel	l'hôtel (*m*)	"otell"
▷ **can you recommend a (cheap) hotel?**	pouvez-vous recommander un hôtel (pas cher)?	"poovay-voo ruhkomoñday un otell (pa shehr)"
hour	l'heure (*f*)	"uhr"
▷ **an hour ago**	il y a une heure	"eel ya oon uhr"
▷ **in 2 hours time**	dans 2 heures	"doñ duhz uhr"
▷ **the journey takes 2 hours**	il y a 2 heures de voyage	"eel ya duhz uhr duh vwayazh"
house	la maison	"mehzoñ"
house wine	la réserve du patron	"rayzehrv doo patroñ"
▷ **a bottle/carafe of house wine**	une bouteille/carafe de la réserve du patron	"oon bootay/karaf duh la raysehrv doo patroñ"
hovercraft	l'aéroglisseur (*m*)	"a-ehrogleesuhr"
▷ **we came by hovercraft**	nous sommes venus en aéroglisseur	"noo som vnoo on a-ehrogleesuhr"
how (*in what way*)	comment	"komoñ"
▷ **how are you?**	comment allez-vous?	"komoñt alay-voo"
▷ **how are you feeling now?**	comment vous sentez-vous maintenant?	"komoñ voo soñtay-voo mañtnoñ"
▷ **how much?**	combien?	"koñbyañ"
▷ **how many?**	combien?	"koñbyañ"
hundred	cent	"soñ"
▷ **about a hundred people**	une centaine de personnes	"oon soñten duh pehrson"
hungry:		
▷ **I am hungry**	j'ai faim	"zhay fañ"
hurry:		
▷ **I'm in a hurry**	je suis pressé	"zhuh swee pressay"
to hurt	blesser	"blassay"
▷ **he is hurt**	il est blessé	"eel eh blessay"

ABSOLUTE ESSENTIALS

I don't understand	je ne comprends pas	"zhuh nuh koñproñ pa"
I don't speak French	je ne parle pas français	"zhuh nuh parl pa froñsay"
do you speak English?	parlez-vous anglais?	"parlay-voo oñglay"
could you help me?	pourriez-vous m'aider?	"pooreeay-voo mayday"

▷ **my back hurts**	j'ai mal au dos	"zhay mal oh doh"
▷ **he has hurt himself**	il s'est fait mal	"eel seh feh mal"
▷ **he has hurt his leg/ arm**	il s'est blessé à la jambe/au bras	"eel seh blessay a la zhoñb/oh bra"
husband	le mari	"maree"
hydrofoil	l'hydrofoil (m)	"eedrofoil"
I	je	"zhuh"
ice	la glace	"glas"
ice cream	la glace	"glas"
iced	glacé(e)	"glassay"
ice lolly	l'esquimau ® (m)	"eskeemo"
ice rink	la patinoire	"pateenwar"
ice skates	les patins (mpl) à glace	"patañ a glas"
ice skating	le patinage sur glace	"pateenazh soor glas"
▷ **can we go ice skating?**	est-ce qu'on peut faire du patinage sur glace?	"es-koñ puh fehr doo pateenazh soor glas"
icy	glacé(e)	"glassay"
▷ **icy roads**	des routes verglacées	"day root vehrglassay"
if	si	"see"
ignition	l'allumage (m)	"aloomazh"
ill	malade	"malad"
immediately	immédiatement	"eemaydyatmoñ"
important	important (m) importante (f)	"añportoñ" "añportoñt"
impossible	impossible	"añposeebl"
in	dans	"doñ"
inch (metric equiv = 2.54 cm)	le pouce	"poos"

included	compris (*m*)	"koñpree"
	comprise (*f*)	"koñpreez"
▷ **is service included?**	est-ce que le service est compris?	"es-kuh luh sehrvees eh koñpree"
indicator (*on car*)	le clignotant	"kleenyotoñ"
▷ **the indicator isn't working**	le clignotant ne marche pas	"luh kleenyotoñ nuh marsh pa"
indigestion	l'indigestion (*f*)	"añdee-zhestyoñ"
indoor:		
▷ **indoor swimming pool**	piscine couverte	"peeseen koovehrt"
▷ **indoor tennis**	tennis couvert	"tennis koovehr"
indoors	à l'intérieur	"a lañtayree-uhr"
infectious	infectieux (*m*)	"añfeksyuh"
	infectieuse (*f*)	"añfeksyuz"
▷ **is it infectious?**	est-ce que c'est contagieux?	"es-kuh seh koñta-zhuh"
information.	les renseignements (*mpl*)	"roñsaynyuh-moñ"
▷ **I'd like some information about ...**	je voudrais des renseignements sur ...	"zhuh voodray day roñsaynyuh-moñ soor"
information office	le bureau de renseignements	"booro duh roñsaynyuh-moñ"
injection	la piqûre	"peekoor"
▷ **please give me an injection**	vous voulez bien me faire une piqûre	"voo voolay byañ muh fehr oon peekoor"
injured	blessé(e)	"blessay"
▷ **he is seriously injured**	il est sérieusement blessé	"eel eh say-ryuzmoñ blessay"
ink	l'encre (*f*)	"oñkr"
insect	l'insecte (*m*)	"añsekt"
insect bite	la piqûre d'insecte	"peekoor dañsekt"

ABSOLUTE ESSENTIALS

do you have ...?	avez-vous ...?	"avay-voo"
is there ...?	y a-t-il ...?	"ya-teel"
are there ...?	y a-t-il ...?	"ya-teel"
how much is ...?	combien coûte ...?	"koñbyañ koot"

insect repellent	la crème anti-insecte	"krem oñtee-añsekt"
inside	l'intérieur (m)	"añtayree-uhr"
▷ inside the car	dans la voiture	"doñ la vwatoor"
▷ let's go inside	allons à l'intérieur	"aloñz a lañtayree-uhr"
instant coffee	le café instantané	"kafay añstoñtanay"
instead of	au lieu de	"oh lyuh duh"
instructor	le moniteur	"moneetuhr"
insulin	l'insuline (f)	"añsooleen"
insurance	l'assurance (f)	"asooroñs"
▷ will the insurance pay for it?	est-ce que l'assurance couvrira cela?	"es-kuh lasooroñs koovreera sla"
insurance certificate	la carte d'assurance (f)	"kart dasooroñs"
▷ can I see your insurance certificate, please?	est-ce que je peux voir votre carte d'assurance, s'il vous plaît?	"es-kuh zhuh puh vwar votre kart dasooroñs seel voo pleh"
to insure:		
▷ can I insure my luggage?	est-ce que je peux assurer mes bagages?	"es-kuh zhuh puh asooray may bagazh"
interesting	intéressant (m) intéressante (f)	"añtayrehsoñ" "añtayrehsoñt"
▷ can you suggest somewhere interesting to go?	pouvez-vous suggérer un endroit intéressant à visiter?	"poovay-voo soo-zhayray un oñdrwa añtayrehsoñ a veezeetay"
international	international(e)	"añtehrnasyonal"
interpreter	l'interprète (m/f)	"añtehrpret"
▷ could you act as an interpreter for us please?	est-ce que vous pourriez nous servir d'interprète s'il vous plaît?	"es-kuh voo pooryay noo sehrveer dañtehrpret seel voo pleh"

into	dans	"doñ"
invitation	l'invitation (f)	"añveetasyoñ"
to invite	inviter	"añveetay"
▷ **it's very kind of you to invite us**	c'est très gentil de votre part de nous inviter	"seh tray zhoñteey duh votr par duh nooz añveetay"
invoice	la facture	"faktoor"
Ireland	l'Irlande (f)	"eerloñd"
▷ **Northern Ireland**	l'Irlande du nord	"eerloñd doo nor"
▷ **Republic of Ireland**	la République d'Irlande	"la raypoobleek deerloñd"
Irish	irlandais (m) irlandaise (f)	"eerloñdeh" "eerloñdez"
▷ **I'm Irish**	je suis irlandais/ irlandaise	"zhuh sweez eerloñdeh/ eerloñdez"
iron[1] n (for clothes)	le fer	"fehr"
▷ **I need an iron**	j'ai besoin d'un fer à repasser	"zhay buhzwañ duñ fehr a ruhpassay"
▷ **I want to use my iron**	je voudrais utiliser mon fer à repasser	"zhuh voodrayz ooteeleezay moñ fehr a ruhpassay"
to iron[2] vb:		
▷ **where can I get this skirt ironed?**	où est-ce que je peux faire repasser cette jupe?	"oo es-kuh zhuh puh fehr ruhpassay set zhoop"
is:		
▷ **he/she/it is**	il/elle est	"eel/el eh"
island	l'île (f)	"eel"
it	il (m) elle (f)	"eel" "el"
Italian	italien (m) italienne (f)	"eetalyañ" "eetalyenn"

ABSOLUTE ESSENTIALS

I don't understand	je ne comprends pas	"zhuh nuh koñproñ pa"
I don't speak French	je ne parle pas français	"zhuh nuh parl pa froñsay"
do you speak English?	parlez-vous anglais?	"parlay-voo oñglay"
could you help me?	pourriez-vous m'aider?	"pooreeay-voo mayday"

Italy	l'Italie (f)	"eetalee"
itch	la démangeaison	"daymoñ-zheh-zoñ"
jack (*for car*)	le cric	"kreek"
jacket	le veste	"vest"
jam (*food*)	la confiture	"koñfeetoor"
▷ **strawberry/apricot jam**	de la confiture de fraise/d'abricot	"duh la koñfeetoor duh frez/dabreeko"
jammed	coincé(e)	"kwañsay"
▷ **the drawer is jammed**	le tiroir est coincé	"luh teerwar eh kwañsay"
▷ **the controls have jammed**	les commandes se sont bloquées	"lay komoñd suh soñ blokay"
January	janvier (m)	"zhoñvee-ay"
jar (*container*)	le pot	"poh"
▷ **a jar of coffee**	un pot de café	"uñ poh duh kafay"
jazz	le jazz	"jaz"
jazz festival	le festival de jazz	"festivall duh jaz"
jeans	le jean	"jeen"
jelly (*dessert*)	la gelée	"zhuhlay"
jellyfish	la méduse	"maydooz"
▷ **I've been stung by a jellyfish**	j'ai été piqué par une méduse	"zhay aytay peekay par oon maydooz"
jersey	le pull-over	"pool-ovehr"
jet lag	le décalage horaire	"daykalazh orehr"
▷ **I'm suffering from jet lag**	je souffre du décalage horaire	"zhuh soofr doo daykaylazh orehr"
jet ski	le jet-ski	"jetskee"
jet skiing:		
▷ **I'd like to go jet skiing**	j'aimerais faire du jet-ski	"zhemray fehr doo jetskee"

ABSOLUTE ESSENTIALS

I would like ...	j'aimerais ...	"zhemray"
I need ...	j'ai besoin de ...	"zhay buhswañ duh"
where is ...?	où se trouve ...?	"oo suh troov"
I'm looking for ...	je cherche ...	"zhuh shersh"

jeweller's (shop)	la bijouterie	"bee-zhootree"
jewellery	les bijoux (*mpl*)	"bee-zhoo"
▷ **I would like to put my jewellery in a safe**	je voudrais placer mes bijoux dans un coffre-fort	"zhuh voodray plasay may bee-zhoo doñz uñ kofr-for"
Jewish	juif (*m*)	"zhweef"
	juive (*f*)	"zhweev"
job	le travail	"tra-vye"
▷ **what's your job?**	qu'est-ce que vous faites dans la vie?	"kes-kuh voo fet doñ la vee"
jog:		
▷ **to go jogging**	faire du jogging	"fehr doo jogging"
joke	la plaisanterie	"playzoñtree"
journey	le voyage	"vwayazh"
▷ **how was your journey?**	comment s'est passé votre voyage?	"komoñ seh passay votr vwayazh"
jug	la cruche	"kroosh"
▷ **a jug of water**	une cruche d'eau	"oon kroosh doh"
juice	le jus	"zhoo"
July	juillet (*m*)	"zhwee-ay"
jump leads	les câbles (*mpl*) de raccordement de batterie	"kabl duh rakordmoñ duh batree"
junction (*road*)	la bifurcation	"beefoorkasyoñ"
▷ **go left at the next junction**	tournez à gauche au prochain croisement	"toornay a gohsh oh proshañ krwazmoñ"
June	juin (*m*)	"zhwañ"
just:		
▷ **just two**	deux seulement	"duh sulmoñ"

ABSOLUTE ESSENTIALS

do you have ...?	avez-vous ...?	"avay-voo"
is there ...?	y a-t-il ...?	"ya-teel"
are there ...?	y a-t-il ...?	"ya-teel"
how much is ...?	combien coûte ...?	"koñbyañ koot"

▷ I've just arrived	je viens d'arriver	"zhuh vyañ dareevay"
to keep (retain)	garder	"garday"
▷ keep the door locked	fermez la porte à clé	"fehrmay la port a clay"
▷ may I keep it?	est-ce que je peux le garder?	"es-kuh zhuh puh luh garday"
▷ could you keep me a loaf of bread?	est-ce que vous pourriez me mettre de côté un pain?	"es-kuh voo pooryay muh metr duh kohtay uñ pañ"
▷ how long will it keep?	combien de temps peut-on le conserver?	"koñbyañ duh toñ puht-oñ luh koñsehrvay"
▷ keep to the path	ne vous écartez pas du chemin	"nuh vooz aykartay pa doo shmañ"
kettle	la bouilloire	"booy-war"
key	la clé	"klay"
▷ which is the key for the front door?	quelle est la clé de la porte d'entrée?	"kel eh la klay duh la port doñtray"
▷ I've lost my key	j'ai perdu ma clé	"zhay pehrdoo ma klay"
▷ my key, please	ma clé, s'il vous plaît	"ma klay seel voo pleh"
kidneys (part of body)	les reins (mpl)	"rañ"
(as food)	les rognons (mpl)	"ronyoñ"
kilo	le kilo	"keelo"
kilometre	le kilomètre	"keelometr"
kind¹ n (sort, type)	la sorte	"sort"
▷ what kind of ...?	quelle sorte de ...?	"kel sort duh"
kind² adj (person)	gentil(le)	"zhoñteey"
▷ that's very kind of you	c'est très gentil de votre part	"seh treh zhoñteey duh votr par"
to kiss	embrasser	"oñbrassay"
kitchen	la cuisine	"kweezeen"
knife	le couteau	"kooto"
to know (facts)	savoir	"savwar"

ABSOLUTE ESSENTIALS

yes (please)	oui (merci)	"wee (mehrsee)"
no (thank you)	non (merci)	"noñ (mehrsee)"
hello	bonjour	"boñzhoor"
goodbye	au revoir	"o ruhvwar"

(person)	connaître	"konehtr"
▷ **do you know a good place to go?**	connaissez-vous un bon endroit où nous pourrions aller?	"konessay-voo uñ bon oñdrwa oo noo pooryoñ alay"
▷ **do you know where I can ...?**	savez-vous où je pourrais ...?	"savay-voo oo zhuh pooray"
▷ **do you know Paul?**	connaissez-vous Paul?	"konessay-voo Paul"
▷ **do you know how to do this?**	savez-vous comment faire cela?	"savay-voo komoñ fehr sla"
▷ **I don't know**	je ne sais pas	"zhuh nuh say pa"
kosher	kascher	"kashehr"
lace	la dentelle	"doñtell"
laces *(for shoes)*	les lacets *(mpl)*	"lasay"
ladder	l'échelle *(f)*	"ayshell"
ladies'	les toilettes *(fpl)*	"twalett"
▷ **where is the ladies'?**	où sont les toilettes pour dames?	"oo soñ lay twalett poor dam"
lady	la dame	"dam"
lager	la bière blonde	"byehr bloñd"
lake	le lac	"lak"
lamb	l'agneau *(m)*	"an-yoh"
lamp	la lampe	"loñp"
▷ **the lamp is not working**	la lampe ne marche pas	"la loñp nuh marsh pa"
lane	la ruelle	"rooell"
(of motorway)	la voie	"vwa"
▷ **you're in the wrong lane**	vous êtes sur la mauvaise voie	"vooz et soor la movez vwa"
language	la langue	"loñg"
▷ **what languages do you speak?**	quelles langues parlez-vous?	"kel loñg parlay-voo"

ABSOLUTE ESSENTIALS

I don't understand	je ne comprends pas	"zhuh nuh koñproñ pa"
I don't speak French	je ne parle pas français	"zhuh nuh parl pa froñsay"
do you speak English?	parlez-vous anglais?	"parlay-voo oñglay"
could you help me?	pourriez-vous m'aider?	"pooreeay-voo mayday"

large	grand (*m*)	"groñ"
	grande (*f*)	"groñd"
larger	plus grand (*m*)	"ploo groñ"
	plus grande (*f*)	"ploo groñd"
▷ **do you have a larger one?**	est-ce que vous en avez un plus grand?	"es-kuh vooz on avay uñ ploo groñ"
last¹ *adj*	dernier (*m*)	"dehr-nyay"
	dernière (*f*)	"dehr-nyehr"
▷ **last week**	la semaine dernière	"smen dehr-nyehr"
to last² *vb*	durer	"dooray"
▷ **how long will it last?**	combien de temps cela va-t-il durer?	"koñbyañ duh temps sla va-teel dooray"
late	tard	"tar"
▷ **the train is late**	le train a du retard	"luh trañ a doo ruhtar"
▷ **sorry we are late**	nous sommes désolés d'être en retard	"noo som dayzolay detroñ ruhtar"
▷ **we went to bed late**	nous nous sommes couchés tard	"noo noo som kooshay tar"
▷ **late last night**	tard hier soir	"tar yehr swar"
▷ **it's too late**	il est trop tard	"eel eh troh tar"
▷ **we are 10 minutes late**	nous avons 10 minutes de retard	"nooz avoñ dee meenoot duh ruhtar"
later	plus tard	"ploo tar"
▷ **shall I come back later?**	voulez-vous que je revienne plus tard?	"voolay-voo kuh zhuh ruhvyenn ploo tar"
▷ **see you later**	à tout à l'heure	"a toot a luhr"
launderette	la laverie automatique	"lavree otomateek"
laundry service	le service de blanchisserie	"sehrvees duh bloñsheesree"
▷ **is there a laundry service?**	y a-t-il un service de blanchisserie?	"ya-teel uñ sehrvees duh bloñsheesree"
lavatory	les toilettes (*fpl*)	"twalett"
lawyer	l'avocat (*m*)	"avoka"

ABSOLUTE ESSENTIALS		
I would like ...	j'aimerais ...	"zhemray"
I need ...	j'ai besoin de ...	"zhay buhswañ duh"
where is ...?	où se trouve ...?	"oo suh troov"
I'm looking for ...	je cherche ...	"zhuh shersh"

laxative	le laxatif	"laksateef"
lay-by	l'aire (f) de stationnement	"ehr duh stasyonmoñ"
lead[1] n (electric)	le fil	"feel"
to lead[2] vb	mener	"muhnay"
▷ **you lead the way**	montrez-nous le chemin	"moñtray-noo luh shmañ"
leader (of group)	le chef de groupe	"shef duh groop"
leak (of gas, liquid, in roof)	la fuite	"fweet"
▷ **there is a leak in the petrol tank/radiator**	il y a une fuite dans le réservoir d'essence/ dans le radiateur	"eel ya oon fweet doñ luh rayzehrvwar dessoñs/ doñ luh radyatuhr"
to learn	apprendre	"aproñdr"
least:		
▷ **at least**	au moins	"oh mwañ"
leather	le cuir	"kweer"
to leave	partir	"parteer"
(leave behind)	laisser	"lehsay"
▷ **when does the train leave?**	à quelle heure part le train?	"a kel uhr par luh trañ"
▷ **I shall be leaving tomorrow morning at ...**	je partirai demain matin à ...	"zhuh parteeray duhmañ matañ a"
left[1] n:		
▷ **on/to the left**	à gauche	"a gohsh"
▷ **take the third street on the left**	prenez la troisième rue à gauche	"pruhnay la trwazyem roo a gohsh"
left[2] vb:		
▷ **I've been left behind**	je suis resté en arrière	"zhuh swee restay on aryehr"
▷ **I left my bags in the taxi**	j'ai laissé mes bagages dans le taxi	"zhay lehsay may bagazh doñ luh taxi"

ABSOLUTE ESSENTIALS

do you have ...?	avez-vous ...?	"avay-voo"
is there ...?	y a-t-il ...?	"ya-teel"
are there ...?	y a-t-il ...?	"ya-teel"
how much is ...?	combien coûte ...?	"koñbyañ koot"

▷ **I left the keys in the car**	j'ai laissé les clés dans la voiture	"zhah lehsay lay klay doñ la vwatoor"
left-luggage (office)	la consigne	"koñseenyuh"
leg	la jambe	"zhoñb"
lemon	le citron	"seetroñ"
lemonade	la limonade	"leemonad"
lemon tea	le thé au citron	"tay oh seetroñ"
to lend	prêter	"pretay"
▷ **could you lend me some money?**	est-ce que vous pourriez me prêter de l'argent?	"es-kuh voo pooryay muh pretay duh larzhoñ"
▷ **could you lend me a towel?**	est-ce que vous pourriez me prêter une serviette?	"es-kuh voo pooryay muh pretay oon sehrvyett"
lens	l'objectif (m)	"ob-zhekteef"
▷ **I wear contact lenses**	je porte des lentilles de contact	"zhuh port day loñteey duh koñtakt"
less	moins	"mwañ"
lesson	la leçon	"luhsoñ"
▷ **do you give lessons?**	est-ce que vous donnez des leçons?	"es-kuh voo donay day luhsoñ"
▷ **can we take lessons?**	est-ce qu'on peut prendre des leçons?	"es-koñ puh proñdr day luhsoñ"
to let (allow)	permettre	"pehrmetr"
(hire out)	louer	"looay"
letter	la lettre	"letr"
▷ **how much is a letter to England?**	c'est combien pour envoyer une lettre en Angleterre?	"seh koñbyañ poor oñvwayay oon letr on oñgluhtehr"
▷ **are there any letters for me?**	est-ce qu'il y a du courrier pour moi?	"es-keel ya doo kooryay poor mwa"
lettuce	la laitue	"laytoo"

light bulb

level crossing	le passage à niveau	"pasazh a neevo"
library	la bibliothèque	"beebleeotek"
licence	le permis	"pehrmee"
lid	le couvercle	"koovehrkl"
to **lie down**	se coucher	"suh kooshay"
lifeboat	le canot de sauvetage	"kano duh sohvtazh"
▷ **call out the lifeboat!**	appelez le secours en mer!	"aplay luh skoor oñ mehr"
lifeguard	le surveillant de baignade	"soorvay-yoñ duh baynyad"
▷ **get the lifeguard!**	allez chercher le surveillant de baignade!	"alay shehrshay luh soorvayoñ duh baynyad"
life jacket	le gilet de sauvetage	"zheeleh duh sohvtazh"
lift	l'ascenseur (m)	"asoñsuhr"
▷ **is there a lift in the building?**	est-ce qu'il y a un ascenseur dans le bâtiment?	"es-keel ya un asoñsuhr doñ luh bateemoñ"
▷ **can you give me a lift to the garage?**	est-ce que vous pouvez me conduire jusqu'au garage?	"es-kuh voo poovay muh koñdweer zhoosko garazh"
lift pass (*on ski slopes*)	l'abonnement (m) aux remontées	"abonmoñ oh ruhmoñtay"
light	la lumière	"loomyehr"
▷ **have you got a light?**	avez-vous du feu?	"avay-voo doo fuh"
▷ **may I take it over to the light?**	est-ce que je peux la voir à la lumière?	"es-kuh zhuh puh la vwar a la loomyehr"
▷ **light blue/green**	bleu/vert clair	"bluh/vehr klehr"
▷ **do you mind if I turn off the light?**	est-ce que cela vous dérangerait si j'éteignais la lumière?	"es-kuh sla voo dayroñzh-ray see zhay-tenyay la loomyehr"
light bulb	l'ampoule (f)	"oñpool"

ABSOLUTE ESSENTIALS

I don't understand	je ne comprends pas	"zhuh nuh koñproñ pa"
I don't speak French	je ne parle pas français	"zhuh nuh parl pa froñsay"
do you speak English?	parlez-vous anglais?	"parlay-voo oñglay"
could you help me?	pourriez-vous m'aider?	"pooreeay-voo mayday"

lighter	le briquet	"breekeh"
lighter fuel	le gaz à briquet	"gaz a breekeh"
like¹ *prep*	comme	"kom"
▷ **like you**	comme vous	"kom voo"
▷ **like this**	comme ça	"kom sa"
to like² *vb*	aimer	"aymay"
▷ **I like coffee**	j'aime le café	"zhem luh kafay"
▷ **I would like a newspaper**	je voudrais un journal	"zhuh voodray uñ zhoornal"
lime (*fruit*)	le citron vert	"seetroñ vehr"
line	la ligne	"leenyuh"
▷ **I'd like an outside line, please**	c'est pour une communication extérieure, s'il vous plaît	"seh poor oon komooneeka-syoñ ekstayree-uhr seel voo pleh"
▷ **the line's engaged**	c'est occupé	"set okoopay"
▷ **it's a bad line**	la ligne est mauvaise	"la leenyuh eh movez"
lip salve	la pommade pour les lèvres	"pomad poor lay lehvr"
lipstick	le rouge à lèvres	"roozh a lehvr"
liqueur	la liqueur	"leekuhr"
▷ **what liqueurs do you have?**	qu'est-ce que vous avez comme liqueurs?	"kes-kuh vooz avay kom leekuhr"
Lisbon	Lisbonne	"leezbonn"
to listen	écouter	"aykootay"
▷ **listen!**	écoutez!	"aykootay"
to listen to	écouter	"aykootay"
litre	le litre	"leetr"
little	petit (*m*) petite (*f*)	"puhtee" "puhteet"

ABSOLUTE ESSENTIALS

I would like ...	j'aimerais ...	"zhemray"
I need ...	j'ai besoin de ...	"zhay buhswañ duh"
where is ...?	où se trouve ...?	"oo suh troov"
I'm looking for ...	je cherche ...	"zhuh shersh"

| ▷ **a little milk** | un peu de lait | "uñ puh duh leh" |

to live	vivre	"veevr"
▷ **I live in London**	j'habite à Londres	"zhabeet a loñdr"
▷ **where do you live?**	où habitez-vous?	"oo abeetay-voo"

| **liver** | le foie | "fwa" |

| **living room** | la salle de séjour | "sal duh say-zhoor" |

| **loaf** | le pain | "pañ" |

| **lobby** | le hall | "ohl" |
| ▷ **I'll meet you in the lobby** | je vous rejoindrai dans le hall | "zhuh voo ruh-zhwañdray doñ luh ohl" |

| **lobster** | le homard | "omar" |

local (*wine, speciality*)	local(e)	"lokall"
▷ **what's the local speciality?**	quelle est la spécialité du coin?	"kel eh la spay-syaleetay doo kwañ"
▷ **I'd like to order something local**	j'aimerais quelque chose de local	"zhemray kelkuh shohz duh lokall"

| **lock¹** *n* (*on door, box*) | la serrure | "sehroor" |
| ▷ **the lock is broken** | la serrure est cassée | "la sehroor eh kassay" |

| **to lock²** *vb* (*door*) | fermer à clé | "fehrmay a klay" |
| ▷ **I have locked myself out of my room** | je me suis enfermé dehors | "zhuh muh sweez oñfehrmay duh-or" |

locker	la consigne automatique	"koñseenyuh otomateek"
▷ **are there any luggage lockers?**	est-ce qu'il y a des casiers de consigne automatique?	"es-keel ya day kazyay duh koñseenyuh otomateek"
▷ **where are the clothes lockers?**	où sont les casiers pour vêtements?	"oo soñ lay kazyay poor vetmoñ"

| **lollipop** | la sucette | "soosett" |

| **London** | Londres | "loñdr" |

| **long** | long (*m*) | "loñ" |
| | longue (*f*) | "loñg" |

ABSOLUTE ESSENTIALS

do you have ...?	avez-vous ...?	"avay-voo"
is there ...?	y a-t-il ...?	"ya-teel"
are there ...?	y a-t-il ...?	"ya-teel"
how much is ...?	combien coûte ...?	"koñbyañ koot"

▷ **for a long time**	longtemps	"loñtoñ"
▷ **how long will it take to get there?**	combien de temps faut-il pour y aller?	"koñbyañ duh toñ foht-eel poor ee alay"
▷ **will it be long?**	est-ce que ce sera long?	"es-kuh suh sra loñ"
▷ **how long will it be?**	combien de temps cela va mettre?	"koñbyañ duh toñ sla va metr"

long-sighted:

▷ **I'm long-sighted**	je suis presbyte	"zhuh swee prehzbeet"

to look	regarder	"ruhgarday"
▷ **I'm just looking**	je regarde seulement	"zhuh ruhgard suhlmoñ"

to look after	garder	"garday"
▷ **could you look after my case for a minute please?**	est-ce que vous pourriez surveiller ma malette pendant une minute s'il vous plaît?	"es-kuh voo pooreeay soorvayay ma malett poñdoñ oon meenoot seel voo pleh"
▷ **I need someone to look after the children tonight**	j'ai besoin de quelqu'un pour s'occuper des enfants ce soir	"zhay buhzwañ duh kelkuñ poor sokoopay dayz oñfoñ suh swar"

to look for	chercher	"shehr-shay"
▷ **we're looking for a hotel/an apartment**	nous cherchons un hôtel/un appartement	"noo shehrshoñz un otell/ un apartmoñ"

lorry	le camion	"kamyoñ"
to lose	perdre	"pehrdr"
lost (*object*)	perdu(e)	"pehrdoo"
▷ **I have lost ...**	j'ai perdu ...	"zhay pehrdoo"
▷ **I am lost**	je suis perdu	"zhuh swee pehrdoo"
▷ **my son is lost**	mon fils a disparu	"moñ fees a deesparoo"
lost property office	le bureau des objets trouvés	"booro dayz op-zhay troovay"

lot:

▷ **a lot**	beaucoup	"bohkoo"
lotion	la lotion	"losyoñ"

loud	fort (*m*)	"for"
	forte (*f*)	"fort"
▷ **it's too loud**	c'est trop fort	"seh troh for"
lounge (*in hotel*)	le salon	"saloñ"
▷ **could we have coffee in the lounge?**	est-ce que nous pourrions avoir le café dans le salon?	"es-kuh noo pooryoñ avwar luh kafay doñ luh saloñ"
to love (*person*)	aimer	"aymay"
▷ **I love swimming**	j'aime nager	"zhem nazhay"
▷ **I love seafood**	j'adore les fruits de mer	"zhador lay frwee duh mehr"
lovely	charmant (*m*)	"sharmoñ"
	charmante (*f*)	"sharmoñt"
▷ **it's a lovely day!**	qu'il fait beau!	"keel feh boh"
low	bas (*m*)	"ba"
	basse (*f*)	"bas"
low tide	la marée basse	"maray bas"
lucky:		
▷ **I am lucky**	j'ai de la chance	"zhay duh la shoñs"
luggage	les bagages (*mpl*)	"bagazh"
▷ **can you help me with my luggage, please?**	est-ce que vous pouvez m'aider à porter mes bagages, s'il vous plaît?	"es-kuh voo poovay mayday a portay may bagazh seel voo pleh"
▷ **please take my luggage to a taxi**	est-ce que vous pouvez porter mes bagages jusqu'à un taxi?	"es-kuh voo poovay portay may bagazh zhooska uñ taxi"
▷ **I sent my luggage on in advance**	j'ai envoyé mes bagages à l'avance	"zhay oñvwayay may bagazh a lavoñs"
▷ **our luggage has not arrived**	nos bagages ne sont pas arrivés	"noh bagazh nuh soñ paz areevay"
▷ **where do I check in my luggage?**	où est-ce qu'on enregistre les bagages?	"oo es-koñ oñruh-zheestr lay bagazh"
▷ **could you have my luggage taken up?**	vous pouvez faire monter mes bagages?	"voo poovay fehr moñtay may bagazh"

ABSOLUTE ESSENTIALS

I don't understand	je ne comprends pas	"zhuh nuh koñproñ pa"
I don't speak French	je ne parle pas français	"zhuh nuh parl pa froñsay"
do you speak English?	parlez-vous anglais?	"parlay-voo oñglay"
could you help me?	pourriez-vous m'aider?	"pooreeay-voo mayday"

▷ please send someone to collect my luggage	vous voulez bien envoyer quelqu'un pour prendre mes bagages	"voo voolay byañ oñvwayay kelkuñ poor proñdr may bagazh"
luggage allowance	le poids maximum autorisé	"pwa makseemum otoreezay"
▷ what's the luggage allowance?	quel est le poids maximum de bagages autorisé?	"kel eh luh pwa makseemum duh bagazh otoreezay"
luggage rack (on car, in train)	le porte-bagages	"port-bagazh"
luggage tag	l'étiquette (f) à bagages	"ayteekett a bagazh"
luggage trolley	le chariot à bagages	"sharyo a bagazh"
▷ are there any luggage trolleys?	est-ce qu'il y a des chariots à bagages?	"es-keel ya day shayryo a bagazh"
lunch	le déjeuner	"day-zhuhnay"
▷ what's for lunch?	qu'est-ce qu'il , a pour le déjeuner?	"kes-keel ya poor luh day-zhuhnay"
Luxembourg	le Luxembourg	"looksoñboor"
luxury	de luxe	"duh loox"
macaroni	les macaroni (mpl)	"makaronee"
machine	la machine	"masheen"
mackerel	le maquereau	"makro"
madam	madame	"madamm"
Madrid	Madrid	"madreed"
magazine	la revue	"ruhvoo"
▷ do you have any English magazines?	est-ce que vous avez des revues en anglais?	"es-kuh vooz avay day ruhvoo on oñglay"
maid	la domestique	"domesteek"

ABSOLUTE ESSENTIALS		
I would like ...	j'aimerais ...	"zhemray"
I need ...	j'ai besoin de ...	"zhay buhswañ duh"
where is ...?	où se trouve ...?	"oo suh troov"
I'm looking for ...	je cherche ...	"zhuh shersh"

▷ **when does the maid come?**	quand vient la domestique?	"koñ vyañ la domesteek"
main	principal(e)	"prañseepal"
▷ **the main station**	la gare principale	"la gar prañseepal"
main course	le plat de résistance	"pla duh rayzeestoñs"
mains (*electric*)	le secteur	"sektuhr"
▷ **turn it off at the mains**	coupez le courant au secteur	"koopay luh kooroñ oh sektuhr"
to make	faire	"fehr"

I make	je fais	"zhuh feh"
you make	vous faites	"voo fet"
he/she/it makes	il/elle fait	"eel/el feh"
we make	nous faisons	"noo fuhzoñ"
they make	ils/elles font	"eel/el foñ"

make-up	le maquillage	"makeeyazh"
make-up remover	le démaquillant	"dayma-keeyoñ"
mallet	le maillet	"mye-yay"
man	l'homme (*m*)	"om"
manager	le directeur	"deerektuhr"
▷ **I'd like to speak to the manager**	je voudrais parler au directeur	"zhuh voodray parlay oh deerektuhr"
many	beaucoup	"bohkoo"
map	la carte	"kart"
▷ **can you show me on the map?**	est-ce que vous pouvez me montrer sur la carte?	"es-kuh voo poovay muh moñtray soor la kart"
▷ **I want a street map of the city**	je voudrais un plan de la ville	"zhuh voodrayz uñ ploñ duh la veel"

do you have ...?	avez-vous ...?	"avay-voo"
is there ...?	y a-t-il ...?	"ya-teel"
are there ...?	y a-t-il ...?	"ya-teel"
how much is ...?	combien coûte ...?	"koñbyañ koot"

▷ I need a road map of ...	j'ai besoin d'une carte routière de ...	"zhay buhzwañ doon kart roo-tyehr duh"
▷ where can I buy a map of the area?	où est-ce que je peux acheter une carte de la région?	"oo es-kuh zhuh puh ashtay oon kart duh la ray-zhyoñ"
March	mars *(m)*	"mars"
margarine	la margarine	"margareen"
mark *(currency)*	le mark	"mark"
(symbol, stain)	la marque	"mark"
market	le marché	"marshay"
market day	le jour de marché	"zhoor duh marshay"
▷ when is market day?	quel est le jour de marché?	"kel eh luh zhoor duh marshay"
marmalade	la confiture d'oranges	"koñfeetoor doroñzh"
married	marié(e)	"maryay"
marzipan	la pâte d'amandes	"paht damoñd"
mascara	le mascara	"maskara"
mass *(in church)*	la messe	"mess"
▷ when is mass?	à quelle heure est la messe?	"a kel uhr eh la mess"
matches	les allumettes *(fpl)*	"aloomett"
material *(cloth)*	le tissu	"teesoo"
▷ what is the material?	c'est fait en quoi?	"seh feh oñ kwa"
to **matter**:		
▷ it doesn't matter	ça ne fait rien	"sa nuh feh ryañ"
▷ what's the matter?	qu'est-ce qu'il y a?	"kes-keel ya"
May	mai *(m)*	"may"
mayonnaise	la mayonnaise	"mayonez"
meal	le repas	"ruhpa"

to **mean** (*signify*)	signifier	"seenyee-fyay"
▷ **what does this mean?**	qu'est-ce que cela signifie?	"kes-kuh sla seenyeefee"
measles	la rougeole	"roo-zholl"
to **measure**	mesurer	"muhzooray"
▷ **can you measure me please?**	est-ce que vous pouvez prendre mes mesures, s'il vous plaît?	"es-kuh voo poovay proñdr may muhzoor seel voo pleh"
meat	la viande	"vyoñd"
▷ **I don't eat meat**	je ne mange pas de viande	"zhuh nuh moñzh pa duh vyoñd"
mechanic	le mécanicien	"maykaneesyañ"
▷ **can you send a mechanic?**	est-ce que vous pouvez envoyer un mécanicien?	"es-kuh voo poovay oñvwayay uñ maykaneesyañ"
medicine	le médicament	"maydeekamoñ"
medium (*steak*)	moyen (*m*)	"mwayañ"
	moyenne (*f*)	"mwayenn"
medium rare	à point	"a pwañ"
to **meet**	rencontrer	"roñkoñtray"
▷ **pleased to meet you**	enchanté	"oñshoñtay"
▷ **shall we meet afterwards?**	nous pourrions peut-être nous voir après?	"noo pooryoñ puh-tetr noo vwar apreh"
▷ **where can we meet?**	où pouvons-nous nous voir?	"oo poovoñ-noo noo vwar"
melon	le melon	"mloñ"
member (*of club etc*)	le membre	"moñbr"
▷ **do we need to be members?**	est-ce qu'il faut être membre?	"es-keel foh etr moñbr"
men	les hommes (*mpl*)	"om"
to **mention**	mentionner	"moñsyonnay"

ABSOLUTE ESSENTIALS

I don't understand	je ne comprends pas	"zhuh nuh koñproñ pa"
I don't speak French	je ne parle pas français	"zhuh nuh parl pa froñsay"
do you speak English?	parlez-vous anglais?	"parlay-voo oñglay"
could you help me?	pourriez-vous m'aider?	"pooreeay-voo mayday"

▷ **don't mention it**	je vous en prie	"zhuh vooz oñ pree"
menu	le menu	"mnoo"
▷ **may we see the menu?**	le menu, s'il vous plaît	"luh mnoo seel voo pleh"
▷ **do you have a special menu for children?**	est-ce que vous avez un menu spécial pour les enfants?	"es-kuh vooz avay uñ mnoo spaysyal poor layz oñfoñ"
▷ **we'll have the menu at ... francs**	le menu à ... francs	"luh mnoo a ... froñ"
message	le message	"messazh"
▷ **can I leave a message with his secretary?**	est-ce que je peux laisser un message à sa secrétaire?	"es-kuh zhuh puh lessay uñ messazh a sa suhkray-tehr"
▷ **could you take a message please?**	pourriez-vous prendre un message s'il vous plaît?	"pooryay-voo proñdruñ messazh seel voo pleh"
metal	le métal	"maytal"
meter (*for electricity, gas*)	le compteur	"koñtuhr"
(*parking meter*)	le parcmètre	"parkmetr"
▷ **the parking meter is broken**	le parcmètre ne marche pas	"luh parkmetr nuh marsh pa"
▷ **do you have change for the parking meter?**	est-ce que vous avez de la monnaie pour le parcmètre?	"es-kuh vooz avay duh la moneh poor le parkmetr"
metre	le mètre	"metr"
migraine	la migraine	"meegrenn"
mile (*metric equiv = 1.60 km*)	le mille	"meel"
milk	le lait	"leh"
▷ **semi-skimmed milk**	le lait demi-écrémé	"leh duhmee-aykraymay"
▷ **skimmed milk**	le lait écrémé	"leh aykraymay"
milkshake	le milk-shake	"meelkshake"
millilitre	le millilitre	"meeleeleetr"

millimetre	le millimètre	"meeleemetr"
million	le million	"meelyoñ"
mince	le bifteck haché	"beeftek ashay"
to mind:		
▷ **do you mind if ...?**	est-ce que cela vous gêne si ...?	"es-kuh sla voo zhen see"
▷ **I don't mind**	cela ne me gêne pas	"sla nuh muh zhen pa"
mine	le mien	"myañ"
▷ **this is not mine**	ce n'est pas le mien	"suh neh pa luh myañ"
mineral water	l'eau (f) minérale	"oh meenayrall"
minimum	le minimum	"meeneemum"
minister (*church*)	le pasteur	"pastuhr"
minor road	la route secondaire	"root zgoñdehr"
mint (*herb*)	la menthe	"moñt"
(*sweet*)	le bonbon à la menthe	"boñboñ a la moñt"
minute	la minute	"meenoot"
▷ **wait a minute**	attendez une minute	"atoñday oon meenoot"
mirror	la glace	"glas"
Miss	mademoiselle	"madmwazell"
to miss (*train etc*)	rater	"ratay"
▷ **I've missed my train**	j'ai raté mon train	"zhay ratay moñ trañ"
missing:		
▷ **my son is missing**	mon fils a disparu	"moñ fees a deesparoo"
▷ **my handbag is missing**	mon sac a disparu	"moñ sak a deesparoo"
mistake	l'erreur (f)	"eh-ruhr"
▷ **there must be a mistake**	ce doit être une erreur	"suh dwat etr oon eh-ruhr"
▷ **you've made a mistake in the change**	vous ne m'avez pas bien rendu la monnaie	"voo nuh mavay pa byañ roñdoo la moneh"

ABSOLUTE ESSENTIALS

do you have ...?	avez-vous ...?	"avay-voo"
is there ...?	y a-t-il ...?	"ya-teel"
are there ...?	y a-t-il ...?	"ya-teel"
how much is ...?	combien coûte ...?	"koñbyañ koot"

misty	brumeux (*m*)	"broomuh"
	brumeuse (*f*)	"broomuz"
misunderstanding:		
▷ **there's been a misunderstanding**	il y a eu une méprise	"eel ya oo oon maypreez"
modern	moderne	"modehrn"
moisturizer	le lait hydratant	"leh eedratoñ"
Monaco	le Monaco	"monako"
monastery	le monastère	"monastehr"
Monday	lundi (*m*)	"luñdee"
money	l'argent (*m*)	"ar-zhoñ"
▷ **I have run out of money**	je n'ai plus d'argent	"zhuh nay ploo dar-zhoñ"
▷ **I have no money**	je n'ai pas d'argent	"zhuh nay pa dar-zhoñ"
▷ **can I borrow some money?**	est-ce que je peux emprunter de l'argent?	"es-kuh zhuh puh oñpruntay duh lar-zhoñ"
▷ **can you arrange to have some money sent over urgently?**	est-ce que vous pouvez me faire envoyer de l'argent d'urgence?	"es-kuh voo poovay muh fehr oñvwayay duh lar-zhoñ door-zhoñs"
money belt	la ceinture porte-monnaie	"sañtoor port-moneh"
money order	le mandat	"moñda"
month	le mois	"mwa"
monument	le monument	"monoomoñ"
mop (*for floor*)	le balai à laver	"balay a lavay"
more (than)	plus (de)	"ploos (duh)"
▷ **more wine, please**	plus de vin, s'il vous plaît	"ploos duh vañ seel voo pleh"
morning	le matin	"matañ"

▷ in the morning	le matin	"luh matañ"
mosquito	le moustique	"moosteek"
mosquito bite	la piqûre de moustique	"peekoor duh moosteek"

most:

▷ the most popular discotheque	la boîte de nuit la plus populaire	"la bwat duh nwee la ploo popoolehr"
mother	la mère	"mehr"
motor	le moteur	"motuhr"
motor boat	le bateau à moteur	"bato a motuhr"
▷ can we rent a motor boat?	est-ce qu'on peut louer un bateau à moteur?	"es-koñ puh loo-ay uñ bato a motuhr"
motor cycle	la moto	"moto"
motorway	l'autoroute (f)	"otoroot"
▷ how do I get onto the motorway?	pour rejoindre l'autoroute, s'il vous plaît?	"poor ruh-zhwañdruh lotoroot seel voo pleh"
▷ is there a toll on this motorway?	est-ce que c'est une autoroute à péage?	"es-kuh set oon otoroot a pay-yazh"
mountain	la montagne	"moñtanyuh"
mountain bike	le VTT	"vay tay tay"
mousse	la mousse	"moos"
mouth	la bouche	"boosh"
to move	bouger	"boozhay"
▷ he can't move	il ne peut pas bouger	"eel nuh puh pa boozhay"
▷ he can't move his leg	il ne peut pas bouger la jambe	"eel nuh puh pa boozhay la zhoñb"
▷ don't move him	ne le bougez pas	"nuh luh boozhay pa"
▷ could you move your car please?	pouvez-vous déplacer votre voiture s'il vous plaît?	"poovay-voo dayplasay votr vwatoor seel voo pleh"

ABSOLUTE ESSENTIALS

I don't understand	je ne comprends pas	"zhuh nuh koñproñ pa"
I don't speak French	je ne parle pas français	"zhuh nuh parl pa froñsay"
do you speak English?	parlez-vous anglais?	"parlay-voo oñglay"
could you help me?	pourriez-vous m'aider?	"pooreeay-voo mayday"

Mr	Monsieur	"muhsyuh"
Mrs	Madame	"madamm"
much	beaucoup	"bohkoo"
▷ it costs too much	ça coûte trop cher	"sa koot troh shehr"
▷ that's too much	c'est trop	"seh troh"
▷ there's too much ...	il y a trop de ...	"eel ya troh duh"
muesli	le muesli	"moozlee"
mumps	les oreillons (mpl)	"oray-yoñ"
museum	le musée	"moozay"
▷ is the museum open in the morning/ afternoon?	le musée est ouvert le matin/l'après-midi?	"luh moozay et oovehr luh matañ/lapray-meedee"
mushroom	le champignon	"shoñpeenyoñ"
music	la musique	"moozeek"
▷ the music is too loud	la musique est trop forte	"la moozeek eh troh fort"
Muslim	musulman (m) musulmane (f)	"moozoolmoñ" "moozoolman"
mussel	la moule	"mool"
must:		

I must	je dois	"zhuh dwa"
you must	vous devez	"voo dvay"
he/she/it must	il/elle doit	"eel/el dwa"
we must	nous devons	"noo dvoñ"
they must	ils/elles doivent	"eel/el dwav"

▷ I must make a phone call	je dois donner un coup de téléphone	"zhuh dwa donay uñ kood taylayfonn"
mustard	la moutarde	"mootard"
mutton	le mouton	"mootoñ"

ABSOLUTE ESSENTIALS		
I would like ...	j'aimerais ...	"zhemray"
I need ...	j'ai besoin de ...	"zhay buhswañ duh"
where is ...?	où se trouve ...?	"oo suh troov"
I'm looking for ...	je cherche ...	"zhuh shersh"

my:
▷ **my father**	mon père	"moñ pehr"
▷ **my mother**	ma mère	"ma mehr"
▷ **my parents**	mes parents	"may paroñ"

nail (*finger*)	l'ongle (*m*)	"oñgl"
(*metal*)	le clou	"kloo"

nail file	la lime à ongles	"leem a oñgl"
nail polish	le vernis à ongles	"vehrnee a oñgl"
nail polish remover	le dissolvant	"deessolvoñ"
naked	nu(e)	"noo"
name	le nom	"noñ"
▷ **what's your name?**	quel est votre nom?	"kel eh votr noñ"
▷ **my name is ...**	je m'appelle ...	"zhuh mapel"
napkin	la serviette	"sehr-vyet"
nappy	la couche	"koosh"
narrow	étroit (*m*)	"aytrwa"
	étroite (*f*)	"aytrwat"
nationality	la nationalité	"nasyonaleetay"
navy blue	bleu marine	"bluh mareen"
near	près	"preh"
▷ **near the bank/hotel**	près de la banque/près de l'hôtel	"preh duh la boñk/preh duh lotell"
necessary	nécessaire	"naysessehr"
neck	le cou	"koo"
necklace	le collier	"kolyay"

to need:
▷ **do you need anything?**	est-ce que vous avez besoin de quelque chose?	"es-kuh vooz avay buhzwañ duh kelkuh shohz"

ABSOLUTE ESSENTIALS

do you have ...?	avez-vous ...?	"avay-voo"
is there ...?	y a-t-il ...?	"ya-teel"
are there ...?	y a-t-il ...?	"ya-teel"
how much is ...?	combien coûte ...?	"koñbyañ koot"

▷ I need an aspirin	j'ai besoin d'une aspirine	"zhay buhzwañ doon aspeereen"
needle	l'aiguille (f)	"aygweey"
▷ do you have a needle and thread?	est-ce que vous avez du fil et une aiguille?	"es-kuh vooz avay doo feel ay oon aygweey"
negative (photography)	le négatif	"naygateef"
neighbour	le voisin / la voisine	"vwazañ" / "vwazeen"
never	jamais	"zhamay"
▷ I never drink wine	je ne bois jamais de vin	"zhuh nuh bwa zhamay duh vañ"
▷ I've never been to Italy	je ne suis jamais allé en Italie	"zhuh nuh swee zhamay alay on eetalee"
new	nouveau (m) / nouvelle (f)	"noovo" / "noovell"
news	la nouvelle	"noovell"
newsagent	le marchand de journaux	"marshoñd zhoorno"
newspaper	le journal	"zhoornal"
▷ do you have any English newspapers?	est-ce que vous avez des journaux en anglais?	"es-kuh vooz avay day zhoorno on oñgleh"
New Year	le Nouvel An	"noovell oñ"
▷ Happy New Year!	Bonne Année!	"bonn anay"
New Zealand	la Nouvelle-Zélande	"noovell zayloñd"
next	prochain (m) / prochaine (f)	"proshañ" / "proshenn"
▷ the next stop	le prochain arrêt	"luh proshen areh"
▷ next week	la semaine prochaine	"la smen proshenn"
▷ when's the next bus to town?	quand passe le prochain bus pour la ville?	"koñ pass luh proshañ boos poor la veel"

▷ **take the next turning on the left**	prenez le prochain tournant à gauche	"pruhnay luh proshañ toornoñ a gohsh"
nice	bien	"byañ"
(*person*)	gentil(le)	"zhoñteey"
(*picture, house*)	joli(e)	"zholee"
▷ **we are having a nice time**	nous nous amusons bien	"noo nooz amoozoñ byañ"
▷ **it doesn't taste very nice**	ce n'est pas très bon	"suh neh pa treh boñ"
▷ **nice to have met you**	enchanté de vous avoir rencontré	"oñshoñtay duh vooz avwar roñkoñtray"
night	la nuit	"nwee"
▷ **at night**	la nuit	"la nwee"
▷ **on Saturday night**	samedi soir	"samdee swar"
▷ **last night**	hier soir	"yehr swar"
▷ **tomorrow night**	demain soir	"duhmañ swar"
night club	la boîte de nuit	"bwat duh nwee"
nightdress	la chemise de nuit	"shmeez duh nwee"
nine	neuf	"nuhf"
nineteen	dix-neuf	"deez-nuhf"
ninety	quatre-vingt-dix	"katr-vañ-dees"
no	non	"noñ"
▷ **no thank you**	non merci	"noñ mehrsee"
▷ **there's no coffee**	il n'y a pas de café	"eel nya pa duh kafay"
nobody	personne	"pehrsonn"
noisy	bruyant (*m*)	"brwee-yoñ"
	bruyante (*f*)	"brwee-yoñt"
▷ **it's too noisy**	c'est trop bruyant	"seh troh brwee-yoñ"
non-alcoholic	non alcoolisé(e)	"non alkoleezay"

ABSOLUTE ESSENTIALS

I don't understand	je ne comprends pas	"zhuh nuh koñproñ pa"
I don't speak French	je ne parle pas français	"zhuh nuh parl pa froñsay"
do you speak English?	parlez-vous anglais?	"parlay-voo oñglay"
could you help me?	pourriez-vous m'aider?	"pooreeay-voo mayday"

▷ **what non-alcoholic drinks do you have?**	qu'est-ce que vous avez comme boissons non alcoolisées?	"kes-kuh vooz avay kom bwasoñ non alkoleezay"
none	aucun (m)	"ohkuñ"
	aucune (f)	"ohkoon"
▷ **there's none left**	il n'en reste plus	"eel noñ rest ploo"
non-smoking (compartment)	non-fumeurs	"noñ-foomuhr"
▷ **is there a non-smoking area?**	est-ce qu'il y a une zone non-fumeurs?	"es-keel ya oon zohn noñ-foomuhr"
▷ **I want to book a seat in a non-smoking compartment**	je voudrais réserver une place dans un compartiment non-fumeurs	"zhuh voodray rayzehrvay oon plas doñz uñ koñparteemoñ noñ-foomuhr"
Normandy	la Normandie	"normoñdee"
north	le nord	"nor"
Northern Ireland	l'Irlande (f) du Nord	"eerloñd doo nor"
not	pas	"pa"
▷ **I don't know**	je ne sais pas	"zhuhn seh pas"
▷ **I am not coming**	je ne viens pas	"zhuh nuh vyañ pa"
note	le billet	"beeyeh"
▷ **do you have change of this note?**	est-ce que vous avez la monnaie de ce billet?	"es-kuh vooz avay la moneh duh suh beeyeh"
note pad	le bloc-notes	"blok-not"
nothing	rien	"ryañ"
▷ **nothing to declare**	rien à déclarer	"ryañ a dayklaray"
notice (sign)	la pancarte	"poñkart"
November	novembre (m)	"novoñbr"
now	maintenant	"mañtnoñ"
number	le nombre	"noñbr"

ABSOLUTE ESSENTIALS		
I would like ...	j'aimerais ...	"zhemray"
I need ...	j'ai besoin de ...	"zhay buhswañ duh"
where is ...?	où se trouve ...?	"oo suh troov"
I'm looking for ...	je cherche ...	"zhuh shersh"

▷ **car number**	le numéro d'immatriculation	"noomayro deematreekoo-lasyoñ"
▷ **what's your room number?**	quel est le numéro de votre chambre?	"kel eh luh noomayro duh votr shoñbr"
▷ **what's the telephone number?**	quel est le numéro de téléphone?	"kel eh luh noomayro duh taylayfonn"
▷ **sorry, wrong number**	désolé, vous avez fait le mauvais numéro	"dayzolay, vooz avay feh luh moveh noomayro"
nurse	l'infirmière (f)	"añfeerm-yehr"
nursery slope	la piste pour débutants	"peest poor daybootoñ"
nut (to eat)	la noix	"nwa"
(for bolt)	l'écrou (m)	"aykroo"
occasionally	de temps en temps	"duh toñz oñ toñ"
o'clock:		
▷ **it's 10 o'clock**	il est 10 heures	"eel eh deez uhr"
▷ **at 2 o'clock**	à 2 heures	"a duhz uhr"
October	octobre (m)	"oktobr"
of	de	"duh"
of course	bien sûr	"byañ soor"
off (light)	éteint (m)	"aytañ"
	éteinte (f)	"aytañt"
(rotten)	mauvais (m)	"mohveh"
	mauvaise (f)	"movez"
▷ **let me off here, please**	je voudrais descendre ici, s'il vous plaît	"zhuh voodray dessoñdr eesee seel voo pleh"
▷ **the lights are off**	les lumières sont éteintes	"lay loomyehr soñt aytañt"
to **offer**	offrir	"ofreer"
office	le bureau	"booro"
▷ **I work in an office**	je travaille dans un bureau	"zhuh travye doñz uñ booro"

ABSOLUTE ESSENTIALS

do you have ...?	avez-vous ...?	"avay-voo"
is there ...?	y a-t-il ...?	"ya-teel"
are there ...?	y a-t-il ...?	"ya-teel"
how much is ...?	combien coûte ...?	"koñbyañ koot"

often	souvent	"soovoñ"
oil	l'huile (f)	"weel"
oil filter	le filtre à huile	"feeltra weel"
ointment	la pommade	"pomad"
OK	bien	"byañ"
old	vieux (m)	"vyuh"
	vieille (f)	"vyay"
▷ **how old are you?**	quel âge avez-vous?	"kel azh avay-voo"
old-age pensioner	le retraité	"ruhtrettay"
	la retraitée	"ruhtrettay"
olive oil	l'huile (f) d'olive	"weel doleev"
olives	les olives (fpl)	"oleev"
omelette	l'omelette (f)	"omlett"
on¹ adj (light)	allumé(e)	"aloomay"
(engine etc)	en marche	"oñ marsh"
on² prep	sur	"soor"
▷ **on the table**	sur la table	"soor la tabl"
once	une fois	"oon fwa"
▷ **once a day/year**	une fois par jour/an	"oon fwa par zhoor/oñ"
one	un (m)	"uñ"
	une (f)	"oon"
one-way street	le sens unique	"soñs ooneek"
onion	l'oignon (m)	"onyoñ"
only	seulement	"suhlmoñ"
▷ **we only want 3**	nous n'en voulons que 3	"noo noñ vooloñ kuh trwa"
open¹ adj	ouvert (m)	"oovehr"
	ouverte (f)	"oovehrt"
▷ **are you open?**	êtes-vous ouvert?	"et-voo oovehr"

ABSOLUTE ESSENTIALS

yes (please)	oui (merci)	"wee (mehrsee)"
no (thank you)	non (merci)	"noñ (mehrsee)"
hello	bonjour	"boñzhoor"
goodbye	au revoir	"o ruhvwar"

▷ **is the castle open to the public?**	est-ce que le château est ouvert au public?	"es-kuh luh shato et oovehr oh poobleek"
to open² *vb*	ouvrir	"oovreer"
▷ **what time does the museum open?**	le musée ouvre à quelle heure?	"luh moozay oovr a kel uhr"
▷ **I can't open the window**	je ne peux pas ouvrir la fenêtre	"zhuh nuh puh pa oovreer la fuhnehtr"
opera	l'opéra (*m*)	"opayra"
operator	le/la téléphoniste	"taylayfoneest"
opposite:		
▷ **opposite the hotel**	en face de l'hôtel	"oñ fas duh lotell"
or	ou	"oo"
orange¹ *n*	l'orange (*f*)	"oroñzh"
orange² *adj*	orange	"oroñzh"
orange juice	le jus d'orange	"zhoo doroñzh"
(*freshly-squeezed*)	l'orange (*f*) pressée	"oroñzh presay"
to order	commander	"komoñday"
▷ **can you order me a taxi, please?**	pouvez-vous m'appeler un taxi, s'il vous plaît?	"poovay voo maplay uñ taxi seel voo pleh"
▷ **can I order now please?**	est-ce que je peux commander maintenant, s'il vous plaît?	"es-kuh zhuh puh komoñday mañtnoñ seel voo pleh"
oregano	l'origan (*m*)	"oreegoñ"
original	original(e)	"oree-zheenall"
other	autre	"ohtr"
▷ **the other one**	l'autre	"lohtr"
▷ **do you have any others?**	est-ce que vous en avez d'autres?	"es-kuh vooz on avay dohtr"
▷ **where are the others?**	où sont les autres?	"oo soñ layz ohtr"
ounce	≈ 25 grammes	"vañ-sañ gram"

ABSOLUTE ESSENTIALS

I don't understand	je ne comprends pas	"zhuh nuh koñproñ pa"
I don't speak French	je ne parle pas français	"zhuh nuh parl pa froñsay"
do you speak English?	parlez-vous anglais?	"parlay-voo oñglay"
could you help me?	pourriez-vous m'aider?	"pooreeay-voo mayday"

our:

▷ our father/mother	notre père/mère	"notr pehr/mehr"
▷ our parents	nos parents	"noh paroñ"

| **ours** | le nôtre | "nohtr" |

| **out** (*light*) | éteinte | "aytañt" |
| ▷ she's out | elle est sortie | "el eh sortee" |

| **outdoor** (*pool etc*) | en plein air | "oñ plen ehr" |
| ▷ what are the outdoor activities? | qu'y a-t-il comme activités en plein air? | "kee ya-teel kom akteeveetay oñ plen ehr" |

outside	à l'extérieur	"a lekstayree-uhr"
▷ let's go outside	allons à l'extérieur	"aloñz a lekstayree-uhr"
▷ an outside line please	une ligne extérieure s'il vous plaît	"oon leenyuh ekstayree-uhr seel voo pleh"

| **oven** | le four | "foor" |

| **over** (*on top of*) | au-dessus de | "oh duhsoo duh" |

| **to overcharge** | faire payer trop cher | "fehr pay-yay troh shehr" |
| ▷ I've been overcharged | on m'a fait payer trop cher | "oñ ma feh pay-yay troh shehr" |

overheating:

| ▷ the engine is overheating | le moteur chauffe | "luh motuhr shohf" |

| **overnight** (*travel*) | de nuit | "duh nwee" |

to owe	devoir	"duhvwar"
▷ you owe me ...	vous me devez ...	"voo muh duhvay"
▷ what do I owe you?	combien est-ce que je vous dois?	"koñbyañ es-kuh zhuh voo dwa"

| **owner** | le/la propriétaire | "propree-aytehr" |
| ▷ could I speak to the owner please? | pourrais-je parler au propriétaire s'il vous plaît? | "poorayzh parlay oh propree-aytehr seel voo pleh" |

| **oyster** | l'huître (*f*) | "weetr" |

ABSOLUTE ESSENTIALS		
I would like ...	j'aimerais ...	"zhemray"
I need ...	j'ai besoin de ...	"zhay buhswañ duh"
where is ...?	où se trouve ...?	"oo suh troov"
I'm looking for ...	je cherche ...	"zhuh shersh"

to pack:

▷ **I need to pack now**	je dois faire mes bagages maintenant	"zhuh dwa fehr may bagazh mañtnoñ"
package	le paquet	"pakeh"
package tour	le voyage organisé	"vwayazh organeezay"
packed lunch	le panier repas	"panyay ruhpa"
packet	le paquet	"pakeh"
▷ **a packet of cigarettes**	un paquet de cigarettes	"uñ pakeh duh seegarett"
paddling pool	le petit bassin pour enfants	"puhtee bassañ poor oñfoñ"
▷ **is there a paddling pool for the children?**	est-ce qu'il y a un petit bassin pour les enfants?	"es-keel ya uñ puhtee bassañ poor layz oñfoñ"
paid	payé(e)	"payay"
pain	la douleur	"dooluhr"
▷ **I have a pain here/in my chest**	j'ai mal ici/dans la poitrine	"zhay mal eesee/doñ la pwatreen"
painful	douloureux (m) douloureuse (f)	"doolooruh" "doolooruz"
painkiller	le calmant	"kalmoñ"
painting	le tableau	"tablo"
pair	la paire	"pehr"
▷ **a pair of sandals**	une paire de sandales	"oon pehr duh soñdal"
palace	le palais	"paleh"
▷ **is the palace open to the public?**	est-ce que le palais est ouvert au public?	"es-kuh luh paleh et oovehr oh poobleek"
pan	la casserole	"kasrol"
pancake	la crêpe	"krep"
pants	le slip	"sleep"

paper	le papier	"papyay"
paraffin	le pétrole	"paytrol"
paragliding:		
▷ where can we go paragliding?	où est-ce qu'on peut faire du parapente?	"oo es-koñ puh fehr doo parapoñt"
parascending:		
▷ we'd like to go parascending	nous aimerions faire du parachute ascensionnel	"nooz ehmryoñ fehr doo parashoot asoñsyonnell"
parasol	le parasol	"parasol"
parcel	le colis	"kolee"
▷ I want to send this parcel	je voudrais envoyer ce paquet	"zhuh voodrayz oñvwayay suh pakeh"
pardon (*I didn't understand*)	comment?	"komoñ"
▷ I beg your pardon!	pardon!	"pardoñ"
parent	le parent	"paroñ"
Paris	Paris	"paree"
park[1] *n*	le parc	"park"
to **park**[2] *vb*	stationner	"stasyonay"
▷ can we park our caravan here?	pouvons-nous garer notre caravane ici?	"poovoñ noo garay notr karavann eesee"
▷ where can I park?	où est-ce que je peux me garer?	"oo es-kuh zhuh puh muh garay"
▷ can I park here?	est-ce que je peux me garer ici?	"es-kuh zhuh puh muh garay eesee"
parking disc	le disque de stationnement	"deesk duh stasyonmoñ"
parking meter	le parcmètre	"parkmetr"
▷ the parking meter is broken	le parcmètre ne marche pas	"luh parkmetr nuh marsh pa"

ABSOLUTE ESSENTIALS

yes (please)	oui (merci)	"wee (mehrsee)"
no (thank you)	non (merci)	"noñ (mehrsee)"
hello	bonjour	"boñzhoor"
goodbye	au revoir	"o ruhvwar"

| ▷ do you have change for the parking meter? | est-ce que vous avez de la monnaie pour le parcmètre? | "es-kuh vooz avay duh la moneh poor luh parkmetr" |

parsley	le persil	"perseey"
part	la partie	"partee"
party (*group*)	le groupe	"groop"
passenger	le passager	"passa-zhay"
	la passagère	"passa-zhyehr"
passport	le passeport	"paspor"
▷ I have forgotten my passport	j'ai oublié mon passeport	"zhay ooblee-ay moñ paspor"
▷ please give me my passport back	mon passeport, s'il vous plaît	"moñ paspor seel voo pleh"
▷ my wife/husband and I have a joint passport	ma femme/mon mari et moi sommes sur le même passeport	"ma fam/moñ maree ay mwa som soor luh mem paspor"
▷ the children are on this passport	les enfants sont sur ce passeport	"layz oñfoñ soñ soor suh paspor"
▷ my passport number is ...	le numéro de mon passeport est ...	"luh noomayro duh moñ paspor eh"
▷ I've lost my passport	j'ai perdu mon passeport	"zhay pehrdoo moñ paspor"
▷ my passport has been stolen	je me suis fait voler mon passeport	"zhuhm swee feh volay moñ paspor"
▷ I've got a visitor's passport	j'ai un passeport temporaire	"zhay uñ paspor toñporehr"
passport control	le contrôle des passeports	"koñtrohl day paspor"
pasta	les pâtes (*fpl*)	"paht"
pastry	la pâte	"paht"
(*cake*)	la pâtisserie	"pateesree"
pâté	le pâté	"pahtay"
path	le chemin	"shmañ"

ABSOLUTE ESSENTIALS

I don't understand	je ne comprends pas	"zhuh nuh koñproñ pa"
I don't speak French	je ne parle pas français	"zhuh nuh parl pa froñsay"
do you speak English?	parlez-vous anglais?	"parlay-voo oñglay"
could you help me?	pourriez-vous m'aider?	"pooreeay-voo mayday"

pay

▷ where does this path lead?	où mène ce chemin?	"oo men suh shmañ"
to pay	payer	"pay-yay"
▷ do I pay now or later?	dois-je payer maintenant ou plus tard?	"dwazh pay-yay mañtnoñ oo ploo tar"
payment	le paiement	"paymoñ"
peach	la pêche	"pesh"
peanut	la cacahuète	"kakawet"
pear	la poire	"pwar"
peas	les petits pois	"puhtee pwa"
peg (for clothes)	la pince	"pañs"
(for tent)	la cheville	"shveey"
pen	le stylo	"steelo"
▷ do you have a pen I could borrow?	est-ce que je peux vous emprunter un stylo?	"es-kuh zhuh puh vooz oñpruñtay uñ steelo"
pencil	le crayon	"krayoñ"
penicillin	la pénicilline	"payneeseeleen"
▷ I am allergic to penicillin	je suis allergique à la pénicilline	"zhuh swee alehr-zheek a la payneeseeleen"
penknife	la canif	"kaneef"
pensioner	le retraité / la retraitée	"ruhtrehtay" / "ruhtrehtay"
▷ are there reductions for pensioners?	est-ce qu'il y a des réductions pour les personnes du troisième âge?	"es-keel ya day raydooksyoñ poor lay pehrsonn doo trwazyem azh"
pepper (spice)	le poivre	"pwavr"
(vegetable)	le poivron	"pwavroñ"
per:		
▷ per hour	à l'heure	"a luhr"

ABSOLUTE ESSENTIALS

I would like ...	j'aimerais ...	"zhemray"
I need ...	j'ai besoin de ...	"zhay buhswañ duh"
where is ...?	où se trouve ...?	"oo suh troov"
I'm looking for ...	je cherche ...	"zhuh shersh"

▷ **per week**	par semaine	"par smen"
▷ **60 miles per hour**	95 kilomètres à l'heure	"95 keelometr a luhr"
perfect	parfait (*m*)	"parfeh"
	parfaite (*f*)	"parfeht"
performance	la représentation	"ruhprayzoñtasyoñ"
▷ **what time does the performance begin?**	le spectacle commence à quelle heure?	"luh spektakl komoñs a kel uhr"
▷ **how long does the performance last?**	le spectacle dure combien de temps?	"luh spektakl door koñbyañ duh toñ"
perfume	le parfum	"parfuñ"
perhaps	peut-être	"puh-tehtr"
period (*menstruation*)	les règles (*fpl*)	"rehgl"
perm	la permanente	"pehrmanoñt"
▷ **my hair is permed**	j'ai une permanente	"zhay oon pehrmanoñt"
permit	le permis	"pehrmee"
▷ **do I need a fishing permit?**	est-ce qu'il me faut un permis de pêche?	"es-keel muh foht uñ pehrmee duh pesh"
person	la personne	"pehrsonn"
petrol	l'essence (*f*)	"essoñs"
▷ **20 litres of unleaded petrol**	20 litres d'essence sans plomb	"vañ leetr dessoñs soñ ploñ"
▷ **I have run out of petrol**	je suis en panne d'essence	"zhuh sweez oñ pann dessoñs"
petrol station	la station-service	"stasyoñ sehrvees"
pheasant	le faisan	"fuhzoñ"
phone[1] *n*	le téléphone	"taylayfonn"
to **phone**[2] *vb*	téléphoner	"taylayfonay"
▷ **can I phone from here?**	est-ce que je peux téléphoner d'ici?	"es-kuh zhuh puh taylayfonay deesee"
phone box	la cabine téléphonique	"kabeen taylayfoneek"

ABSOLUTE ESSENTIALS

do you have ...?	avez-vous ...?	"avay-voo"
is there ...?	y a-t-il ...?	"ya-teel"
are there ...?	y a-t-il ...?	"ya-teel"
how much is ...?	combien coûte ...?	"koñbyañ koot"

phone card	la télécarte	"taylaykart"
▷ do you sell phone cards?	est-ce que vous vendez des télécartes?	"es-kuh voo voñday day taylaykart"
photocopy [1] *n*	la photocopie	"fotokopee"
▷ I'd like a photocopy of this please	je voudrais une photocopie de ceci s'il vous plaît	"zhuh voodrayz oon fotokopee duh suhsee seel voo pleh"
to **photocopy** [2] *vb*	photocopier	"fotokopyay"
▷ where can I get some photocopying done?	où est-ce que je pourrais faire faire des photocopies?	"oo es-kuh zhuh pooray fehr fehr day fotokopee"
photo(graph)	la photo	"foto"
▷ when will the photos be ready?	les photos seront prêtes quand?	"lay foto sroñ pret koñ"
▷ can I take photos in here?	est-ce que je peux prendre des photos ici?	"es-kuh zhuh puh proñdr day foto eesee"
▷ would you take a photo of us?	est-ce que vous pourriez prendre une photo de nous?	"es-kuh voo pooryay proñdr oon foto duh noo"
picnic	le pique-nique	"peek-neek"
▷ a picnic lunch	un pique-nique	"uñ peek-neek"
picture (*painting, photo*)	le tableau	"tablo"
pie	la tourte	"toort"
piece	le morceau	"morso"
▷ a piece of cake	un morceau de gâteau	"uñ morso duh gato"
▷ a 10 franc piece	une pièce de 10 francs	"oon pyess duh dee frañ"
pill	la pilule	"peelool"
pillow	l'oreiller (*m*)	"orayay"
▷ I would like an extra pillow	je voudrais un oreiller supplémentaire	"zhuh voodrayz oon orayay sooplaymoñtehr"
pillowcase	la taie d'oreiller	"tay dorayay"

pin	l'épingle (*f*)	"aypañgl"
pineapple	l'ananas (*m*)	"anana"
pink	rose	"rohz"
pint	le demi-litre	"duhmee-leetr"
pipe	la pipe	"peep"
pipe tobacco	le tabac à pipe	"taba a peep"
pistachio	la pistache	"peestash"
plane	l'avion (*m*)	"avyoñ"
▷ **my plane leaves at ...**	mon avion décolle à ...	"mon avyoñ daycoll a"
▷ **I've missed my plane**	j'ai raté mon avion	"zhay ratay mon avyoñ"
plaster (*sticking plaster*)	le sparadrap	"sparadra"
plastic	le plastique	"plasteek"
plate	l'assiette (*f*)	"asyet"
platform	le quai	"kay"
▷ **which platform for the train to ...?**	pour ..., c'est quel quai?	"poor ... seh kel kay"
to **play** (*games*)	jouer	"zhoo-ay"
▷ **we'd like to play tennis**	nous aimerions jouer au tennis	"nooz ehmryoñ zhoo-ay oh tenees"
playing cards	les cartes à jouer	"kart a zhooay"
playroom	la salle de jeux	"sal duh zhuh"
please	s'il vous plaît	"seel voo pleh"
▷ **yes, please**	oui merci	"wee mehrsee"
pleased	content (*m*)	"koñtoñ"
	contente (*f*)	"koñtoñt"
▷ **pleased to meet you**	enchanté	"oñshoñtay"
pliers	la pince	"pañs"
plug (*electrical*)	la prise	"preez"

ABSOLUTE ESSENTIALS

I don't understand	je ne comprends pas	"zhuh nuh koñproñ pa"
I don't speak French	je ne parle pas français	"zhuh nuh parl pa froñsay"
do you speak English?	parlez-vous anglais?	"parlay-voo oñglay"
could you help me?	pourriez-vous m'aider?	"pooreeay-voo mayday"

plum	la prune	"proon"
plumber	le plombier	"ploñbyay"
points (*in car*)	les vis (*fpl*) platinées	"vees plateenay"
police	la police	"polees"
▷ **get the police!**	appelez la police!	"aplay la polees"
▷ **we will have to report it to the police**	il faut avertir la police	"eel foh avehrteer la polees"
policeman	l'agent (*m*) de police	"azhoñ duh polees"
police station	le commissariat de police	"komeesar-ya duh polees"
▷ **where is the police station?**	où est le commissariat de police?	"oo eh luh komeesar-ya duh polees"
polish (*for shoes*)	le cirage	"seerazh"
polluted	pollué(e)	"poloo-ay"
pony trekking	la randonnée à cheval	"roñdonay a shval"
▷ **we'd like to go pony trekking**	nous aimerions faire de la randonnée équestre	"nooz ehmryoñ fehr duh la roñdonay aykestr"
pool (*swimming*)	la piscine	"peeseen"
▷ **is there a children's pool?**	est-ce qu'il y a une piscine pour enfants?	"es-keel ya oon peeseen poor oñfoñ"
▷ **is the pool heated?**	est-ce que la piscine est chauffée?	"es-kuh la peeseen eh shohfay"
▷ **is it an outdoor pool?**	est-ce que c'est une piscine en plein air?	"es-kuh say oon peeseen oñ plen ehr"
popular	populaire	"popoolehr"
pork	le porc	"por"
port (*seaport*)	le port	"por"
(*wine*)	le porto	"porto"
porter (*in hotel*)	le porteur	"portuhr"
Portugal	le Portugal	"portoogall"

Portuguese	portugais (*m*)	"portoogeh"
	portugaise (*f*)	"portoogez"
possible	possible	"poseebl"
▷ as soon as possible	aussitôt que possible	"ohseeto kuh poseebl"
to **post**	poster	"postay"
▷ where can I post these cards?	où est-ce que je peux poster ces cartes postales?	"oo es-kuh zhuh puh postay say kart postall"
postbox	la boîte aux lettres	"bwat oh letr"
postcard	la carte postale	"kart postall"
▷ do you have any postcards?	avez-vous des cartes postales?	"avay-voo day kart postall"
▷ where can I buy some postcards?	où est-ce que je peux acheter des cartes postales?	"oo es-kuh zhuh puh ashtay day kart postall"
postcode	le code postale	"cod postall"
post office	le bureau de poste	"booro duh post"
pot (*for cooking*)	le pot	"poh"
potato	la pomme de terre	"pom duh tehr"
pottery	la poterie	"potree"
pound (*sterling*)	la livre	"leevr"
(*metric equiv = 0.45 kg*)	la livre	"leevr"
powdered milk	le lait en poudre	"leh oñ poodr"
pram	le landeau	"loñdo"
prawn	la crevette	"kruhvett"
to **prefer**	préférer	"prayfayray"
▷ I'd prefer to go ...	je préférerais aller ...	"zhuh prayfayruhray alay"
▷ I prefer ... to ...	je préfère ... à ...	"zhuh prayfehr ... a"
pregnant	enceinte	"oñsañt"
to **prepare**	préparer	"prayparay"

prescription	l'ordonnance (f)	"ordonoñs"
▷ where can I get this prescription made up?	où est-ce que je peux obtenir cette ordonnance?	"oo es-kuh zhuh puhz optneer set ordonoñs"
present (gift)	le cadeau	"kado"
▷ I want to buy a present for my husband/my wife	je voudrais acheter un cadeau pour mon mari/ma femme	"zhuh voodray ashtay uñ kado poor moñ maree/ma fam"
pretty	joli(e)	"zholee"
price	le prix	"pree"
price list	le tarif	"tareef"
priest	le prêtre	"pretr"
▷ I want to see a priest	je voudrais voir un prêtre	"zhuh voodray vwar uñ pretr"
private	privé(e)	"preevay"
▷ can I speak to you in private?	est-ce que je peux vous parler en privé?	"es-kuh zhuh puh voo parlay oñ preevay"
▷ this is private	c'est confidentiel	"seh koñfeedoñsyell"
▷ I have private health insurance	j'ai une assurance maladie privée	"zhay oon asooroñs maladee preevay"
probably	probablement	"probabluh-moñ"
problem	le problème	"problemm"
programme	le programme	"programm"
to pronounce	prononcer	"pronoñsay"
▷ how do you pronounce it?	comment ça se prononce?	"komoñ sas pronoñs"
Protestant	protestant (m)	"protestoñ"
	protestante (f)	"protestoñt"
prunes	les pruneaux	"proono"
public	public (m)	"poobleek"
	publique (f)	"poobleek"

ABSOLUTE ESSENTIALS

yes (please)	oui (merci)	"wee (mehrsee)"
no (thank you)	non (merci)	"noñ (mehrsee)"
hello	bonjour	"boñzhoor"
goodbye	au revoir	"o ruhvwar"

▷ **is the castle open to the public?**	est-ce que le château est ouvert au public?	"es-kuh luh shato et oovehr oh poobleek"
public holiday	le jour férié	"zhoor fayr-yay"
pudding	le dessert	"dessehr"
to pull	tirer	"teeray"
pullover	le pull	"pool"
puncture	la crevaison	"kruhvehzoñ"
▷ **I have a puncture**	j'ai crevé	"zhay kruhvay"
purple	violet (*m*)	"vyoleh"
	violette (*f*)	"vyolet"
purse	le porte-monnaie	"port-moneh"
▷ **my purse has been stolen**	je me suis fait voler mon porte-monnaie	"zhum swee feh volay moñ port-moneh"
▷ **I've lost my purse**	j'ai perdu mon porte-monnaie	"zhay pehrdoo moñ port-moneh"
push[1] *n*:		
▷ **my car's broken down, can you give me a push?**	ma voiture est en panne, est-ce que vous pouvez m'aider à la pousser?	"ma vwatoor et oñ pann es-kuh voo poovay mayday a la poosay"
to push[2] *vb*	pousser	"poosay"
to put (*place*)	mettre	"metr"
to put down	déposer	"daypoh-zay"
▷ **put it down over there please**	posez-le là s'il vous plaît	"pohzay-luh la seel voo pleh"
pyjamas	le pyjama	"pee-zhama"
the Pyrenees	les Pyrénées (*fpl*)	"peeraynay"
quarter	le quart	"kar"
▷ **quarter to 10**	10 heures moins le quart	"deez uhr mwañ luh kar"
▷ **quarter past 3**	3 heures et quart	"trwaz uhr ay kar"

ABSOLUTE ESSENTIALS

I don't understand	je ne comprends pas	"zhuh nuh koñproñ pa"
I don't speak French	je ne parle pas français	"zhuh nuh parl pa froñsay"
do you speak English?	parlez-vous anglais?	"parlay-voo oñglay"
could you help me?	pourriez-vous m'aider?	"pooreeay-voo mayday"

queue	la queue	"kuh"
▷ is this the end of the queue?	est-ce ici que l'on fait la queue?	"es eesee kuh loñ feh la kuh"
quick	rapide	"rapeed"
quickly	vite	"veet"
quiet (place)	tranquille	"troñkeel"
quilt	l'édredon (m)	"aydruhdoñ"
quite (rather)	assez	"assay"
(completely)	complètement	"koñpletmoñ"
rabbit	le lapin	"lapañ"
racket	la raquette	"rakett"
▷ can we hire rackets?	est-ce qu'on peut louer des raquettes?	"es-koñ puh loo-ay day rakett"
radiator	le radiateur	"radya-tuhr"
radio	la radio	"radyo"
▷ is there a radio/radio cassette in the car?	est-ce qu'il y a une radio/un radiocassette dans la voiture?	"es-keel ya oon radyo/uñ radyo-kasett doñ la vwatoor"
radish	le radis	"radee"
railway station	la gare	"gar"
rain¹ n	la pluie	"plwee"
to rain² vb	pleuvoir	"pluhvwar"
▷ is it going to rain?	est-ce qu'il va pleuvoir?	"es-keel va pluhvwar"
▷ it's raining	il pleut	"eel pluh"
raincoat	l'imperméable (m)	"añpehrmayabl"
raisin	le raisin sec	"rayzañ sek"
rare (unique)	rare	"rar"
(steak)	saignant	"say-nyoñ"

rash:

▷ I have a rash	j'ai une éruption de boutons	"zhay oon ayroopsyoñ duh bootoñ"

raspberry	la framboise	"froñbwaz"

rate	le taux	"toh"
▷ what is the daily/ weekly rate?	quels sont vos prix par jour/par semaine?	"kel soñ voh pree par zhoor/par smen"
▷ do you have a special rate for children?	y a-t-il une réduction pour les enfants?	"ya-teel oon raydooksyoñ poor layz oñfoñ"
▷ what is the rate for sterling/dollars?	combien vaut la livre/le dollar?	"koñbyañ voh la leevr/luh dollar"
▷ rate of exchange	le taux de change	"tohd shoñzh"

raw	cru(e)	"kroo"

razor	le rasoir	"razwar"

razor blades	les lames (fpl) de rasoir	"lam duh razwar"

ready	prêt (m)	"preh"
	prête (f)	"pret"
▷ are you ready?	êtes-vous prêt?	"et-voo preh"
▷ I'm ready	je suis prêt	"zhuh swee preh"
▷ when will lunch/dinner be ready?	quand est-ce que le déjeuner/dîner sera prêt?	"koñt es-kuh luh dayzhuh-nay/deenay suhra preh"

real	vrai(e)	"vray"

receipt	le reçu	"ruhsoo"
▷ I'd like a receipt, please	un reçu, s'il vous plaît	"uñ ruhsoo seel voo pleh"

recently	récemment	"raysmoñ"

reception	la réception	"raysepsyoñ"

recipe	la recette	"ruhsett"

to recommend	recommander	"ruhkomoñday"

ABSOLUTE ESSENTIALS

do you have ...?	avez-vous ...?	"avay-voo"
is there ...?	y a-t-il ...?	"ya-teel"
are there ...?	y a-t-il ...?	"ya-teel"
how much is ...?	combien coûte ...?	"koñbyañ koot"

▷ what do you recommend?	qu'est-ce que vous nous conseillez?	"kes-kuh voo noo koñsay-yay"
▷ can you recommend a cheap hotel/a good restaurant?	pouvez-vous recommander un hôtel pas cher/un bon restaurant?	"poovay-voo ruhkomoñday un otell pa shehr/uñ boñ restoroñ"
record (music etc)	le disque	"deesk"
red	rouge	"roozh"
reduction	la réduction	"raydooksyoñ"
▷ is there a reduction for children/for senior citizens/for a group?	est-ce qu'il y a des réductions pour les enfants/les personnes du troisième âge/les groupes?	"es-keel ya day raydooksyoñ poor layz oñfoñ/lay pehrsonn doo trwazyem azh/lay groop"
refill	la recharge	"ruh-sharzh"
▷ do you have a refill for my gas lighter?	avez-vous une recharge pour mon briquet?	"avay-vooz oon ruh-sharzh poor moñ breekeh"
refund	le remboursement	"roñboorsmoñ"
▷ I'd like a refund	je voudrais me faire rembourser	"zhuh voodray muh fehr roñboorsay"
to **register:**		
▷ where do I register?	où est-ce que je me présente à l'enregistrement?	"oo es-kuh zhuh muh prayzoñt a loñruh-zheestr-moñ"
registered	recommandé(e)	"ruhkomoñday"
registered delivery	l'envoi (m) recommandé	"oñvwa ruhkomoñday"
regulation	le règlement	"raygluhmoñ"
▷ I'm very sorry, I didn't know the regulations	je suis désolé, je ne connaissais pas le règlement	"zhuh swee dayzolay, zhuh nuh konessay pa luh raygluhmoñ"
to **reimburse**	rembourser	"roñboorsay"
relation (family)	le parent	"paroñ"

ABSOLUTE ESSENTIALS

yes (please)	oui (merci)	"wee (mehrsee)"
no (thank you)	non (merci)	"noñ (mehrsee)"
hello	bonjour	"boñzhoor"
goodbye	au revoir	"o ruhvwar"

to **relax**	se détendre	"suh daytoñdr"
reliable (*company, service*)	sérieux (*m*) sérieuse (*f*)	"sayreeuh" "sayreeuz"
to **remain**	rester	"restay"
to **remember**	se rappeler	"suh raplay"
to **rent**	louer	"loo-ay"
▷ **I'd like to rent a room/a villa**	je voudrais louer une chambre/une villa	"zhuh voodray loo-ay oon shoñbr/oon veela"
rental	la location	"lokasyoñ"
to **repair**	réparer	"rayparay"
▷ **can you repair this?**	pouvez-vous réparer ça?	"poovay-voo rayparay sa"
to **repeat**	répéter	"raypaytay"
▷ **please repeat that**	répétez, s'il vous plaît	"raypaytay seel voo pleh"
reservation	la réservation	"rayzehrvasyoñ"
▷ **I'd like to make a reservation for 7.30/ for 2 people**	je voudrais faire une réservation pour 7 heures et demie/pour 2 personnes	"zhuh voodray fehr oon rayzehrvasyoñ poor set uhr ay duhmee/poor duh pehrsonn"
to **reserve**	réserver	"rayzehrvay"
▷ **we'd like to reserve 2 seats for tonight**	nous désirons réserver 2 places pour ce soir	"noo dayzeeroñ rayzehrvay duh plas poor suh swar"
▷ **I have reserved a room in the name of ...**	j'ai réservé une chambre au nom de ...	"zhay rayzehrvay oon shoñbr oh noñ duh"
▷ **I want to reserve a single/double room**	je voudrais réserver une chambre pour une personne/deux personnes	"zhuh voodray rayzehrvay oon shoñbr poor oon pehrsonn/duh pehrsonn"
rest[1] *n* (*repose*)	le repos	"ruhpo"
(*stop*)	l'arrêt (*m*)	"areh"
(*remainder*)	le reste	"rest"

ABSOLUTE ESSENTIALS

I don't understand	je ne comprends pas	"zhuh nuh koñproñ pa"
I don't speak French	je ne parle pas français	"zhuh nuh parl pa froñsay"
do you speak English?	parlez-vous anglais?	"parlay-voo oñglay"
could you help me?	pourriez-vous m'aider?	"pooreeay-voo mayday"

▷ the rest of the wine	le reste du vin	"luh rest doo vañ"
to **rest**[2] vb	se reposer	"suh ruhpohzay"
restaurant	le restaurant	"restoroñ"
restaurant car	le wagon-restaurant	"vagoñrestoroñ"
to **return** (go back)	retourner	"ruhtoornay"
(give back)	rendre	"roñdr"
return ticket	le billet aller et retour	"beeyeh alay ay ruhtoor"
▷ a return ticket to ..., first class	un aller-retour pour ..., en première classe	"uñ alay-ruhtoor poor ... oñ pruh-myehr klas"
reverse charge call	l'appel (m) en PCV	"apell oñ pay say vay"
▷ I'd like to make a reverse charge call	je voudrais faire un appell en PCV	"zhuh voodray fehr uñ apel oñ pay say vay"
rheumatism	le rhumatisme	"roomateezmuh"
rhubarb	la rhubarbe	"roobarb"
rice	le riz	"ree"
ride:		
▷ to go for a ride (on horseback)	faire une promenade à cheval	"fehr oon promnad a shval"
riding	l'équitation (f)	"aykeetasyoñ"
▷ can we go horse riding?	est-ce qu'on peut faire du cheval?	"es-koñ puh fehr doo shval"
right[1] n:		
▷ on/to the right	à droite	"a drwat"
right[2] adj (correct)	exact(e)	"egzakt"
right of way	la priorité	"la preeoreetay"
ring	la bague	"bag"
ripe	mûr(e)	"moor"
river	la rivière	"reevyehr"

ABSOLUTE ESSENTIALS		
I would like ...	j'aimerais ...	"zhemray"
I need ...	j'ai besoin de ...	"zhay buhswañ duh"
where is ...?	où se trouve ...?	"oo suh troov"
I'm looking for ...	je cherche ...	"zhuh shersh"

▷ **can one swim in the river?**	peut-on se baigner dans la rivière?	"puh-toñ suh baynyay doñ la reevyehr"
▷ **am I allowed to fish in the river?**	est-ce que je peux pêcher dans la rivière?	"es-kuh zhuh puh peshay doñ la reevyehr"
the **Riviera**	la Côte d'Azur	"koht dazoor"
road	la route	"root"
▷ **is the road to ... snowed up?**	est-ce que la route de ... est enneigée?	"es-kuh la root duh ... et oñneh-zhay"
▷ **which road do I take for ..., please?**	la route pour aller à ..., s'il vous plaît?	"la root poor alay a ... seel voo pleh"
▷ **when will the road be clear?**	quand est-ce que la route sera dégagée?	"koñt es-kuh la root suhra dayga-zhay"
road map	la carte routière	"kart rootyehr"
roast	rôti(e)	"rohtee"
to **rob**	voler	"volay"
▷ **I've been robbed**	on m'a volé quelque chose	"oñ ma volay kelkuh shohz"
rock climbing:		
▷ **to go rock climbing**	faire de l'escalade	"fehr duh leskalad"
roll (*bread*)	le petit pain	"puhtee pañ"
roller skates	les patins (*mpl*) à roulettes	"patañ a roolett"
roller skating:		
▷ **where can we go roller skating?**	où est-ce qu'on peut faire du patin à roulettes?	"oo es-koñ puh fehr doo patañ a roolett"
Rome	Rome	"rom"
roof	le toit	"twa"
▷ **the roof leaks**	il y a des fuites dans le toit	"eel ya day fweet doñ luh twa"
roof rack	la galerie	"galree"

ABSOLUTE ESSENTIALS

do you have ...?	avez-vous ...?	"avay-voo"
is there ...?	y a-t-il ...?	"ya-teel"
are there ...?	y a-t-il ...?	"ya-teel"
how much is ...?	combien coûte ...?	"koñbyañ koot"

room (*in house, hotel*)	la pièce	"pyess"
(*space*)	la place	"plas"
room service	le service des chambres	"sehrvees day shoñbr"
rope	la corde	"kord"
rosé (*wine*)	le rosé	"rozay"
rough (*surface*)	rugueux (*m*)	"rooguh"
	rugueuse (*f*)	"rooguz"
▷ **is the sea rough today?**	est-ce que la mer est agitée aujourd'hui?	"es-kuh la mehr et azheetay oh-zhoordwee"
▷ **the crossing was rough**	la traversée a été agitée	"la travehrsay a aytay azheetay"
round[1] *n*:		
▷ **whose round is it?**	qui est-ce qui paye la tournée?	"kee es-kee pay la toornay"
▷ **a round of golf**	une partie de golf	"oon partee duh golf"
round[2] *adj* (*object*)	rond (*m*)	"roñ"
	ronde (*f*)	"roñd"
round[3] *prep*:		
▷ **round the corner**	après le coin	"apreh luh kwañ"
route	la route	"root"
▷ **is there a route that avoids the traffic?**	est-ce qu'il y a un itinéraire qui évite les encombrements?	"es-keel ya un eeteenayrehr kee ayveet layz oñkoñbruhmoñ"
rowing boat	le canot à rames	"kano a ram"
▷ **can we rent a rowing boat?**	est-ce qu'on peut louer un bateau à rames?	"es-koñ puh loo-ay uñ bato a ram"
rubber	le caoutchouc	"kaoot-shoo"
rubber band	l'élastique (*m*)	"aylasteek"
rubbish	les ordures (*fpl*)	"ordoor"
rucksack	le sac à dos	"sak a doh"

ABSOLUTE ESSENTIALS		
yes (please)	oui (merci)	"wee (mehrsee)"
no (thank you)	non (merci)	"noñ (mehrsee)"
hello	bonjour	"boñzhoor"
goodbye	au revoir	"o ruhvwar"

rug	le petit tapis	"puhtee tapee"
rugby	le rugby	"roogbee"
ruins	les ruines (fpl)	"rween"
rum	le rhum	"rom"
run[1] n (skiing)	la piste	"peest"
▷ **which are the easiest runs?**	quelles sont les pistes les plus faciles?	"kel soñ lay peest lay ploo faseel"
to run[2] vb	courir	"kooreer"
▷ **the bus runs every 20 minutes**	le bus passe toutes les 20 minutes	"luh boos pas toot leh vañ meenoot"
▷ **he runs the hotel**	il tient l'hôtel	"eel tyañ lotell"
▷ **she runs her own business**	elle dirige sa propre entreprise	"el deereezh sa propr oñtruhpreez"
▷ **I run courses in marketing**	je donne des cours de marketing	"zhuh don day koor duh marketeeng"
running:		
▷ **to go running**	aller courir	"alay kooreer"
rush hour	les heures (fpl) d'affluence	"uhr dafloo-oñs"
saccharine	la saccharine	"sakareen"
safe[1] n	le coffre-fort	"kofr-for"
▷ **please put this in the hotel safe**	mettez cela dans le coffre-fort de l'hôtel s'il vous plaît	"metay sla doñ luh kofr-for duh lotell seel voo pleh"
safe[2] adj (beach, medicine)	sans danger	"soñ doñ-zhay"
▷ **is it safe to swim here?**	est-ce qu'on peut se baigner ici sans danger?	"es-koñ puh suh baynyay eesee soñ doñ-zhay"
▷ **is it safe for children?** (medicine)	c'est sans danger pour les enfants?	"seh soñ doñ-zhay poor layz oñfoñ"
safe sex	les rapports (mpl) sexuels protégés	"rapor sexooell protay-zhay"

ABSOLUTE ESSENTIALS

I don't understand	je ne comprends pas	"zhuh nuh koñproñ pa"
I don't speak French	je ne parle pas français	"zhuh nuh parl pa froñsay"
do you speak English?	parlez-vous anglais?	"parlay-voo oñglay"
could you help me?	pourriez-vous m'aider?	"pooreeay-voo mayday"

safety pin	l'épingle (*f*) de sûreté	"aypañgl duh soortay"
▷ **I need a safety pin**	j'ai besoin d'une épingle de sûreté	"zhay buhzwañ doon aypañgl duh soortay"
sail[1] *n*	la voile	"vwal"
to sail[2] *vb*:		
▷ **when do we sail?**	à quelle heure part le bateau?	"a kel uhr par luh bato"
sailboard	la planche à voile	"ploñsh a vwal"
▷ **I'd like to go sailboarding**	je voudrais faire de la planche à voile	"zhuh voodray fehr de la ploñsh a vwal"
sailing (*sport*)	la voile	"vwal"
▷ **what time is the next sailing?**	la prochaine traversée est à quelle heure?	"la proshen travehrsay et a kel uhr"
▷ **I'd like to go sailing**	je voudrais faire de la voile	"zhuh voodray fehr duh la vwal"
salad	la salade	"saladd"
▷ **a mixed salad**	une salade composée	"oon saladd koñpoh-zay"
salad dressing	la vinaigrette	"veenaygrett"
saline solution (for contact lenses)	la solution saline (pour lentilles de contact)	"soloosyoñ saleen (poor loñteey duh koñtakt)"
salmon	le saumon	"sohmoñ"
salt	le sel	"sel"
▷ **pass the salt, please**	passez-moi le sel, s'il vous plaît	"passay-mwa luh sel seel voo pleh"
same	même	"mem"
▷ **I'll have the same**	je vais prendre la même chose	"zhuh vay proñdr la mem shohz"
sand	le sable	"sabl"
sandals	les sandales (*fpl*)	"soñdal"
sandwich	le sandwich	"soñdweech"

▷ **what kind of sandwiches do you have?**	quels types de sandwichs avez-vous?	"kel teep duh soñdweech avay-voo"
sandy:		
▷ **a sandy beach**	une plage de sable	"oon plazh duh sabl"
sanitary towel	la serviette hygiénique	"sehrvyet ee-zhayneek"
sardine	la sardine	"sardeen"
Saturday	samedi (*m*)	"samdee"
sauce	la sauce	"sohs"
saucepan	la casserole	"kasroll"
saucer	la soucoupe	"sookoop"
sauna	le sauna	"sohna"
sausage	la saucisse	"sohsees"
savoury (*not sweet*)	salé(e)	"salay"
to **say**	dire	"deer"
scallop	la coquille Saint-Jacques	"kokeey sañ-zhak"
scampi	les langoustines (*fpl*) frites	"loñgoosteen freet"
scarf	l'écharpe (*f*)	"aysharp"
school	l'école (*f*)	"aykol"
scissors	les ciseaux (*mpl*)	"seezoh"
Scotland	l'Écosse (*f*)	"aykoss"
Scottish	écossais (*m*)	"aykoseh"
	écossaise (*f*)	"aykosez"
▷ **I'm Scottish**	je suis écossais/ écossaise	"zhuh sweez aykoseh/ aykosez"
screw	la vis	"vees"

ABSOLUTE ESSENTIALS

do you have ...?	avez-vous ...?	"avay-voo"
is there ...?	y a-t-il ...?	"ya-teel"
are there ...?	y a-t-il ...?	"ya-teel"
how much is ...?	combien coûte ...?	"koñbyañ koot"

▷ **the screw has come loose**	la vis s'est défaite	"la vees seh dayfet"
screwdriver	le tournevis	"toornvees"
scuba diving:		
▷ **where can we go scuba diving?**	où est-ce qu'on peut faire de la plongée sous-marine?	"oo es-koñ puh fehr duh la ploñ-zhay soo-mareen"
sculpture (*object*)	la sculpture	"skoolptoor"
sea	la mer	"mehr"
seafood	les fruits (*mpl*) de mer	"frwee duh mehr"
▷ **do you like seafood?**	est-ce que vous aimez les fruits de mer?	"es-kuh vooz ehmay lay frwee duh mehr"
seasickness	le mal de mer	"mal duh mehr"
seaside:		
▷ **at the seaside**	au bord de la mer	"oh bor duh la mehr"
season ticket	l'abonnement (*m*)	"abonmoñ"
seat (*chair*)	le siège	"syezh"
(*in train, theatre*)	la place	"plas"
▷ **is this seat free?**	est-ce que cette place est libre?	"es-kuh set plas eh leebr"
▷ **is this seat taken?**	est-ce que cette place est prise?	"es-kuh set plas eh preez"
▷ **we'd like to reserve 2 seats for tonight**	nous désirons réserver 2 places pour ce soir	"noo dayzeeroñ rayzehrvay duh plas poor suh swar"
▷ **I have a seat reservation**	j'ai une place réservée	"zhay oon plas raysehrvay"
second	second (*m*)	"zgoñ"
	seconde (*f*)	"zgoñd"
second class	en deuxième	"oñ duhzyem"
to see	voir	"vwar"

▷ see you soon	à bientôt	"a byañto"
▷ what is there to see here?	qu'est-ce qu'il y a à voir dans la région?	"kes-keel ya a vwar doñ la ray-zhoñ"
self-service	le libre-service	"leebr-sehrvees"
to **sell**	vendre	"voñdr"
▷ do you sell stamps?	est-ce que vous vendez des timbres?	"es-kuh voo voñday day tañbr"
Sellotape®	le Scotch®	"scotch"
semi-skimmed milk	le lait demi-écrémé	"leh duhmee-aykraymay"
to **send**	envoyer	"oñvwayay"
▷ please send my mail/ luggage on to this address	faites suivre mon courrier/mes bagages à cette adresse s'il vous plaît	"fet sweevr moñ kooryay/ may bagazh a set adress seel voo pleh"
senior citizen	le retraité la retraitée	"ruhtrehtay" "ruhtrehtay"
▷ is there a reduction for senior citizens?	est-ce qu'il y a des réductions pour les personnes du troisième âge?	"es-keel ya day raydooksyoñ poor lay pehrsonn doo trwazyem azh"
separate	séparé(e)	"sayparay"
September	septembre (m)	"septoñbr"
serious	grave	"grav"
seriously:		
▷ he is seriously injured	il est sérieusement blessé	"eel eh sayree-uhzmoñ blessay"
to **serve**	servir	"sehrveer"
▷ we are still waiting to be served	on ne nous a pas encore servis	"oñ nuh nooz a pa oñkor sehrvee"
service (in restaurant)	le service	"sehrvees"

ABSOLUTE ESSENTIALS

I don't understand	je ne comprends pas	"zhuh nuh koñproñ pa"
I don't speak French	je ne parle pas français	"zhuh nuh parl pa froñsay"
do you speak English?	parlez-vous anglais?	"parlay-voo oñglay"
could you help me?	pourriez-vous m'aider?	"pooreeay-voo mayday"

is service included?	est-ce que le service est compris?	"es-kuh luh sehrvees eh koñpree"
what time is the service? (*church*)	a quelle heure est le service religieux?	"a kel uhr eh luh sehrvees ruhleezhyuh"
service charge	le service	"sehrvees"
service station	la station-service	"stasyoñ-sehrvees"
set menu	le menu	"mnoo"
we'll take the set menu	nous prendrons le menu	"noo proñdroñ luh mnoo"
do you have a set menu?	est-ce que vous avez un menu à prix fixe?	"es-kuh vooz avay uñ mnoo a pree feeks"
how much is the set menu?	combien fait le menu à prix fixe?	"koñbyañ feh luh mnoo a pree feeks"
seven	sept	"set"
seventeen	dix-sept	"dee-set"
seventy	soixante-dix	"swasoñt-dees"
shade	l'ombre (*f*)	"oñbr"
in the shade	à l'ombre	"a loñbr"
shallow	peu profond (*m*) peu profonde (*f*)	"puh profoñ" "puh profoñd"
shampoo	le shampooing	"shoñpwañ"
a shampoo and set, please	shampooing et mise en plis, s'il vous plaît	"shoñpwañ ay meez oñ plee seel voo pleh"
shandy	le panaché	"panashay"
to share	partager	"parta-zhay"
we could share a taxi	nous pourrions prendre un taxi ensemble	"noo pooryoñ proñdr uñ taxi oñsoñbl"
to shave	se raser	"suh razay"
shaving brush	le blaireau	"blayro"
shaving cream	la crème à raser	"krem a razay"

ABSOLUTE ESSENTIALS

I would like ...	j'aimerais ...	"zhemray"
I need ...	j'ai besoin de ...	"zhay buhswañ duh"
where is ...?	où se trouve ...?	"oo suh troov"
I'm looking for ...	je cherche ...	"zhuh shersh"

she	elle	"el"
sheet	le drap	"dra"
shellfish	le crustacé	"kroostassay"
sherry	le sherry	"shehree"
ship	le navire	"naveer"
shirt	la chemise	"shmeez"
shock absorber	l'amortisseur (m)	"amorteessuhr"
shoe	la chaussure	"shohsoor"
▷ **can you reheel these shoes?**	pouvez-vous remettre un talon à ces chaussures?	"poovay-voo ruhmetr uñ taloñ a say shohsoor"
shoe laces	les lacets (mpl) de chaussures	"laseh duh shohsoor"
shoe polish	le cirage	"seerazh"
shop	le magasin	"magazañ"
▷ **what time do the shops close?**	les magasins ferment à quelle heure?	"lay magazañ fehrm a kel uhr"
shopping:		
▷ **to go shopping**	faire des courses	"fehr day koors"
▷ **where is the main shopping area?**	où se trouvent la plupart des magasins?	"oo suh troov la ploopar day magazañ"
shopping centre	le centre commercial	"soñtr komehr-syal"
shop window	la vitrine	"la veetreen"
▷ **in the (shop) window**	dans la vitrine	"doñ la veetreen"
short	court (m)	"koor"
	courte (f)	"koort"
short cut	le raccourci	"rakoorsee"
shorts	le short	"short"

ABSOLUTE ESSENTIALS

do you have ...?	avez-vous ...?	"avay-voo"
is there ...?	y a-t-il ...?	"ya-teel"
are there ...?	y a-t-il ...?	"ya-teel"
how much is ...?	combien coûte ...?	"koñbyañ koot"

short-sighted:

▷ **I'm short-sighted**	je suis myope	"zhuh swee myop"
shoulder	l'épaule (f)	"aypoll"
▷ **I've hurt my shoulder**	je me suis fait mal à l'épaule	"zhuh muh swee feh mal a laypoll"
show¹ n	le spectacle	"spektakl"
to show² vb	montrer	"moñtray"
▷ **could you show me please?**	est-ce que vous pourriez me le montrer?	"es-kuh voo pooryay muh luh moñtray"
▷ **could you show us around?**	est-ce que vous pourriez nous faire visiter?	"es-kuh voo pooryay noo fehr veezeetay"
shower	la douche	"doosh"
▷ **how does the shower work?**	la douche marche comment?	"la doosh marsh komoñ"
▷ **I'd like a room with a shower**	je voudrais une chambre avec douche	"zhuh voodrayz oon shoñbr avek doosh"
shrimp	la crevette grise	"kruhvet greez"
sick (ill)	malade	"malad"
▷ **she has been sick**	elle a vomi	"el a vomee"
▷ **I feel sick**	j'ai envie de vomir	"zhay oñvee duh vomeer"
sightseeing	le tourisme	"tooreezmuh"
▷ **are there any sightseeing tours?**	y a-t-il des excursions organisées?	"ee a-teel dayz ekskoorsyoñ organeezay"
sign¹ n	le panneau	"pano"
to sign² vb	signer	"seenyay"
▷ **where do I sign?**	où est-ce que je dois signer?	"oo es-kuh zhuh dwa seenyay"
signature	la signature	"seenyatoor"

silk	la soie	"swa"
silver	l'argent (m)	"ar-zhoñ"
similar	semblable	"soñblabl"
simple	simple	"sañpl"
single (unmarried)	célibataire	"sayleebatehr"
(not double)	simple	"sañpl"
(bed, room)	pour une personne	"poor oon pehrsonn"
▷ **a single to ..., second class**	un aller simple pour ..., en seconde classe	"un alay sañpl poor ... oñ zgoñd klas"
single bed	le lit pour une personne	"lee poor oon pehrsonn"
single room	la chambre pour une personne	"shoñbr poor oon pehrsonn"
▷ **I want to reserve a single room**	je voudrais réserver une chambre pour une personne	"zhuh voodray rayzehrvay oon shoñbr poor oon pehrsonn"
sir	Monsieur	"muhsyuh"
sister	la sœur	"suhr"
to sit	s'asseoir	"saswar"
▷ **please sit down**	asseyez-vous s'il vous plaît	"assayay-voo seel voo pleh"
six	six	"sees"
sixteen	seize	"sehz"
sixty	soixante	"swasoñt"
size	la taille	"tye"
▷ **I take a continental size 40**	je prends du 40	"zhuh proñ doo karoñt"
▷ **do you have this in a bigger/smaller size?**	est-ce que vous avez ceci dans une plus grande/plus petite taille?	"es-kuh vooz avay suhsee doñz oon ploo groñd/ploo puhteet tye"

ABSOLUTE ESSENTIALS

I don't understand	je ne comprends pas	"zhuh nuh koñproñ pa"
I don't speak French	je ne parle pas français	"zhuh nuh parl pa froñsay"
do you speak English?	parlez-vous anglais?	"parlay-voo oñglay"
could you help me?	pourriez-vous m'aider?	"pooreeay-voo mayday"

skate	le patin	"patañ"
▷ **where can we hire skates?**	où est-ce que nous pouvons louer des patins?	"oo es-kuh noo poovoñ loo-ay day patañ"
skateboard	le skateboard	"skateboard"
skateboarding:		
▷ **I'd like to go skateboarding**	je voudrais faire du skateboard	"zhuh voodray fehr doo skateboard"
skating:		
▷ **where can we go (ice) skating?**	où est-ce qu'on peut faire du patin à glace?	"oo es-koñ puh fehr doo patañ a glas"
▷ **where can we go (roller) skating?**	où est-ce qu'on peut faire du patin à roulettes?	"oo es-koñ puh fehr doo patañ a roolett"
ski¹ *n*	le ski	"skee"
▷ **can we hire skis here?**	est-ce qu'on peut louer des skis ici?	"es-koñ puh loo-ay day skee eesee"
to ski² *vb*	faire du ski	"fehr doo skee"
ski boots	les chaussures *(fpl)* de ski	"shohsoor duh skee"
skid:		
▷ **the car skidded**	la voiture a dérapé	"la vwatoor a dayrapay"
skiing (downhill) (cross-country)	le ski alpin le ski di fond	"skee alpañ" "skee duh foñ"
▷ **to go skiing**	faire du ski	"fehr doo skee"
▷ **to go cross-country skiing**	faire du ski de fond	"fehr doo skee duh foñ"
skiing lessons	les cours *(mpl)* de ski	"koor duh skee"
▷ **do you organize skiing lessons?**	est-ce que vous organisez des cours de ski?	"es-kuh vooz organeezay day koor duh skee"
ski instructor	le moniteur de ski	"moneetuhr duh skee"

ski jacket	le blouson de ski	"bloozoñ duh skee"
ski lift	la remontée mécanique	"ruhmoñtay maykaneek"
skimmed milk	le lait écrémé	"leh aykraymay"
skin	la peau	"poh"
skin diving	la plongée sous-marine	"ploñzhay soo-mareen"
ski pants	le fuseau	"foozo"
ski pass	le forfait de ski	"forfeh duh skee"
ski pole	le bâton de ski	"bahtoñ duh skee"
ski resort	la station de ski	"stasyon duh skee"
skirt	la jupe	"zhoop"
ski run	la piste	"peest"
ski suit	la combinaison de ski	"koñbee-nehzoñ duh skee"
sledge	la luge	"loozh"
sledging:		
▷ **where can we go sledging?**	où est-ce qu'on peut faire de la luge?	"oo es-koñ puh fehr duh la loozh"
to sleep	dormir	"dormeer"
▷ **I can't sleep for the noise**	je ne peux pas dormir à cause du bruit	"zhuh nuh puh pa dormeer a kohz doo brwee"
sleeper:		
▷ **can I reserve a sleeper?**	est-ce que je peux réserver une place dans une voiture-lit?	"es-kuh zhuh puh rayzehrvay oon plas doñs oon vwatoor-lee"
sleeping bag	le sac de couchage	"sak duh kooshazh"
sleeping car	le voiture-lit	"vwatoor-lee"
sleeping pill	le somnifère	"somneefehr"
slice	la tranche	"troñsh"

ABSOLUTE ESSENTIALS

do you have ...?	avez-vous ...?	"avay-voo"
is there ...?	y a-t-il ...?	"ya-teel"
are there ...?	y a-t-il ...?	"ya-teel"
how much is ...?	combien coûte ...?	"koñbyañ koot"

slide (*photograph*)	la diapositive	"dyapozeeteev"
slow	lent (*m*)	"loñ"
	lente (*f*)	"loñt"
slow down	ralentissez	"raloñtissay"
slowly	lentement	"loñtmoñ"
▷ **please speak slowly**	parlez lentement s'il vous plaît	"parlay loñtmoñ seel voo pleh"
small	petit (*m*)	"puhtee"
	petite (*f*)	"puhteet"
smaller (than)	plus petit (que)	"ploo puhtee (kuh)"
	plus petite (que)	"ploo puhteet (kuh)"
smell	l'odeur (*f*)	"oduhr"
smoke[1] *n*	la fumée	"foomay"
to **smoke**[2] *vb*	fumer	"foomay"
▷ **do you mind if I smoke?**	est-ce que cela vous dérange si je fume?	"es-kuh sla voo dayroñzh see zhuh foom"
▷ **do you smoke?**	est-ce que vous fumez?	"es-kuh voo foomay"
smoked	fumé(e)	"foomay"
smoking:		
▷ **I'd like a seat in the smoking area**	je voudrais une place dans la zone fumeurs	"zhuh voodrayz oon plas doñ la zohn foomuhr"
▷ **I'd like a no smoking room**	je voudrais une chambre non-fumeurs	"zhuh voodrayz oon shoñbr noñ-foomuhr"
smoky:		
▷ **it's too smoky here**	c'est trop enfumé ici	"seh troh oñfoomay eesee"
snack bar	le snack	"snack"
snorkel	le tuba	"tooba"
snorkelling:		
▷ **to go snorkelling**	faire de la plongée avec tuba	"fehr duh la ploñzhay avek tooba"

snow[1] *n*	la neige	"nezh"
▷ **what are the snow conditions?**	quelles sont les conditions d'enneigement?	"kel soñ lay koñdeesyoñ doñnezh-moñ"
to snow[2] *vb*	neiger	"neh-zhay"
▷ **is it going to snow?**	est-ce qu'il va neiger?	"es-keel va neh-zhay"
snowboard	le snowboard	"snowboard"
snowboarding:		
▷ **to go snowboarding**	faire du snowboard	"fehr doo snowboard"
snowed up	enneigé(e)	"oñneh-zhay"
snowing:		
▷ **it's snowing**	il neige	"eel nezh"
snowplough	le chasse-neige	"shass-nezh"
so:		
▷ **so much**	tant	"toñ"
soaking solution (for contact lenses)	la solution de conservation (pour lentilles de contact)	"soloosyoñ duh koñsehrvasyoñ (poor loñteey duh koñtakt)"
soap	le savon	"savoñ"
▷ **there is no soap**	il n'y a pas de savon	"eel nya pa duh savoñ"
soap powder	la lessive	"leseev"
sober (*not drunk*)	pas ivre	"paz eevr"
sock	la chaussette	"shohsett"
socket	la prise de courant	"preez duh kooroñ"
▷ **where is the socket for my electric razor?**	où se trouve la prise pour rasoir électrique?	"oo suh troov la preez poor razwar aylektreek"
soda	l'eau (*f*) de Seltz	"oh duh selts"

ABSOLUTE ESSENTIALS

I don't understand	je ne comprends pas	"zhuh nuh koñproñ pa"
I don't speak French	je ne parle pas français	"zhuh nuh parl pa froñsay"
do you speak English?	parlez-vous anglais?	"parlay-voo oñglay"
could you help me?	pourriez-vous m'aider?	"pooreeay-voo mayday"

soft

soft	doux (m)	"doo"
	douce (f)	"doos"
soft drink	la boisson non alcoolisée	"bwasoñ non alkoleezay"
sole	la sole	"sol"
soluble aspirin	l'aspirine (f) soluble	"aspeereen sooloobl"

solution:

▷ saline solution for contact lenses	la solution saline pour lentilles de contact	"sooloosyoñ saleen poor loñteey duh koñtakt"
▷ cleansing solution for contact lenses	la solution d'aseptisation pour lentilles de contact	"sooloosyoñ dasepteezasyoñ poor loñteey duh koñtakt"
▷ soaking solution for contact lenses	la solution de conservation pour lentilles de contact	"sooloosyoñ duh koñsehrvasyoñ poor loñteey duh koñtakt"
some	quelques	"kelkuh"
someone	quelqu'un	"kelkuñ"
something	quelque chose	"kelkuh shohz"
sometimes	quelquefois	"kelkuhfwa"
son	le fils	"fees"
song	la chanson	"shoñsoñ"
soon	bientôt	"byañto"
sore	douloureux (m)	"doolooruh"
	douloureuse (f)	"doolooruz"
▷ I have a sore throat	j'ai mal à la gorge	"zhay mal a la gorzh"
▷ my feet/eyes are sore	j'ai mal aux pieds/aux yeux	"zhay mal oh pyay/ohz yuh"

sorry:

| ▷ I'm sorry! | excusez-moi | "exkoozay-mwa" |

ABSOLUTE ESSENTIALS

I would like ...	j'aimerais ...	"zhemray"
I need ...	j'ai besoin de ...	"zhay buhswañ duh"
where is ...?	où se trouve ...?	"oo suh troov"
I'm looking for ...	je cherche ...	"zhuh shersh"

sort:

▷ **what sort of cheese?** | quelle sorte de fromage? | "kel sort duh fromazh"

soup | le potage | "potazh"

▷ **what is the soup of the day?** | quel est le potage du jour? | "kel eh luh potazh doo zhoor"

south | le sud | "sood"

souvenir | le souvenir | "soovneer"

space:

▷ **parking space** | la place de stationnement | "plas duh stasyonmoñ"

spade | la pelle | "pel"

Spain | l'Espagne (f) | "espanyuh"

Spanish | espagnol(e) | "espanyol"

spanner | la clé | "klay"

spare wheel | la roue de rechange | "roo duh ruhshoñzh"

sparkling wine | le vin pétillant | "vañ payteeyoñ"

spark plug | la bougie | "boozhee"

to speak | parler | "parlay"

▷ **can I speak to ...?** | est-ce que je peux parler à ...? | "es-kuh zhuh puh parlay a"

▷ **please speak louder** | parlez plus fort s'il vous plaît | "parlay ploo for seel voo pleh"

special | spécial(e) | "spaysyal"

▷ **do you have a special menu for children?** | est-ce que vous avez un menu spécial pour les enfants? | "es-kuh vooz avay uñ mnoo spaysyal poor layz oñfoñ"

speciality | la spécialité | "spaysya-leetay"

▷ **is there a local speciality?** | est-ce qu'il y a une spécialité régionale? | "es-keel ya oon spaysya-leetay ray-zhonal"

ABSOLUTE ESSENTIALS

do you have ...?	avez-vous ...?	"avay-voo"
is there ...?	y a-t-il ...?	"ya-teel"
are there ...?	y a-t-il ...?	"ya-teel"
how much is ...?	combien coûte ...?	"koñbyañ koot"

▷ **what is the chef's speciality?**	quelle est la spécialité du chef?	"kel eh la spaysya-leetay doo shef"
speed	la vitesse	"veetes"
speed limit	la limitation de vitesse	"leemeetasyoñ duh veetes"
▷ **what is the speed limit on this road?**	sur cette route, la vitesse est limitée à combien?	"soor set root la veetes eh leemeetay a koñbyañ"
speedometer	le compteur de vitesse	"koñtuhr duh veetes"
to **spell:**		
▷ **how do you spell it?**	comment ça s'écrit?	"komoñ sa saykree"
spicy	épicé(e)	"aypeesay"
spinach	l'épinard (m)	"aypeenar"
spirits	les spiritueux (mpl)	"speereetwuh"
sponge	l'éponge (f)	"aypoñzh"
spoon	la cuiller	"kweeyehr"
sport	le sport	"spor"
▷ **which sports activities are available here?**	on peut pratiquer quels sports ici?	"oñ puh prateekay kel spor eesee"
spring (season)	le printemps	"prañtoñ"
square (in town)	la place	"plas"
squash (game)	le squash	"skwosh"
(lemon drink)	la citronnade	"seetronad"
(orange drink)	l'orangeade	"oroñ-zhad"
stain	la tache	"tash"
▷ **this stain is coffee/ blood**	c'est une tache de café/ sang	"set oon tash duh kafay/ soñ"
▷ **can you remove this stain?**	est-ce que vous pouvez faire partir cette tache?	"es-kuh voo poovay fehr parteer set tash"

ABSOLUTE ESSENTIALS

yes (please)	oui (merci)	"wee (mehrsee)"
no (thank you)	non (merci)	"noñ (mehrsee)"
hello	bonjour	"boñzhoor"
goodbye	au revoir	"o ruhvwar"

stairs	l'escalier (m)	"eskalyay"
stalls (theatre)	l'orchestre (m)	"orkestr"
stamp	le timbre	"tañbr"
▷ **do you sell stamps?**	est-ce que vous vendez des timbres?	"es-kuh voo voñday day tañbr"
▷ **I'd like 6 stamps for postcards to America, please**	je voudrais 6 timbres pour affranchir des cartes postales pour l'Amérique, s'il vous plaît	"zhuh voodray see tañbr poor afroñsheer day kart postall poor lamayreek seel voo pleh"
▷ **12 3 franc stamps, please**	12 timbres à 3 francs, s'il vous plaît	"dooz tañbr a trwa froñ seel voo pleh"
▷ **where can I buy stamps?**	où est-ce que je peux acheter des timbres?	"oo es-kuh zhuh puh ashtay day tañbr"
to start	commencer	"komoñsay"
▷ **when does the film start?**	quand commence le film?	"koñ komoñs luh feelm"
starter (in meal)	le hors d'œuvre	"or duhvr"
(in car)	le démarreur	"daymaruhr"
station	la gare	"gar"
▷ **to the main station, please**	à la gare, s'il vous plaît	"a la gar seel voo pleh"
stationer's	la papeterie	"paptree"
to stay (remain)	rester	"restay"
▷ **I'm staying at the hotel ...**	je suis à l'hôtel ...	"zhuh sweez a lotell"
▷ **I want to stay an extra night**	je voudrais rester une nuit supplémentaire	"zhuh voodray restay oon nwee sooplaymoñtehr"
▷ **where are you staying?**	où est-ce que vous logez?	"oo es-kuh voo lozhay"
steak	le bifteck	"beeftek"
steep	raide	"red"

ABSOLUTE ESSENTIALS

I don't understand	je ne comprends pas	"zhuh nuh koñproñ pa"
I don't speak French	je ne parle pas français	"zhuh nuh parl pa froñsay"
do you speak English?	parlez-vous anglais?	"parlay-voo oñglay"
could you help me?	pourriez-vous m'aider?	"pooreeay-voo mayday"

sterling:

▷ **pounds sterling**	le sterling	"stehrling"
▷ **what is the rate for sterling?**	combien vaut la livre?	"koñbyañ voh la leevr"

stew	le ragoût	"ragoo"
steward	le steward	"steward"
stewardess	l'hôtesse (f)	"ohtess"
sticking plaster	le sparadrap	"sparadra"
still (*motionless*)	immobile	"eemobeel"
▷ **is he still there?**	est-ce qu'il est toujours là?	"es-keel eh too-zhoor la"
sting	la piqûre	"peekoor"
stockings	les bas (*mpl*)	"ba"
stolen	volé(e)	"volay"
▷ **my passport/my watch has been stolen**	on m'a volé mon passeport/ma montre	"oñ ma volay moñ paspor/ ma moñtr"
stomach	l'estomac (*m*)	"estoma"
stomach ache	les maux (*mpl*) d'estomac	"moh destoma"
stomach upset	l'estomac (*m*) dérangé	"estoma dayroñ-zhay"
▷ **I have a stomach upset**	j'ai l'estomac dérangé	"zhay lestoma dayroñ-zhay"
to stop	arrêter	"arehtay"
▷ **stop here**	arrêtez-vous ici	"arehtay-vooz eesee"
▷ **does the train stop at ...?**	est-ce que le train s'arrête à ...?	"es-kuh luh trañ saret a"
▷ **where do we stop for lunch?**	où nous arrêtons-nous pour déjeuner?	"oo nooz arehtoñ-noo poor dayzhuh-nay"
▷ **please stop the bus**	arrêtez-le bus, s'il vous plaît	"arehtay luh boos seel voo pleh"
stopover	la halte	"alt"

ABSOLUTE ESSENTIALS

I would like ...	j'aimerais ...	"zhemray"
I need ...	j'ai besoin de ...	"zhay buhswañ duh"
where is ...?	où se trouve ...?	"oo suh troov"
I'm looking for ...	je cherche ...	"zhuh shersh"

storm	l'orage (m)	"orazh"
stormy:		
▷ it's (very) stormy	le temps est (très) orageux	"luh toñ eh trehz ora-zhuh"
straight on	tout droit	"too drwa"
strap (of suitcase, bag)	la lanière	"lanyehr"
▷ I need a new strap for my watch	j'ai besoin d'un nouveau bracelet pour ma montre	"zhay buhzwañ duñ noovo braslay poor ma moñtr"
straw (for drinking)	la paille	"pye"
strawberry	la fraise	"frez"
street	la rue	"roo"
street map	le plan des rues	"ploñ day roo"
string	la ficelle	"feesell"
striped	rayé(e)	"rayay"
strong	fort (m)	"for"
	forte (f)	"fort"
stuck	bloqué(e)	"blokay"
student	l'étudiant (m)	"aytoodyoñ"
	l'étudiante (f)	"aytoodyoñt"
stung	piqué(e)	"peekay"
▷ he has been stung	il a été piqué	"eel a aytay peekay"
stupid	stupide	"stoopeed"
suddenly	soudain	"soodañ"
suede	le daim	"dañ"
sugar	le sucre	"sookr"
suit (man's)	le costume	"kostoom"
(women's)	le tailleur	"tye-yuhr"

ABSOLUTE ESSENTIALS

do you have ...?	avez-vous ...?	"avay-voo"
is there ...?	y a-t-il ...?	"ya-teel"
are there ...?	y a-t-il ...?	"ya-teel"
how much is ...?	combien coûte ...?	"koñbyañ koot"

suitcase	la valise	"valeez"
▷ **my suitcase was damaged in transit**	ma valise a été endommagé pendant le voyage	"ma valeez a aytay oñdomazhay poñdoñ luh vwayazh"
▷ **my suitcase is missing**	ma valise est égarée	"ma valeez et aygaray"
summer	l'été (m)	"aytay"
sun	le soleil	"solay"
to sunbathe	prendre un bain de soleil	"proñdr uñ bañ duh solay"
sunbed (lounger)	le lit bain de soleil	"lee bañ duh solay"
(with sunray lamp)	le lit à ultra-violets	"lee a ooltra-vyoleh"
sunburn	le coup de soleil	"koo duh solay"
▷ **can you give me anything for sunburn?**	est-ce que vous pouvez me donner quelque chose pour les coups de soleil?	"es-kuh voo poovay muh donay kelkuh shohz poor lay koo duh solay"
sunburnt:		
▷ **I am sunburnt**	j'ai attrapé des coups de soleil	"zhay atrapay day koo duh solay"
Sunday	dimanche (m)	"deemoñsh"
sunglasses	les lunettes (fpl) de soleil	"loonett duh solay"
sun lounger	le lit bain de soleil	"lee bañ duh solay"
sunny:		
▷ **it's sunny**	il fait du soleil	"eel feh doo solay"
sunshade	le parasol	"parasoll"
sunstroke	l'insolation (f)	"añsolasyoñ"
suntan lotion	le lait solaire	"leh solehr"
supermarket	le supermarché	"soopehr-marshay"

supper (*dinner*)	le souper	"soopay"
supplement	le supplément	"sooplaymoñ"
▷ **is there a supplement to pay?**	est-ce qu'il faut payer un supplément?	"es-keel foh payay uñ sooplaymoñ"
sure	sûr(e)	"soor"
surface mail:		
▷ **by surface mail**	par voie de terre	"par vwa duh tehr"
surfboard	la planche de surf	"ploñsh duh surf"
▷ **can I rent a surfboard?**	est-ce que je peux louer une planche de surf?	"es-kuh zhuh puh loo-ay oon ploñsh duh surf"
surfer	le surfeur	"surfuhr"
surfing:		
▷ **to go surfing**	faire du surf	"fehr doo surf"
surname	le nom de famille	"noñ duh fameey"
sweater	le pull	"pool"
sweet	sucré(e)	"sookray"
sweetener	l'édulcorant (*m*)	"aydoolkoroñ"
sweets	les bonbons (*mpl*)	"boñboñ"
to swim	nager	"na-zhay"
▷ **can one swim in the river?**	peut-on se baigner dans la rivière?	"puh-toñ suh baynyay doñ la reevyehr"
▷ **is it safe to swim here?**	est-ce que l'on peut nager ici sans danger?	"es-kuh loñ puh na-zhay eesee soñ doñ-zhay"
▷ **can you swim?**	savez-vous nager?	"savay-voo na-zhay"
swimming:		
▷ **to go swimming**	aller nager	"alay na-zhay"
swimming pool	la piscine	"peeseen"
▷ **is there a swimming pool?**	est-ce qu'il y a une piscine?	"es-keel ya oon peeseen"

ABSOLUTE ESSENTIALS

I don't understand	je ne comprends pas	"zhuh nuh koñproñ pa"
I don't speak French	je ne parle pas français	"zhuh nuh parl pa froñsay"
do you speak English?	parlez-vous anglais?	"parlay-voo oñglay"
could you help me?	pourriez-vous m'aider?	"pooreeay-voo mayday"

▷ where is the municipal swimming pool?	où est la piscine municipale?	"oo eh la peeseen mooneeseepal"
swimsuit	le maillot de bain	"mye-yo duh bañ"
Swiss	suisse	"swees"
switch	le bouton	"bootoñ"
to switch off	éteindre	"aytañdr"
▷ can I switch the light/ radio off?	est-ce que je peux éteindre la lumière/la radio?	"es-kuh zhuh puhz aytañdr la loomyehr/la radyo"
to switch on	allumer	"aloomay"
▷ can I switch the light/ radio on?	est-ce que je peux allumer la lumière/la radio?	"es-kuh zhuh puhz aloomay la loomyehr/la radyo"
Switzerland	la Suisse	"swees"
synagogue	la synagogue	"seenagog"
table	la table	"tabl"
▷ a table for four, please	une table pour quatre, s'il vous plaît	"oon tabl poor katr seel voo pleh"
▷ the table is booked for ... o'clock this evening	on a réservé une table pour ... heures ce soir	"oñ a rayzehrvay oon tabl poor ... uhr suh swar"
tablecloth	la nappe	"nap"
tablespoon	la cuiller de service	"kweeyehr duh sehrvees"
tablet	le comprimé	"koñpreemay"
table tennis	le ping-pong	"pingpong"
to take	prendre	"proñdr"
▷ how long does the journey take?	la visite prend combien de temps?	"la veezeet proñ koñbyañ duh toñ"
▷ I take a continental size 40	je prends du 40	"zhuh proñ doo karoñt"
▷ I'd like to take a shower	je voudrais prendre une douche	"zhuh voodray proñdr oon doosh"

▷ **could you take a photograph of us?**	est-ce que vous pourriez nous prendre en photo?	"es-kuh voo pooryay noo proñdr oñ foto"
talc	le talc	"talc"
to **talk**	parler	"parlay"
tall	grand (m) grande (f)	"groñ" "groñd"
▷ **how tall are you?**	quelle taille faites-vous?	"kel tye fet-voo"
▷ **how tall is it?**	quelle est sa taille?	"kel eh sa tye"
▷ **I am I m 80 tall**	je mesure I m 80	"zhuh muhzoor uñ metr katr-vañ"
▷ **it is 10 m tall**	il fait 10 m de haut	"eel fay dee metr duh oh"
tampons	les tampons (mpl)	"toñpoñ"
tap	le robinet	"robeenay"
tape (cassette)	la cassette	"kasett"
(video)	la vidéo	"veedayo"
(ribbon)	le ruban	"rooboñ"
tape-recorder	le magnétophone	"man-yetofon"
tart	la tarte	"tart"
tartar sauce	la sauce tartare	"sohs tartar"
taste[1] n	le goût	"goo"
to **taste**[2] vb	goûter	"gootay"
▷ **can I taste it?**	est-ce que je peux le goûter?	"es-kuh zhuh puh luh gootay"
tax	l'impôt (m)	"añpo"
taxi	le taxi	"taxi"
▷ **can you order me a taxi, please?**	pouvez-vous m'appeler un taxi, s'il vous plaît?	"poovay-voo maplay uñ taxi seel voo pleh"
taxi rank	la station de taxis	"stasyoñ duh taxi"

ABSOLUTE ESSENTIALS

do you have ...?	avez-vous ...?	"avay-voo"
is there ...?	y a-t-il ...?	"ya-teel"
are there ...?	y a-t-il ...?	"ya-teel"
how much is ...?	combien coûte ...?	"koñbyañ koot"

tea	le thé	"tay"
tea bag	le sachet de thé	"sashay duh tay"
to **teach**	enseigner	"oñsehnyay"
teacher	le professeur	"professuhr"
team	l'équipe (f)	"aykeep"
team games	les jeux (mpl) d'équipes	"zhuh daykeep"
teapot	la théière	"tay-yehr"
teaspoon	la cuiller à café	"kweeyehr a kafay"
teat	la tétine	"tayteen"
tee shirt	le tee-shirt	"tee-shirt"
teeth	les dents (mpl)	"doñ"
telegram	le télégramme	"taylaygram"
▷ **can I send a telegram from here?**	est-ce que je peux envoyer un télégramme d'ici?	"es-kuh zhuh puh oñvwayay uñ taylaygram deesee"
telephone[1] n	le téléphone	"taylayfonn"
to **telephone**[2] vb	téléphoner	"taylayfonay"
▷ **how much is it to telephone Britain?**	ça coûte combien pour téléphoner en Grande-Bretagne?	"sa koot koñbyañ poor taylayfonay oñ groñd-bruhtanyuh"
telephone book	l'annuaire (m)	"anwehr"
telephone box	la cabine téléphonique	"kabeen taylayfoneek"
telephone call	le coup de téléphone	"koo duh taylayfonn"
▷ **I'd like to make a telephone call**	je voudrais téléphoner	"zhuh voodray taylayfonay"
telephone directory	l'annuaire (m)	"anwehr"
television	la télévision	"taylayveezyoñ"
television lounge	la salle de télé	"sal duh taylay"

▷ is there a television lounge?	est-ce qu'il y a une salle de télé?	"es-keel ya oon sal duh taylay"
television set	le poste de télévision	"post duh taylayveezyoñ"
telex	le télex	"tayleks"
to tell	dire	"deer"
temperature	la température	"toñpayratoor"
▷ to have a temperature	avoir de la fièvre	"avwar duh la fyehvr"
▷ what is the temperature?	quelle est la température?	"kel eh la toñpayratoor"
temporary	provisoire	"proveezwar"
ten	dix	"dees"
tennis	le tennis	"tenees"
▷ where can we play tennis?	où est-ce qu'on peut jouer au tennis?	"oo es-koñ puh zhoo-ay oh tenees"
tennis ball	la balle de tennis	"bal duh tenees"
tennis court	le court de tennis	"koor duh tenees"
▷ how much is it to hire a tennis court?	combien faut-il compter pour louer un court de tennis?	"koñbyañ foh-teel koñtay poor loo-ay uñ koor duh tenees"
tennis racket	la raquette de tennis	"rakett duh tenees"
tent	la tente	"toñt"
▷ can we pitch our tent here?	est-ce que nous pouvons planter notre tente ici?	"es-kuh noo poovoñ ploñtay notr toñt eesee"
tent peg	le piquet de tente	"peekeh duh toñt"
terminus	le terminus	"tehrmeenoos"
terrace	la terrasse	"tehras"
▷ can I eat on the terrace?	est-ce que je peux manger sur la terrasse?	"es-kuh zhuh puh moñzhay soor la tehras"

ABSOLUTE ESSENTIALS

I don't understand	je ne comprends pas	"zhuh nuh koñproñ pa"
I don't speak French	je ne parle pas français	"zhuh nuh parl pa froñsay"
do you speak English?	parlez-vous anglais?	"parlay-voo oñglay"
could you help me?	pourriez-vous m'aider?	"pooreeay-voo mayday"

than	que	"kuh"
▷ **better than this**	mieux que ceci	"myuh kuh suhsee"
thank you	merci	"mehrsee"
▷ **thank you very much**	merci beaucoup	"mehrsee bohkoo"
▷ **no thank you**	non merci	"noñ mehrsee"
that	cela	"sla"
▷ **that one**	celui-là (m)	"suhlwee-la"
	celle-là (f)	"sel-la"
thaw:		
▷ **it's thawing**	ça fond	"sa foñ"
theatre	le théâtre	"tayatr"
their	leur	"luhr"
theirs	le leur	"luhr"
then	alors	"alor"
there	là	"la"
▷ **there is/there are**	il y a	"eel ya"
thermometer	le thermomètre	"tehrmomehtr"
these	ceux-ci (m)	"suh-see"
	celles-ci (f)	"sel-see"
they	ils (m)	"eel"
	elles (f)	"el"
thief	le voleur	"voluhr"
thing	la chose	"shohz"
▷ **my things**	mes affaires	"mayz afehr"
to **think**	penser	"poñsay"
third	troisième	"trwazyem"
thirsty:		
▷ **I'm thirsty**	j'ai soif	"zhay swaf"

ABSOLUTE ESSENTIALS

I would like ...	j'aimerais ...	"zhemray"
I need ...	j'ai besoin de ...	"zhay buhswañ duh"
where is ...?	où se trouve ...?	"oo suh troov"
I'm looking for ...	je cherche ...	"zhuh shersh"

thirteen	treize	"trehz"
thirty	trente	"troñt"
this	ceci	"suhsee"
▷ **this one**	celui-ci (*m*)	"suhlwee-see"
	celle-ci (*f*)	"sel-see"
those	ceux-là (*m*)	"suh-la"
	celles-là (*f*)	"sel-la"
thousand	mille	"meel"
thread	le fil	"feel"
three	trois	"trwa"
throat	la gorge	"gorzh"
▷ **I want something for a sore throat**	je voudrais quelque chose pour le mal de gorge	"zhuh voodray kelkuh shohz poor luh mal duh gorzh"
throat lozenges	les pastilles (*fpl*) pour la gorge	"pasteey poor la gorzh"
through	à travers	"a travehr"
▷ **I can't get through** (*on telephone*)	je n'arrive pas à obtenir la communication	"zhuh nareev pa a optneer la komooneekasyoñ"
▷ **is it/this a through train?**	est-ce que c'est un train direct?	"es-kuh set uñ trañ deerekt"
thunder:		
▷ **I think it's going to thunder**	je pense qu'il va y avoir du tonnerre	"zhuh poñs keel va yavwar doo tonehr"
thunderstorm	l'orage (*m*)	"orazh"
▷ **will there be a thunderstorm?**	est-ce qu'il va y avoir un orage?	"es-keel va yavwar un orazh"
Thursday	jeudi (*m*)	"zhuhdee"
ticket	le billet	"beeyeh"
▷ **a single ticket**	un aller simple	"un alay sañpl"
▷ **a return ticket**	un aller-retour	"un alay-ruhtoor"

ABSOLUTE ESSENTIALS

do you have ...?	avez-vous ...?	"avay-voo"
is there ...?	y a-t-il ...?	"ya-teel"
are there ...?	y a-t-il ...?	"ya-teel"
how much is ...?	combien coûte ...?	"koñbyañ koot"

▷ a book of tickets	un carnet de tickets	"uñ karneh duh teekeh"
▷ 2 tickets for the opera/theatre	2 billets d'opéra/de théâtre	"duh beeyeh dopayra/duh tayatr"
▷ can you book the tickets for us?	pouvez-vous nous réserver les billets?	"poovay-voo noo rayzehrvay lay beeyeh"
▷ where do I buy a ticket?	où est-ce qu'on achète un ticket?	"oo es-kon ashet uñ teekeh"
▷ can I buy the tickets here?	est-ce que je peux acheter les billets ici?	"es-kuh zhuh puh ashtay lay beeyeh eesee"
ticket collector	le contrôleur	"koñtroluhr"
ticket office	le guichet	"geesheh"
tide	la marée	"maray"
tie	la cravate	"kravatt"
tights	le collant	"koloñ"
till¹ n	la caisse	"kes"
till² prep	jusqu'à	"zhooska"
▷ I want to stay 3 nights from ... till ...	je désire rester 3 nuits du ... au ...	"zhuh dayzeer restay trwah nwee doo ... oh"
time	le temps	"toñ"
▷ this time	cette fois	"set fwa"
▷ what time is it?	quelle heure est-il?	"kel uhr e-teel"
▷ do we have time to visit the town?	est-ce que nous avons le temps de visiter la ville?	"es-kuh nooz avoñ luh toñ duh veezeetay la veel"
▷ what time do we get to ...?	nous arrivons à quelle heure à ...?	"nooz areevoñ a kel uhr a"
▷ is it time to go?	est-ce qu'il est l'heure de partir?	"es-keel eh luhr duh parteer"
timetable (transport)	l'horaire (m)	"orehr"
▷ can I have a timetable?	est-ce que je peux avoir un horaire?	"es-kuh zhuh puh avwar un orehr"
timetable board	le tableau des horaires	"tablo dayz orehr"

ABSOLUTE ESSENTIALS

yes (please)	oui (merci)	"wee (mehrsee)"
no (thank you)	non (merci)	"noñ (mehrsee)"
hello	bonjour	"boñzhoor"
goodbye	au revoir	"o ruhvwar"

tin	la boîte	"bwat"
tinfoil	le papier d'étain	"papyay daytañ"
tin-opener	l'ouvre-boîtes (m)	"oovr-bwat"
tinted	coloré(e)	"koloray"
▷ my hair is tinted	j'ai une coloration	"zhay oon kolorasyoñ"
tip (to waiter etc)	le pourboire	"poorbwar"
▷ is it usual to tip?	est-ce qu'on donne habituellement un pourboire?	"es-koñ don abeetwelmoñ uñ poorbwar"
▷ how much should I tip?	je devrais donner un pourboire de combien?	"zhuh duhvray donay uñ poorbwar duh koñbyañ"
▷ is the tip included?	est-ce que le service est compris?	"es-kuh luh sehrvees eh koñpree"
tipped (cigarettes)	filtre	"filtr"
tired	fatigué(e)	"fateegay"
tiring	fatigant (m)	"fateegoñ"
	fatigante (f)	"fateegoñt"
tissue	le kleenex ®	"kleeneks"
to	à	"a"
(with name of country)	en	"oñ"
toast	le toast	"toast"
▷ 2 slices of toast	2 toasts	"duh toast"
tobacco	le tabac	"taba"
tobacconist's	le bureau de tabac	"booro duh taba"
today	aujourd'hui	"oh-zhoordwee"
▷ is it open today?	est-ce que c'est ouvert aujourd'hui?	"es-kuh set oovehr oh-zhoordwee"
together	ensemble	"oñsoñbl"

ABSOLUTE ESSENTIALS

I don't understand	je ne comprends pas	"zhuh nuh koñproñ pa"
I don't speak French	je ne parle pas français	"zhuh nuh parl pa froñsay"
do you speak English?	parlez-vous anglais?	"parlay-voo oñglay"
could you help me?	pourriez-vous m'aider?	"pooreeay-voo mayday"

toilet	les toilettes (fpl)	"twalett"
▷ is there a toilet for the disabled?	est-ce qu'il y a des toilettes pour handicapés?	"es-keel ya day twalett poor oñdeekapay"
▷ where are the toilets, please?	les toilettes, s'il vous plaît?	"lay twalett seel voo pleh"
▷ is there a toilet on board?	est-ce qu'il y a des toilettes à bord?	"es-keel ya day twalett a bor"
▷ the toilet won't flush	la chasse d'eau ne marche pas	"la shas doh nuh marsh pa"
toilet paper	le papier hygiénique	"papyay ee-zhayneek"
▷ there is no toilet paper	il n'y a pas de papier hygiénique	"eel nya pa duh papyay ee-zhayneek"
toll	le péage	"pay-yazh"
▷ is there a toll on this motorway?	est-ce que c'est une autoroute à péage?	"es-kuh set oon otoroot a pay-yazh"
tomato	la tomate	"tomat"
tomato juice	le jus de tomate	"zhoo duh tomat"
tomato soup	la soupe à la tomate	"soop a la tomat"
tomorrow	demain	"duhmañ"
▷ is it open tomorrow?	est-ce que c'est ouvert demain?	"es-kuh set oovehr duhmañ"
tomorrow afternoon	demain après-midi	"duhmañ apray-meedee"
tomorrow morning	demain matin	"duhmañ matañ"
tomorrow night	demain soir	"duhmañ swar"
tongue	la langue	"loñg"
tonic water	le Schweppes®	"shwepps"
tonight	ce soir	"suh swar"
too (also)	aussi	"osee"

ABSOLUTE ESSENTIALS

I would like ...	j'aimerais ...	"zhemray"
I need ...	j'ai besoin de ...	"zhay buhswañ duh"
where is ...?	où se trouve ...?	"oo suh troov"
I'm looking for ...	je cherche ...	"zhuh shersh"

▷ it's too big	c'est trop grand	"seh troh groñ"
tooth	la dent	"doñ"
▷ I've broken a tooth	j'ai une dent de cassée	"zhay oon doñ duh kassay"

toothache:

▷ I have toothache	j'ai mal aux dents	"zhay mal oh doñ"
▷ I want something for toothache	je voudrais quelque chose pour le mal aux dents	"zhuh voodray kelkuh shohz poor luh mal oh doñ"
toothbrush	la brosse à dents	"bros a doñ"
toothpaste	le dentifrice	"doñteefrees"
toothpick	le cure-dent	"koor-doñ"
top[1] *n*	le dessus	"duhsoo"
▷ on top of ...	sur ...	"soor"

top[2] *adj:*

▷ the top floor	le dernier étage	"dehr-nyehr aytazh"
torch	la lampe de poche	"loñp duh posh"
torn	déchiré(e)	"daysheeray"
total	le total	"totall"
tough (*meat*)	dur(e)	"door"
tour	l'excursion (*f*)	"ekskoorsyoñ"
▷ how long does the tour take?	la visite dure combien de temps?	"la veezeet door koñbyañ duh toñ"
▷ when is the bus tour of the town?	la visite guidée de la ville en bus est à quelle heure?	"la veezeet geeday duh la veel oñ boos et a kel uhr"
▷ the tour starts at about ...	la visite guidée commence vers ...	"la veezeet geeday komoñs vehr"
tourist	le/la touriste	"tooreest"

tourist office	le syndicat d'initiative	"sañdeeka deenee-syateev"
▷ **I'm looking for the tourist information office**	je cherche le syndicat d'initiative	"zhuh shersh luh sañdeeka deenee-syateev"
tourist ticket	le billet touristique	"beeyeh tooreesteek"
to **tow**	remorquer	"ruhmorkay"
▷ **can you tow me to a garage?**	pouvez-vous me remorquer jusqu'à un garage?	"poovay-voo muh ruhmorkay zhooska uñ garazh"
towel	la serviette	"sehr-vyett"
▷ **the towels have run out**	les essuie-mains sont finis	"layz eswee-mañ soñ feenee"
town	la ville	"veel"
town centre	le centre-ville	"soñtr-veel"
town plan	le plan de la ville	"ploñ duh la veel"
tow rope	le câble de remorque	"kahbl duh ruhmork"
toy	le jouet	"zhoo-eh"
toy shop	le magasin de jouets	"magazañ duh zhoo-eh"
traditional	traditionnel(e)	"tra-deesyonell"
traffic	la circulation	"seerkoolasyoñ"
▷ **is the traffic heavy on the motorway?**	est-ce qu'il y a beaucoup de circulation sur l'autoroute?	"es-keel ya bohkoo duh seerkoolasyoñ soor lotoroot"
▷ **is there a route that avoids the traffic?**	est-ce qu'il y a un itinéraire qui évite les encombrements?	"es-keel ya un eetee-nayrehr kee ayveet layz oñkoñ-bruhmoñ"
traffic jam	l'embouteillage (m)	"oñbootay-yazh"
trailer	la remorque	"ruhmork"

ABSOLUTE ESSENTIALS		
yes (please)	oui (merci)	"wee (mehrsee)"
no (thank you)	non (merci)	"noñ (mehrsee)"
hello	bonjour	"boñzhoor"
goodbye	au revoir	"o ruhvwar"

train	le train	"trañ"
▷ **what times are the trains to ...?**	quel est l'horaire des trains pour ...?	"kel eh lorehr day trañ poor"
▷ **when is the first/next/ last train to ...?**	à quelle heure est le premier/le prochain/le dernier train pour ...?	"a kel uhr eh luh pruhmyay/luh proshañ/ luh dehr-nyay trañ poor"
▷ **is this the train for ...?**	est-ce que c'est le train pour ...?	"es-kuh seh luh trañ poor"
▷ **does this train go to ...?**	est-ce que ce train va à ...?	"es-kuh suh trañ va a"
▷ **does this train stop at ...?**	est-ce que ce train s'arrête à ...?	"es-kuh suh trañ sarett a"
▷ **how frequent are the trains to town?**	il y a des trains pour le centre-ville tous les combien?	"eel ya day trañ poor luh soñtr-veel too lay koñbyañ"
▷ **are there any cheap train fares?**	est-ce qu'il y a des tarifs ferroviaires réduits?	"es-keel ya day tareef fehrov-yehr ray-dwee"
training shoes	les chaussures (fpl) de sport	"shohsoor duh spor"
tram	le tramway	"tramway"
trampoline	le trampolino	"trampoleeno"
to transfer	transférer	"troñsfayray"
▷ **I should like to transfer some money from my bank in ...**	je voudrais transférer de l'argent de ma banque à ...	"zhuh voodray troñsfayray duh lar-zhoñ duh ma boñk a"
to translate	traduire	"tradweer"
▷ **could you translate this for me?**	est-ce que vous pourriez traduire cela pour moi?	"es-kuh voo pooryay tradweer sla poor mwa"
translation	la traduction	"tradooksyoñ"
to travel	voyager	"vwaya-zhay"
▷ **I am travelling alone**	je voyage seul	"zhuh vwayazh suhl"
travel agent	l'agent (m) de voyages	"azhoñ duh vwayazh"

ABSOLUTE ESSENTIALS

I don't understand	je ne comprends pas	"zhuh nuh koñproñ pa"
I don't speak French	je ne parle pas français	"zhuh nuh parl pa froñsay"
do you speak English?	parlez-vous anglais?	"parlay-voo oñglay"
could you help me?	pourriez-vous m'aider?	"pooreeay-voo mayday"

traveller's cheques	le chèque de voyage	"shek duh vwayazh"
▷ do you accept traveller's cheques?	est-ce que vous acceptez les chèques de voyage?	"es-kuh vooz akseptay lay shek duh vwayazh"
▷ can I change my traveller's cheques here?	est-ce que je peux changer ici mes chèques de voyage?	"es-kuh zhuh puh shoñzhay eesee may shek duh vwayazh"
travel-sick:		
▷ I get travel-sick	je suis malade pendant les transports	"zhuh swee malad poñdoñ lay troñspor"
tray	le plateau	"plato"
tree	l'arbre (m)	"arbr"
trim:		
▷ can I have a trim?	est-ce que vous pouvez me faire une coupe d'entretien?	"es-kuh voo poovay muh fehr oon koop doñtr-tyañ"
trip	l'excursion (f)	"ekskoorsyoñ"
▷ this is my first trip to ...	c'est la première fois que je viens à ...	"seh la pruhmyehr fwa kuh zhuh vyañ a"
▷ a business trip	un voyage d'affaires	"uñ vwayazh dafehr"
▷ do you run day trips to ...?	est-ce que vous organisez des excursions à la journée à ...?	"es-kuh vooz organeezay dayz ekskoorsyoñ a la zhoornay a"
trolley	le chariot	"sharyo"
trouble	les ennuis (mpl)	"oñnwee"
▷ I am in trouble	j'ai un problème	"zhay uñ problemm"
▷ I'm sorry to trouble you	je suis désolé de vous déranger	"zhuh swee dayzolay duh voo dayroñ-zhay"
▷ I'm having trouble with the phone/key	j'ai des problèmes avec le téléphone/la clé	"zhay day problemm avek luh taylayfonn/la klay"
trousers	le pantalon	"poñtaloñ"
trout	la truite	"trweet"

ABSOLUTE ESSENTIALS		
I would like ...	j'aimerais ...	"zhemray"
I need ...	j'ai besoin de ...	"zhay buhswañ duh"
where is ...?	où se trouve ...?	"oo suh troov"
I'm looking for ...	je cherche ...	"zhuh shersh"

true	vrai(e)	"vray"
trunk (*luggage*)	la malle	"mal"
▷ I'd like to send my trunk on ahead	je voudrais faire envoyer ma malle	"zhuh voodray fehr oñvwayay ma mal"
trunks (*for swimming*)	le slip de bain	"sleep duh bañ"
to **try**	essayer	"essay-yay"
to **try on**	essayer	"essay-yay"
▷ may I try on this dress?	est-ce que je peux essayer cette robe?	"es-kuh zhuh puh essay-yay set rob"
T-shirt	le T-shirt	"tee-shirt"
Tuesday	mardi (*m*)	"mardee"
tuna	le thon	"toñ"
tunnel	le tunnel	"toonell"
▷ the Channel tunnel	le tunnel sous la Manche	"luh toonell soo la moñsh"
turkey	le dindon	"dañdoñ"
turn[1] *n*:		
▷ it's my/her turn	c'est mon/son tour	"seh moñ/soñ toor"
to **turn**[2] *vb* (*handle, wheel*)	tourner	"toornay"
to **turn down** (*sound, heating etc*)	diminuer	"deemeenoo-ay"
turning	le tournant	"toornoñ"
▷ is this the turning for ...?	est-ce que c'est là que je tourne pour ...?	"es-kuh seh la kuh zhuh toorn poor"
▷ take the second turning on your left	prenez le deuxième tournant à gauche	"pruhnay luh duhzyem toornoñ a gohsh"
turnip	le navet	"naveh"
to **turn off** (*light etc*)	éteindre	"aytañdr"

ABSOLUTE ESSENTIALS

do you have ...?	avez-vous ...?	"avay-voo"
is there ...?	y a-t-il ...?	"ya-teel"
are there ...?	y a-t-il ...?	"ya-teel"
how much is ...?	combien coûte ...?	"koñbyañ koot"

(engine)	couper	"koopay"
▷ I can't turn the heating off	je ne peux pas fermer le chauffage	"zhuh nuh puh pa fehrmay luh shofazh"
to **turn on** (light etc)	allumer	"aloomay"
(engine)	mettre en marche	"metroñ marsh"
▷ I can't turn the heating on	je ne peux pas ouvrir le chauffage	"zhuh nuh puh paz oovreer luh shofazh"
to **turn up** (sound, heating etc)	augmenter	"ohgmoñtay"
tweezers	la pince à épiler	"pañs a aypeelay"
twelve	douze	"dooz"
twenty	vingt	"vañ"
▷ about twenty people	une vingtaine de personnes	"oon vañten duh pehrsonn"
twenty-one	vingt et un	"vañt ay uñ"
twenty-two	vingt-deux	"vañ-duh"
twice	deux fois	"duh fwa"
twin-bedded room	la chambre à deux lits	"shoñbra duh lee"
two	deux	"duh"
typical	typique	"teepeek"
▷ have you anything typical of this region?	avez-vous quelque chose qui soit typique de cette région?	"avay-voo kelkuh shohz kee swa teepeek duh set ray-zhoñ"
tyre	le pneu	"pnuh"
tyre pressure	la pression des pneus	"pressyoñ day pnuh"
▷ what should the tyre pressure be?	quelle devrait être la pression des pneus?	"kel duhvret etr la pressyoñ day pnuh"
UK	le Royaume-Uni	"rwye-ohm oonee"
umbrella (for rain)	le parapluie	"paraplwee"
(on beach)	le parasoll	"parasol"

uncomfortable	inconfortable	"añkoñfortabl"
▷ the bed is uncomfortable	le lit est inconfortable	"luh lee et añkoñfortabl"
unconscious	sans connaissance	"soñ konehsoñs"
under	sous	"soo"
underground	le métro	"maytro"
underground station	la station de métro	"stasyoñ duh maytro"
underpass	le passage souterrain	"pasazh sootrañ"
to **understand**	comprendre	"koñproñdr"
▷ I don't understand	je ne comprends pas	"zhuh nuh koñproñ pa"
underwear	les sous-vêtements (*mpl*)	"soovetmoñ"
United States	les États Unis (*mpl*)	"aytaz oonee"
university	l'université (*f*)	"ooneevehr-seetay"
unleaded petrol	l'essence (*f*) sans plomb	"essoñs soñ ploñ"
to **unpack**	défaire ses bagages	"dayfehr say bagazh"
upstairs	en haut	"oñ oh"
up there	là-haut	"la-oh"
urgent	urgent (*m*)	"oorzhoñ"
	urgente (*f*)	"oorzhoñt"
USA	les États-Unis (*mpl*)	"aytaz oonee"
to **use**	utiliser	"ooteeleezay"
▷ may I use your phone?	est-ce que je pourrais utiliser votre téléphone?	"es-kuh zhuh pooray ooteeleezay votr taylayfonn"
useful	utile	"ooteell"
usual	habituel(le)	"abeetwell"
usually	habituellement	"abeetwelmoñ"

ABSOLUTE ESSENTIALS

I don't understand	je ne comprends pas	"zhuh nuh koñproñ pa"
I don't speak French	je ne parle pas français	"zhuh nuh parl pa froñsay"
do you speak English?	parlez-vous anglais?	"parlay-voo oñglay"
could you help me?	pourriez-vous m'aider?	"pooreeay-voo mayday"

vacancy *(in hotel)*	la chambre à louer	"shoñbra loo-ay"
▷ **do you have any vacancies?** *(at campsite)*	est-ce que vous avez encore de la place?	"es-kuh vooz avay oñkor duh la plas"
to vacate:		
▷ **when do I have to vacate the room?**	quand est-ce que je dois libérer la chambre?	"koñt es-kuh zhuh dwa leebayray la shoñbr"
vacuum cleaner	l'aspirateur *(m)*	"aspeeratuhr"
valid	valable	"valabl"
valley	la vallée	"valay"
valuable	d'une grande valeur	"doon groñd valuhr"
valuables	les objets *(mpl)* de valeur	"op-zhay duh valuhr"
van	la camionnette	"kamyonett"
vase	le vase	"vaz"
VAT	la TVA	"tay vay a"
▷ **does the price include VAT?**	est-ce que la TVA est comprise dans le prix?	"es-kuh la tay vay a eh koñpreez doñ luh pree"
veal	le veau	"voh"
vegan	végétalien *(m)* végétalienne *(f)*	"vay-zhaytalyañ" "vay-zhaytalyenn"
▷ **is this suitable for vegans?**	est-ce que cela convient aux végétaliens?	"es-kuh sla koñvyañ oh vay-zhaytalyañ"
▷ **do you have any vegan dishes?**	est-ce que vous avez des plats végétaliens?	"es-kuh vooz avay day pla vay-zhaytalyañ"
vegetables	les légumes *(mpl)*	"laygoom"
▷ **are the vegetables included?**	est-ce que les légumes sont compris?	"es-kuh lay laygoom soñ koñpree"
vegetarian	végétarien *(m)* végétarienne *(f)*	"vay-zhaytaryañ" "vay-zhaytaryenn"
▷ **is this suitable for vegetarians?**	est-ce que cela convient aux végétariens?	"es-kuh sla koñvyañ oh vay-zhaytaryañ"

ABSOLUTE ESSENTIALS

I would like ...	j'aimerais ...	"zhemray"
I need ...	j'ai besoin de ...	"zhay buhswañ duh"
where is ...?	où se trouve ...?	"oo suh troov"
I'm looking for ...	je cherche ...	"zhuh shersh"

▷ **do you have any vegetarian dishes?**	est-ce que vous avez des plats végétariens?	"es-kuh vooz avay day pla vay-zhaytaryañ"
venison	le chevreuil	"shuhv-ruhy"
ventilator	le ventilateur	"voñteelatuhr"
vermouth	le vermouth	"vehrmoot"
vertigo:		
▷ **I suffer from vertigo**	j'ai le vertige	"zhay luh vehrteezh"
very	très	"treh"
vest	le maillot de corps	"mye-yo duh kor"
via	par	"par"
video cassette	la vidéocassette	"veedayokassett"
video (recorder)	le magnétoscope	"manyaytoskop"
Vienna	Vienne	"vyenn"
view	la vue	"voo"
▷ **I'd like a room with a view of the sea**	je voudrais une chambre avec vue sur la mer	"zhuh voodrayz oon shoñbr avek voo soor la mehr"
villa	la maison de campagne	"mehzoñ duh koñpanyuh"
village	le village	"veelazh"
vinegar	le vinaigre	"vee-naygr"
vineyard	le vignoble	"vee-nyobl"
visa	le visa	"veeza"
▷ **I have an entry visa**	j'ai un visa	"zhay uñ veeza"
to visit	visiter	"veezeetay"
▷ **can we visit the vineyard?**	est-ce que nous pouvons visiter le vignoble?	"es-kuh noo poovoñ veezeetay luh vee-nyobl"
vitamin	la vitamine	"veetameen"

ABSOLUTE ESSENTIALS

do you have ...?	avez-vous ...?	"avay-voo"
is there ...?	y a-t-il ...?	"ya-teel"
are there ...?	y a-t-il ...?	"ya-teel"
how much is ...?	combien coûte ...?	"koñbyañ koot"

vodka	la vodka	"vodka"
volleyball	le volley-ball	"volleh-ball"
voltage	le voltage	"voltazh"
▷ **what's the voltage?**	quel est le voltage?	"kel eh luh voltazh"
waist	la taille	"tye"
waistcoat	le gilet	"zheeleh"
to **wait (for)**	attendre	"atoñdr"
▷ **can you wait here for a few minutes?**	est-ce que vous pouvez m'attendre ici quelques instants?	"es-kuh voo poovay matoñdr eesee kelkuhz añstoñ"
▷ **please wait for me**	attendez-moi s'il vous plaît	"atoñday-mwa seel voo pleh"
waiter	le garçon	"garsoñ"
waiting room	la salle d'attente	"sal datoñt"
waitress	la serveuse	"sehrvuz"
to **wake**	réveiller	"rayvay-yay"
▷ **please wake me at 8.00**	réveillez-moi à 8 heures	"rayvay-yay-mwa a weet uhr"
to **wake up**	se réveiller	"suh rayvay-yay"
Wales	le pays de Galles	"payee duh gal"
walk[1] *n*	la promenade	"promnad"
▷ **to go for a walk**	faire une promenade	"fehr oon promnad"
▷ **are there any interesting walks nearby?**	est-ce qu'il y a de belles promenades à faire près d'ici?	"es-keel ya duh bel promnad a fehr preh deesee"
to **walk**[2] *vb*	aller à pied	"alay a pyay"
wallet	le portefeuille	"portfuhy"
walnut	la noix	"nwa"
to **want**	désirer	"dayzeeray"

warm	chaud (*m*)	"shoh"
	chaude (*f*)	"shohd"
warning triangle	le triangle de présignalisation	"treeyoñgl duh pray-seenyal-eeza-syoñ"
to wash	laver	"lavay"
▷ **to wash oneself**	se laver	"slavay"
▷ **where can I wash my clothes/my hands?**	où est-ce que je peux laver mes vêtements/me laver les mains?	"oo es-kuh zhuh puh lavay may vetmoñ/mlavay lay mañ"
washable	lavable	"lavabl"
▷ **is it washable?**	est-ce que c'est lavable?	"es-kuh seh lavabl"
washbasin	le lavabo	"lavabo"
▷ **the washbasin is dirty**	le lavabo est sale	"luh lavabo eh sal"
▷ **do I have to pay extra to use the washbasin?**	est-ce que je dois payer un supplément pour utiliser le lavabo?	"es-kuh zhuh dwa payay uñ sooplaymoñ poor ooteeleezay luh lavabo"
washing	la lessive	"lesseev"
▷ **where can I do some washing?**	où est-ce que je peux faire un peu de lessive?	"oo es-kuh zhuh puh fehr uñ puh duh lesseev"
washing machine	la machine à laver	"masheen a lavay"
▷ **how do you work the washing machine?**	comment fait-on marcher la machine à laver?	"komoñ feh-toñ marshay la masheen a lavay"
washing powder	la lessive	"lesseev"
washing-up liquid	le lave-vaisselle	"lav-vessell"
wasp	la guêpe	"gep"
waste bin	la poubelle	"poobell"
watch[1] *n*	la montre	"moñtr"
▷ **I think my watch is slow/fast**	je pense que ma montre retarde/avance	"zhuh poñs kuh ma moñtr ruhtard/avoñs"

ABSOLUTE ESSENTIALS

I don't understand	je ne comprends pas	"zhuh nuh koñproñ pa"
I don't speak French	je ne parle pas français	"zhuh nuh parl pa froñsay"
do you speak English?	parlez-vous anglais?	"parlay-voo oñglay"
could you help me?	pourriez-vous m'aider?	"pooreeay-voo mayday"

▷ **my watch has stopped**	ma montre s'est arrêtée	"ma moñtr set arehtay"
to **watch**[2] *vb (look at)*	regarder	"ruhgarday"
▷ **could you watch my bag for a minute please?**	est-ce que vous pouvez surveiller mon sac pendant une minute s'il vous plaît?	"es-kuh voo poovay soorvayay moñ sak poñdoñ oon meenoot seel voo pleh"
water	l'eau *(f)*	"oh"
▷ **there is no hot water**	il n'y a pas d'eau chaude	"eel nya pa doh shohd"
▷ **a glass of water**	un verre d'eau	"uñ vehr doh"
waterfall	la chute d'eau	"shoot doh"
water heater	le chauffe-eau	"shoh-foh"
watermelon	la pastèque	"pastek"
waterproof	imperméable	"añpehrmay-yabl"
water-skiing	le ski nautique	"skee noteek"
▷ **is it possible to go water-skiing here?**	est-il possible de faire du ski nautique ici?	"eh-teel poseebl duh fehr doo skee noteek eesee"
wax	la cire	"seer"
way *(manner)*	la manière	"manyehr"
▷ **which is the way to ...?**	comment va-t-on à ...?	"komoñ va-toñ a"
▷ **what's the best way to get to ...?**	quelle est la meilleure façon pour aller à ...?	"kel eh la may-yur fasoñ poor alay a"
▷ **this way**	par ici	"par eesee"
▷ **that way**	par là	"par la"
we	nous	"noo"
weak	faible	"febl"
to **wear**	porter	"portay"
▷ **what should I wear?**	qu'est-ce que je devrais porter?	"kes-kuh zhuh duhvreh portay"
weather	le temps	"toñ"

ABSOLUTE ESSENTIALS

I would like ...	j'aimerais ...	"zhemray"
I need ...	j'ai besoin de ...	"zhay buhswañ duh"
where is ...?	où se trouve ...?	"oo suh troov"
I'm looking for ...	je cherche ...	"zhuh shersh"

▷ **what dreadful weather!**	quel temps affreux!	"kel toñ afruh"
▷ **is the weather going to change?**	est-ce que le temps va changer?	"es-kuh luh toñ va shoñ-zhay"

weather forecast:

▷ **what's the weather forecast for tomorrow?**	quelle est la météo pour demain?	"kel eh la maytayo poor duhmañ"

wedding	le mariage	"mar-yazh"
▷ **we are here for a wedding**	nous sommes ici pour un mariage	"noo somz eesee poor oon mar-yazh"

Wednesday	mercredi (m)	"mehr-kruhdee"
week	la semaine	"smen"
▷ **this week**	cette semaine	"set smen"
▷ **last week**	la semaine dernière	"la smen dehr-nyehr"
▷ **next week**	la semaine prochaine	"la smen proshenn"
▷ **for one/two weeks**	pendant une/deux semaines	"poñdoñ oon/duh smen"

weekday	le jour de semaine	"zhoor duh smen"
weekend	le weekend	"weekend"
weekly rate	le tarif hebdomadaire	"tareef ebdomadehr"
weight	le poids	"pwa"
welcome	bienvenu(e)	"byañvuh-noo"
▷ **you're welcome**	pas de quoi	"pad kwa"
well	en bonne santé	"oñ bon soñtay"
▷ **he's not well**	il ne se porte pas bien	"eel nuh sport pa byañ"
well done (steak)	bien cuit (m)	"byañ kwee"
	bien cuite (f)	"byañ kweet"
Welsh	gallois (m)	"galwa"
	galloise (f)	"galwaz"
▷ **I'm Welsh**	je suis gallois/galloise	"zhuh swee galwa/galwaz"

ABSOLUTE ESSENTIALS

do you have ...?	avez-vous ...?	"avay-voo"
is there ...?	y a-t-il ...?	"ya-teel"
are there ...?	y a-t-il ...?	"ya-teel"
how much is ...?	combien coûte ...?	"koñbyañ koot"

west	l'ouest (m)	"west"
wet	mouillé(e)	"mooyay"
wetsuit	la combinaison de plongée	"koñbeenezoñ duh ploñ-zhay"
what	quoi	"kwa"
▷ **what is it?**	qu'est-ce que c'est?	"kes-kuh seh"
wheel	la roue	"roo"
wheelchair	le fauteuil roulant	"foh-tuhy rooloñ"
when	quand	"koñ"
where	où	"oo"
▷ **where are you from?**	d'où venez-vous?	"doo vnay-voo"
which	quel(le)	"kel"
▷ **which man?**	quel homme?	"kel om"
▷ **which woman?**	quelle femme?	"kel fam"
▷ **which book?**	quel livre?	"kel livr"
▷ **which is it?**	lequel est-ce?	"luhkel es"
while¹ n:		
▷ **in a while**	dans quelque temps	"doñ kelkuh toñ"
while² conj	pendant que	"poñdoñ kuh"
▷ **can you do it while I wait?**	est-ce que vous pouvez le faire pendant que j'attends?	"es-kuh voo poovay luh fehr poñdoñ kuh zhatoñ"
whipped cream	la crème fouettée	"krem fwettay"
whisky	le whisky	"weeskee"
▷ **I'll have a whisky**	un whisky, s'il vous plaît	"uñ weeskee seel voo pleh"
▷ **a whisky and soda**	un whisky soda	"uñ weeskee soda"
white	blanc (m)	"bloñ"
	blanche (f)	"bloñsh"

ABSOLUTE ESSENTIALS

yes (please)	oui (merci)	"wee (mehrsee)"
no (thank you)	non (merci)	"noñ (mehrsee)"
hello	bonjour	"boñzhoor"
goodbye	au revoir	"o ruhvwar"

who	qui	"kee"
▷ who is it?	qui est-ce?	"kee es"
whole	entier (*m*)	"oñtyay"
	entière (*f*)	"oñtyehr"
wholemeal bread	le pain complet	"pañ koñpleh"
whose:		
▷ whose is it?	c'est à qui?	"set a kee"
why	pourquoi	"poorkwa"
wide	large	"larzh"
wife	la femme	"fam"
window	la fenêtre	"fuhnehtr"
▷ I'd like a window seat	je voudrais une place fenêtre	"zhuh voodray oon plas fuhnehtr"
▷ I can't open the window	je ne peux pas ouvrir la fenêtre	"zhuh nuh puh pa oovreer la fuhnehtr"
▷ I have broken the window	j'ai cassé la fenêtre	"zhay kassay la fuhnehtr"
▷ may I open the window?	est-ce que je peux ouvrir la fenêtre?	"es-kuh zhuh puh oovreer la fuhnehtr"
▷ shop window	la vitrine	"la veetreen"
▷ in the window	dans la vitrine	"doñ la veetreen"
windscreen	le pare-brise	"par-breez"
▷ could you clean the windscreen?	faites le pare-brise, s'il vous plaît	"fet luh par-breez seel voo pleh"
▷ the windscreen has shattered	le pare-brise est cassé	"luh par-breez eh kassay"
windscreen washers	les lave-glaces (*mpl*)	"lavglas"
▷ can you top up the windscreen washers?	pouvez-vous remplir les lave-glaces?	"poovay-voo roñpleer lay lavglas"
windscreen wiper	l'essuie-glace (*m*)	"eswee-glas"
windsurfer (*board*)	la planche à voile	"ploñsh a vwal"

windsurfing

▷ can I hire a windsurfer?	est-ce que je peux louer une planche à voile?	"es-kuh zhuh puh loo-ay oon ploñsh a vwal"
windsurfing	la planche à voile	"ploñsh a vwal"
▷ can I go windsurfing?	est-ce que je peux faire de la planche à voile?	"es-kuh zhuh puh fehr duh la ploñsh a vwal"
windy:		
▷ it's (too) windy	il y a trop de vent	"eel ya troh duh voñ"
wine	le vin	"vañ"
▷ this wine is not chilled	ce vin n'est pas assez frais	"suh vañ neh pa assay freh"
▷ red/white wine	du vin rouge/blanc	"doo vañ roozh/bloñ"
▷ rosé wine	du rosé	"doo rozay"
▷ sparkling wine	du vin pétillant	"doo vañ payteeyoñ"
▷ sweet/medium-sweet wine	du vin doux/demi-doux	"doo vañ doo/duhmee-doo"
▷ dry/medium-dry wine	du vin sec/demi-sec	"doo vañ sek/duhmee-sek"
▷ can you recommend a good red/white/rosé wine?	pouvez-vous nous conseiller un bon vin rouge/blanc/rosé?	"poovay-voo noo koñsay-yay uñ boñ vañ roozh/bloñ/rozay"
▷ a bottle/carafe of house wine	une bouteille/carafe de la réserve du patron	"oon bootay/karaf duh la rayzehrv doo patroñ"
wine list	la carte des vins	"kart day vañ"
▷ may we see the wine list, please?	la carte des vins, s'il vous plaît	"la kart day vañ seel voo pleh"
winter	l'hiver (m)	"eevehr"
with	avec	"avek"
without	sans	"soñ"
woman	la femme	"fam"
wood	le bois	"bwa"
wool	la laine	"len"
word	le mot	"moh"

ABSOLUTE ESSENTIALS		
I would like ...	j'aimerais ...	"zhemray"
I need ...	j'ai besoin de ...	"zhay buhzwañ duh"
where is ...?	où se trouve ...?	"oo suh troov"
I'm looking for ...	je cherche ...	"zhuh shersh"

▷ what is the word for ...?	comment dit-on ...?	"komoñ dee-toñ"
to work (*person*)	travailler	"travye-yay"
(*machine, car*)	fonctionner	"foñk-syonay"
▷ this does not work	ça ne marche pas	"sa nuh marsh pa"
▷ how does this work?	comment est-ce que cela fonctionne?	"komoñ es-kuh sla foñksyonn"
▷ where do you work?	où travaillez-vous?	"oo travye-yay-voo"
worried	inquiet (*m*)	"añkyeh"
	inquiète (*f*)	"añkyet"
worse	pire	"peer"
worth:		
▷ it's worth ...	ça vaut ...	"sa voh"
▷ how much is it worth?	combien est-ce que ça vaut?	"koñbyañ es-kuh sa voh"
to wrap (up)	envelopper	"oñvlopay"
▷ could you wrap it up for me, please?	est-ce que vous pouvez me l'envelopper, s'il vous plaît?	"es-kuh voo poovay muh loñvlopay seel voo pleh"
wrapping paper	le papier d'emballage	"papyay doñbalazh"
to write	écrire	"aykreer"
▷ could you write that down, please?	est-ce que vous pourriez écrire cela, s'il vous plaît?	"es-kuh voo pooryay aykreer sla seel voo pleh"
writing paper	le papier à lettres	"papyay a letr"
wrong	faux (*m*)	"foh"
	fausse (*f*)	"fohs"
▷ there is something wrong with the brakes	il y a un problème de freins	"eel ya uñ problemm duh frañ"
▷ I think you've given me the wrong change	je pense que vous ne m'avez pas bien rendu la monnaie	"zhuh poñs kuh voo nuh mavay pa byañ roñdoo la moneh"
▷ what's wrong?	qu'est-ce qui ne va pas?	"kes-kee nuh va pa"

ABSOLUTE ESSENTIALS

do you have ...?	avez-vous ...?	"avay-voo"
is there ...?	y a-t-il ...?	"ya-teel"
are there ...?	y a-t-il ...?	"ya-teel"
how much is ...?	combien coûte ...?	"koñbyañ koot"

yacht	le yacht	"yot"
year	l'an (*m*)	"oñ"
▷ this year	cette année	"set anay"
▷ last year	l'année dernière	"lanay dehr-nyehr"
▷ next year	l'année prochaine	"lanay proshenn"
▷ every year	tous les ans	"too layz oñ"
yellow	jaune	"zhohn"
yes	oui	"wee"
▷ yes please	oui merci	"wee mehrsee"
yesterday	hier	"yehr"
yet:		
▷ not yet	pas encore	"paz oñkor"
yoghurt	le yaourt	"ya-oort"
you	vous	"voo"
young	jeune	"zhuhn"
your:		
▷ your book	votre livre	"votr leevr"
▷ your books	vos livres	"vo leevr"
yours	le vôtre	"votr"
youth hostel	l'auberge (*f*) de jeunesse	"oberzh duh zhuh-ness"
▷ is there a youth hostel?	est-ce qu'il y a une auberge de jeunesse?	"es-keel ya oon oberzh duh zhuh-ness"
zebra crossing	le passage piétons	"pasazh pyaytoñ"
zero	le zéro	"zayro"
zip	la fermeture éclair	"fehrmtoor ayklehr"

In the pronunciation system used in this book, French sounds are represented by spellings of the nearest possible sounds in English. Hence, when you read out the pronunciation – shown in the third column, after the translation – sound the letters as if you were reading an English word. The following notes should help you:

REPRESENTATION	REMARKS	EXAMPLE	PRONUNCIATION
a	As in *cat*	**chat**	*sha*
e/eh	As in *met*	**sec**	*sek*
u/uh	As in *thud*	**repas**	*ruhpa*
oh	As in *go, low*	**bateau**	*batoh*
o	As in *dot*	**colle**	*kol*
oo	As in *moon*	**vous**	*voo*
oñ	Nasalized: let air	**restaurant**	*restoroñ*
añ	out through the	**pain**	*pañ*
uñ	nose as well as the mouth	**lundi**	*luñdee*
zh	As 's' in *measure*	**rouge**	*roozh*
y	As in *yet*	**famille**	*fameey*
ye	As in *fry*	**travailler**	*tra-vye-yay*
ny	As 'ni' in *companion*	**signal**	*seenyal*
s	As in *sit*	**police**	*polees*

Pronouncing French words from their spelling can be made easier by following some fairly precise 'rules'. Final consonants are often silent:

SPELLING	REPRESENTATION	SPELLING	REPRESENTATION
à, â	*a/ah*	**ou, oû, u**	*oo*
e	*e/eh* (see above)	**ui, uî**	*wee*
	uh (see above)	**y**	*ee*
é	*ay*	**g (+e/i), j**	*zh* (see above)
è, ê	*e/eh* (see above)	**gn**	*ny* (see above)
i, î	*ee*	**ch**	*sh*
ô	*o* (see above)	**th**	*t*
û	*oo* (see above)	**tion**	*syoñ* (see above)
ç	*s* (see above)	**qu**	*k*
au(x), eau(x)	*oh* (see above)	**h**	silent
eu(x), œ(u)	*uh* (see above)	**ll**	sometimes *y* (see above)
oi, oî, oy	*wa/wah*		

In the weight and length charts the middle figure can be either metric or imperial. Thus 3.3 feet = 1 metre, 1 foot = 0.3 metres, and so on.

feet		metres	inches		cm	lbs		kg
3.3	1	0.3	0.39	1	2.54	2.2	1	0.45
6.6	2	0.61	0.79	2	5.08	4.4	2	0.91
9.9	3	0.91	1.18	3	7.62	6.6	3	1.4
13.1	4	1.22	1.57	4	10.6	8.8	4	1.8
16.4	5	1.52	1.97	5	12.7	11.0	5	2.2
19.7	6	1.83	2.36	6	15.2	13.2	6	2.7
23.0	7	2.13	2.76	7	17.8	15.4	7	3.2
26.2	8	2.44	3.15	8	20.3	17.6	8	3.6
29.5	9	2.74	3.54	9	22.9	19.8	9	4.1
32.9	10	3.05	3.9	10	25.4	22.0	10	4.5
			4.3	11	27.9			
			4.7	12	30.1			

°C	0	5	10	15	17	20	22	24	26	28	30	35	37	38	40	50	100
°F	32	41	50	59	63	68	72	75	79	82	86	95	98.4	100	104	122	212

Km	10	20	30	40	50	60	70	80	90	100	110	120
Miles	6.2	12.4	18.6	24.9	31.0	37.3	43.5	49.7	56.0	62.0	68.3	74.6

Tyre pressures

lb/sq in	15	18	20	22	24	26	28	30	33	35
kg/sq cm	1.1	1.3	1.4	1.5	1.7	1.8	2.0	2.1	2.3	2.5

Liquids

gallons	1.1	2.2	3.3	4.4	5.5		pints	0.44	0.88	1.76
litres	5	10	15	20	25		litres	0.25	0.5	1

CAR PARTS

accelerator	l'accélérateur *(m)*	"aksaylayratuhr"
air conditioning	la climatisation	"kleemateezasyoñ"
antifreeze	l'antigel *(m)*	"oñtee-zhel"
automatic	automatique	"otomateek"
battery	la batterie	"batree"
boot	le coffre	"kofr"
brake fluid	le liquide pour freins	"leekeed poor frañ"
brakes	les freins *(mpl)*	"frañ"
car	la voiture	"vwatoor"
carburettor	le carburateur	"karbooratuhr"
car number	le numéro d'immatriculation	"noomayro deematreekoo-lasyoñ"
car wash	le lave-auto	"lav-oto"
chain	la chaîne	"shen"
de-ice	dégivrer	"dayzheevray"
diesel	le gas-oil	"gazol"
engine	le moteur	"motuhr"
exhaust pipe	le pot d'échappement	"poh dayshapmoñ"
fan belt	la courroie de ventilateur	"koorwa duh voñteelatuhr"
fuel pump	la pompe d'alimentation	"poñp daleemoñtasyoñ"
garage	le garage	"garazh"
gear	la vitesse	"veetess"
headlight	le phare	"far"
indicator	le clignotant	"kleenyotoñ"
jack	le cric	"kreek"
jump leads	les câbles *(mpl)* de raccordement de batterie	"kabl duh rakordmoñ duh batree"
leak	la fuite	"fweet"
oil filter	le filtre à huile	"feeltra weel"
petrol	l'essence *(f)*	"essoñs"
points	les vis *(fpl)* platinées	"vees plateenay"
radiator	le radiateur	"radya-tuhr"
roof rack	la galerie	"galree"
shock absorber	l'amortisseur *(m)*	"amorteessuhr"
spare wheel	la roue de rechange	"roo duh ruhshoñzh"
spark plug	la bougie	"boozhee"
speedometer	le compteur de vitesse	"koñtuhr duh veetes"
suspension	la suspension	"soospoñsyoñ"
tyre	le pneu	"pnuh"
tyre pressure	la pression des pneus	"pressyoñ day pnuh"
warning triangle	le triangle de présignalisation	"treeyoñgl duh prayseenyal-eeza-syoñ"
windscreen	le pare-brise	"par-breez"
windscreen washers	les lave-glaces *(mpl)*	"lavglas"
windscreen wipers	les essuie-glaces *(mpl)*	"eswee-glas"

COLOURS

black	noir(e)	"nwahr"
blue	bleu(e)	"bluh"
brown	brun	"bruñ"
	brune	"broon"
	marron	"maroñ"
colour	la couleur	"kooluhr"
dark	foncé(e)	"foñsay"
green	vert	"vehr"
	verte	"vehrt"
grey	gris	"gree"
	grise	"greez"
light	clair(e)	"klehr"
navy blue	bleu marine	"bluh mareen"
orange	orange	"oroñzh"
pink	rose	"rohz"
purple	violet	"vyoleh"
	violette	"vyolet"
red	rouge	"roozh"
white	blanc	"bloñ"
	blanche	"bloñsh"
yellow	jaune	"zhohn"

COUNTRIES

America	l'Amérique *(f)*	"amayreek"
Australia	l'Australie *(f)*	"ostralee"
Austria	l'Autriche *(f)*	"otreesh"
Belgium	la Belgique	"bel-zheek"
Britain	la Grande-Bretagne	"groñd bruhtanyuh"
Canada	le Canada	"kanada"
England	l'Angleterre *(f)*	"oñgl-tehr"
Europe	l'Europe *(f)*	"uhrop"
France	la France	"froñs"
Germany	l'Allemagne *(f)*	"almanyuh"
Greece	la Grèce	"gres"
Ireland	l'Irlande *(f)*	"eerloñd"
Italy	l'Italie *(f)*	"eetalee"
Luxembourg	le Luxembourg	"looksoñboor"
New Zealand	la Nouvelle-Zélande	"noovell zayloñd"
Northern Ireland	l'Irlande *(f)* du Nord	"eerloñd doo nor"
Portugal	le Portugal	"portoogall"
Scotland	l'Écosse *(f)*	"aykoss"
Spain	l'Espagne *(f)*	"espanyuh"
Switzerland	la Suisse	"swees"
United States	les États-Unis *(mpl)*	"aytaz oonee"
USA	les États-Unis *(mpl)*	"aytaz oonee"
Wales	le pays de Galles	"payee duh gal"

DRINKS

alcohol	l'alcool *(m)*	"alkol"
alcoholic	alcoolique	"alkoleek"
aperitif	l'apéritif *(m)*	"apayreeteef"
beer	la bière	"byehr"
brandy	le cognac	"konyak"
champagne	le champagne	"shoñpanyuh"
cider	le cidre	"seedr"
cocktail	le cocktail	"koktell"
cocoa	le cacao	"kaka-oh"
coffee	le café	"kafay"
coke®	le coca	"koka"
draught beer	la bière à la pression	"byehr a la presyoñ"
drinking chocolate	le chocolat chaud	"shokola shoh"
drinking water	l'eau *(f)* potable	"oh potabl"
fruit juice	le jus de fruit	"zhoo duh frwee"
gin	le gin	"djeen"
gin and tonic	le gin-tonic	"djeen-toneek"
grapefruit juice	le jus de pamplemousse	"zhoo duh poñpluhmoos"
juice	le jus	"zhoo"
lager	la bière blonde	"byehr bloñd"
lemonade	la limonade	"leemonad"
lemon tea	le thé au citron	"tay oh seetroñ"
liqueur	la liqueur	"leekuhr"
milk	le lait	"leh"
milkshake	le milk-shake	"meelkshake"
mineral water	l'eau *(f)* minérale	"oh meenayrall"
non-alcoholic	non alcoolisé (e)	"non alkoleezay"
orange juice	le jus d'orange	"zhoo doroñzh"
rosé (wine)	le rosé	"rozay"
shandy	le panaché	"panashay"
sherry	le sherry	"shehree"
skimmed milk	le lait écrémé	"leh aykraymay"
soda	l'eau *(f)* de Seltz	"oh duh selts"
soft drink	la boisson non alcoolisée	"bwasoñ non alkoleezay"
spirits	les spiritueux *(mpl)*	"speereetwuh"
squash	la citronnade	"seetronad"
	l'orangeade	"oroñ-zhad"
tea	le thé	"tay"
tomato juice	le jus de tomate	"zhoo duh tomat"
tonic water	le Schweppes®	"shwepps"
vermouth	le vermouth	"vehrmoot"
vodka	le vodka	"vodka"
whisky	le whisky	"weeskee"
wine	le vin	"vañ"

FISH AND SEAFOOD

anchovy	l'anchois *(m)*	"oñshwa"
caviar	le caviar	"kavyar"
cod	le cabillaud	"kabeeyoh"
crab	le crabe	"krab"
fish	le poisson	"pwasoñ"
haddock	l'églefin *(m)*	"aygluhfañ"
hake	le colin	"kolañ"
herring	le hareng	"arañ"
lobster	le homard	"omar"
mackerel	le maquereau	"makro"
mussel	la moule	"mool"
oyster	l'huître *(f)*	"weetr"
prawn	la crevette	"kruhvett"
salmon	le saumon	"sohmoñ"
sardine	la sardine	"sardeen"
scallop	la coquille Saint-Jacques	"kokeey sañ-zhak"
scampi	les langoustines *(fpl)* frites	"loñgoosteen freet"
seafood	les fruits *(mpl)* de mer	"frwee duh mehr"
shellfish	le crustacé	"kroostassay"
shrimp	la crevette grise	"kruhvet greez"
sole	la sole	"sol"
trout	la truite	"trweet"
tuna	le thon	"toñ"

FRUIT AND NUTS

almond	l'amande *(f)*	"amoñd"
apple	la pomme	"pom"
apricot	l'abricot *(m)*	"abreeko"
banana	la banane	"banann"
blackcurrant	le cassis	"kasees"
cherry	la cerise	"sreez"
chestnut	la châtaigne	"sha-tehnyuh"
coconut	la noix de coco	"nwa duh kokoh"
currant	le raisin sec	"rayzañ sek"
date	la datte	"dat"
fig	la figue	"feeg"
fruit	le fruit	"frwee"
grapefruit	le pamplemousse	"poñpluhmoos"
grapes	les raisins *(mpl)*	"rayzañ"
hazelnut	la noisette	"nwazett"
lemon	le citron	"seetroñ"
lime	le citron vert	"seetroñ vehr"
melon	le melon	"mloñ"
nut	la noix	"nwa"
olive	l'olive *(f)*	"oleev"
orange	l'orange *(f)*	"oroñzh"
peach	la pêche	"pesh"
peanut	la cacahuète	"kakawet"
pear	la poire	"pwar"
pineapple	l'ananas *(m)*	"anana"
pistachio	la pistache	"peestash"
plum	la prune	"proon"
prune	le pruneau	"proono"
raisin	le raisin sec	"rayzañ sek"
raspberry	la framboise	"froñbwaz"
strawberry	la fraise	"frez"
walnut	la noix	"nwa"
watermelon	la pastèque	"pastek"

MEATS

bacon	le bacon	"baykon"
beef	le bœuf	"buf"
beefburger	le hamburger	"oñboorgehr"
breast	le blanc	"bloñ"
cheeseburger	le hamburger au fromage	"oñboorgehr oh fromazh"
chicken	le poulet	"pooleh"
chop	la côtelette	"kohtlett"
cold meat	la viande froide	"vyoñd frwad"
duck	le canard	"kanar"
goose	l'oie (f)	"wa"
ham	le jambon	"zhoñboñ"
hamburger	le hamburger	"oñboorgehr"
kidneys	les rognons (mpl)	"ronyoñ"
liver	le foie	"fwa"
meat	la viande	"vyoñd"
mince	le bifteck haché	"beeftek ashay"
mutton	le mouton	"mootoñ"
pâté	le pâté	"pahtay"
pheasant	le faisan	"fuhzoñ"
pork	le porc	"por"
rabbit	le lapin	"lapañ"
salami	le salami	"salamee"
sausage	la saucisse	"sohsees"
steak	le bifteck	"beeftek"
stew	le ragoût	"ragoo"
turkey	le dindon	"dañdoñ"
veal	le veau	"voh"

SHOPS

baker's	la boulangerie	"booloñzh-ree"
barber	le coiffeur	"kwafur"
bookshop	la librairie	"leebrayree"
butcher's	la boucherie	"booshree"
café	le café	"kafay"
chemist's	la pharmacie	"farmasee"
dry-cleaner's	le pressing	"presseeng"
duty-free shop	la boutique hors taxe	"booteek or tax"
grocer's	l'épicerie (f)	"aypeesree"
hairdresser	le coiffeur	"kwafur"
	la coiffeuse	"kwafuz"
health food shop	le magasin de diététique	"magazañ duh deeay-tayteek"
ironmonger's	la quincaillerie	"kañ-kye-yuhree"
jeweller's (shop)	la bijouterie	"bee-zhootree"
launderette	la laverie automatique	"lavree otomateek"
market	le marché	"marshay"
newsagent	le marchand de journaux	"marshoñd zhoorno"
post office	le bureau de poste	"booro duh post"
shop	le magasin	"magazañ"
stationer's	la papeterie	"paptree"
supermarket	le supermarché	"soopehr-marshay"
tobacconist's	le bureau de tabac	"booro duh taba"
toy shop	le magasin de jouets	"magazañ duh zhoo-eh"

VEGETABLES

artichoke	l'artichaut (m)	"arteesho"
asparagus	les asperges (fpl)	"asperzh"
aubergine	l'aubergine (f)	"obehr-zheen"
avocado	l'avocat (m)	"avoka"
bean	le haricot	"areekoh"
beetroot	la betterave	"betrav"
broccoli	le brocoli	"brokolee"
Brussels sprouts	les choux (mpl) de Bruxelles	"shoo duh broosell"
cabbage	le chou	"shoo"
carrot	la carotte	"karott"
cauliflower	le chou-fleur	"shoofluhr"
celery	le céleri	"saylree"
chives	la ciboulette	"seeboolett"
courgette	la courgette	"koor-zhett"
cucumber	le concombre	"koñkoñbr"
French beans	les haricots verts	"areekoh vehr"
garlic	l'ail (m)	"eye"
green pepper	le poivron vert	"pwavroñ vehr"
onion	l'oignon (m)	"onyoñ"
parsley	le persil	"perseey"
peas	les petits pois	"puhtee pwa"
pepper	le poivron	"pwavroñ"
potato	la pomme de terre	"pom duh tehr"
radish	le radis	"radee"
spinach	l'épinard (m)	"aypeenar"
spring onion	la ciboule	"seebool"
tomato	la tomate	"tomat"
turnip	le navet	"naveh"
vegan	végétalien	"vay-zhaytalyañ"
	végétalienne	"vay-zhaytalyenn"
vegetables	les légumes (mpl)	"laygoom"
vegetarian	végétarien	"vay-zhaytaryañ"
	végétarienne	"vay-zhaytaryenn"

FRENCH–ENGLISH

A

à to; at

abats *mpl* offal; giblets

abbaye *f* abbey

abeille *f* bee

abonné(e) *m/f* subscriber; season ticket holder

abonnement *m* subscription; season ticket

abord: d'abord at first

abri *m* shelter

abricot *m* apricot

absence *f*: **absence de signalisation horizontale** no road markings; **absence (partielle) de marquage** no road markings (on some sections)

abstenir: s'abstenir de to refrain from

abus *m*: **tout abus sera puni** penalty for improper use

accélérateur *m* accelerator

accepter to accept

accès *m* access

accessoires *mpl* accessories

accident *m* accident

accidenté(e): un accidenté de la route a road accident victim

accompagnateur(trice) *m/f* guide; courier

accompagner to accompany

accord *m* agreement; understanding

accotement *m* verge

accrocher to hang (up)

accueil *m* welcome; reception; **accueil entre 8h et 21h** opening hours 8am till 9pm

accueillir to greet; to welcome

accusé de réception *m* receipt (*for parcel*); **envoi avec accusé de reception** recorded delivery

A.C.F. *m* Automobile Club de France (similar to the AA)

achat *m* purchase; **achats** shopping

acheter to buy

achever to complete

acier *m* steel; **acier inoxydable** stainless steel

acompte *m* down payment; deposit

action *f* action; special offer (*Switz only*)

actionner: actionnez le signal d'alarme pull the communication cord

activité *f* activity

actualité *f*: **les actualités** the news

addition *f* addition; bill

adhérent(e) *m/f* member

adjoint(e) *m/f* deputy

administration *f* administration; civil service

adresse *f* skill; address

adresser to address;

s'adresser à/adressez-vous à go and see (*person*); enquire at (*office*)

adulte *m/f* adult

aéroclub *m* flying club

aérogare *f* terminal

aéroglisseur *m* hovercraft

aéroport *m* airport

affaire *f* affair; case; deal; **affaires** business; belongings; **bonnes affaires** bargains; **homme/femme d'affaires** businessman/woman; **déjeuner/dîner d'affaires** business lunch/dinner

affectueusement with love (*on letter*)

affiche *f* poster; notice

afficher: défense d'afficher post no bills

affranchissement *m* postage; **dispensé d'affranchissement** postage paid

affreux(euse) awful

afin que in order that

âge *m* age

âgé(e) aged; elderly

agence *f* agency; branch; **agence immobilière** estate agency; **agence de voyages** travel agency

agenda *m* diary

agent *m* agent; **agent immobilier** estate agent; **agent de police** policeman

agir to act; **il s'agit de** it's a question of
agité(e) rough (*sea*)
agiter: agiter avant emploi shake before use
agneau *m* lamb
agrandir to enlarge
agréable pleasant; nice
agréer to accept
agresser to attack
agricole agricultural
aide *f* help; **à l'aide de** with the help of
aider to help
aigle *m* eagle
aiglefin *m* haddock
aigre sour; **à l'aigre-doux** sweet and sour
aiguille *f* needle; **aiguille à tricoter** knitting needle
ail *m* garlic
aile *f* wing
ailleurs elsewhere
aimable pleasant
aimer to love; to like
ainsi thus; this way
aïoli *m* garlic mayonnaise
air *m* tune; air; look; **en plein air** in the open air
aire *f*: **aire de jeux** play area; **aire de services** service area; **aire de stationnement** lay-by
airelles *fpl* bilberries; cranberries
ajouter to add
alarme *f* alarm
alcool *f* alcohol; fruit brandy; **alcool blanc** colourless brandy; **alcool à brûler** methylated spirits
alcoolisé(e) alcoholic; **non alcoolisé(e)** soft
alco(o)test ® *m* Breathalyser ®
algues *fpl* seaweed
aliment *m* food; **aliments pour bébé** baby foods
alimentation *f* food;

groceries; **alimentation générale** grocery shop
allée *f* gangway; driveway
Allemagne *f* Germany
allemand(e) German
aller to go
allergie *f* allergy
allergique à allergic to
aller-retour *m* return ticket
aller (simple) *m* single ticket
allocation *f* allowance
allonger: s'allonger to lie down
allumé(e) on; lit
allume-gaz *m* gas lighter
allumer to turn on; to light; **allumez vos phares** switch on headlights; **allumer la lumière** to put on the light
allumette *f* match; **(pommes) allumettes** matchstick potatoes
allure *f* pace; speed
alors then
aloyau *m* sirloin
Alpes *fpl* Alps
alpinisme *m* mountaineering; climbing
alsacien(ne) Alsatian; **à l'alsacienne** usually served with sauerkraut, ham and sausages
amande *f* almond; **pâte d'amandes** almond paste, marzipan
amandine *f* almond cake
ambassade *f* embassy
ambassadeur *m* ambassador
amélioration *f* improvement
aménager to fit out; to lay out; to develop
amende *f* fine
amener to bring
amer(ère) bitter
américain(e) American

Amérique *f* America
ameublement *m* furniture
ami(e) *m/f* friend
amiable: à l'amiable amicably
amical(e) friendly
amicale *f* association
amincissant(e): crème amincissante slimming cream
amont *m*: **en amont** upstream; uphill
amortisseur *m* shock absorber
amour *m* love
amovible removable
ampoule *f* light bulb; blister (*on skin*); **ampoule buvable/injectable** phial to be taken orally/for injection
amusant(e) funny
amuse-gueule *m* appetizer
amuser to amuse; to entertain
an *m* year
ananas *m* pineapple
anchois *m* anchovy
ancien(ne) old; former; **à l'ancienne** in a wine and cream sauce with mushrooms and onions
ancre *f* anchor
andalouse: à l'andalouse with green peppers, aubergines and tomatoes
andouille *f* sausage made of chitterlings
andouillette *f* small sausage made of chitterlings
âne *m* donkey
angine *f* tonsillitis
anglais(e) English
Angleterre *f* England
anguille *f* eel
animal *m* animal; **animaux admis/non admis** animals/no animals

allowed; **animaux familiers** pets; **animaux sauvages** wildlife

animation f entertainment; compèring

animé(e) busy (place)

anis m aniseed

anisette f aniseed liqueur

année f year; vintage

anniversaire m anniversary; birthday; **joyeux anniversaire** happy birthday

annonce f advertisement; **petites annonces** small ads

annuaire m directory; **annuaire téléphonique** telephone directory

annuel(le) annual; yearly

annulation f cancellation

annuler to cancel

antenne f aerial

antérieur(e) earlier

antibiotique m antibiotic

antibrouillards mpl fog lamps

antigel m antifreeze

antihistaminique m antihistamine

antillais(e) West Indian

Antilles fpl West Indies

antiquaire m/f antique dealer

antiquités fpl antiques

antirides: crème antirides anti-wrinkle cream

antirouille anti-rust

antiseptique m antiseptic

antivol m anti-theft device

A.O.C. see **appellation**

août m August

apercevoir to see; **s'apercevoir de** to notice

apéritif m aperitif

apparaître to appear

appareil m appliance

appareil-photo m camera

appartement m apartment; flat

appartenir à to belong to

appel m call

appeler to call; **s'appeler** to be called

appellation f: **appellation d'origine contrôlée (A.O.C.)** mark guaranteeing the quality and origin of a wine

appendicite f appendicitis

appétit m appetite; **bon appétit!** enjoy your meal!

applaudir to clap

appoint m: **faire l'appoint** exact money please

apporter to bring

apprendre to learn; to teach

approprié(e) suitable; appropriate

approuver to approve of

approximatif(ive) approximate

appuyer: appuyer sur to push; **appuyez sur le bouton** press the button

après afterward(s); after; **après que** after

après-demain the day after tomorrow

après-midi m afternoon

après-rasage m after-shave

après-ski m snow boot; après-ski (evening)

aquarelle f watercolour; watercolours (genre)

arachide f groundnut

araignée f spider

arbitre m referee; umpire

arbre m tree

arène f arena

arête f ridge; bone (of fish)

argent m money; silver (metal); **argent comptant** cash

argenterie f silverware

armagnac m dry brown brandy

arme f weapon; **arme à feu** firearm

armé(e) armed

armée f army

armoire f wardrobe

aromates mpl seasoning

arôme m aroma; fragrance

arracher to pull out; to tear off; to take out

arrêt m stop; **arrêt d'autobus** bus stop; **arrêt facultatif** request stop

arrêté m: **par arrêté préfectoral** by order of the prefect

arrêter to stop; to switch off (engine); to arrest

arrhes fpl deposit (part payment)

arrière rear; back

arrivage m: **arrivage d'huîtres** fresh oysters

arrivée f arrival

arriver to happen; to arrive

arrondissement m (in Paris) district

art m art

artichaut m artichoke; **cœur/fond d'artichaut** artichoke heart

article m item; article; **articles de toilette** toiletries

artificiel(le) artificial

artisan m craftsman

artisanat m arts and crafts

artiste m/f artist

ascenseur m lift

asperge f asparagus

aspirateur m vacuum

cleaner
aspirine f aspirin
assaisonnement m seasoning; dressing
asseoir: s'asseoir to sit down; to sit
assez quite; rather; enough; **j'en ai assez** I have enough; I'm tired of it
assiette f plate; **assiette anglaise** assorted cold roast meats; **assiette charcutière/de charcuterie** assorted cold meats; **assiette de crudités (de saison)** (seasonal) salads and raw vegetables
assis(e) sitting
assister à to attend (*meeting etc*)
association f association; society
associé(e) m/f associate; partner
assorti(e) assorted; matching
assortiment m assortment
assurance f insurance; **assurance complémentaire** supplementary insurance; **assurance tous-risques** comprehensive insurance; **assurance voyages** travel insurance; **compagnie d'assurances** insurance company
assurance-vie f life insurance
assuré(e) confident; insured; **parking assuré** parking facilities; **desserte assurée par autocar** there is a bus service
assurer to assure; to insure; **ce train assure la correspondance avec**

le train de 16.45 this train connects with the 16.45; **s'assurer contre quelque chose** to insure against something
asthme m asthma
atelier m workshop; artist's studio
atomiseur m atomizer
attache f clip
attacher to bind; to fasten; to attach; **attachez vos ceintures** fasten seat belts
attaque f attack
atteindre to reach
attendre to wait; to wait for
attention look out!; **faites attention!** be careful!; **attention à la marche** mind the step
atterrir to land
atterrissage m landing (*of plane*)
attestation f: **attestation d'assurance** insurance certificate
attirer: nous attirons l'attention de notre aimable clientèle sur ... we would ask our customers/guests to note (that) ...
attraper to catch; to trick
au = à + le
aube f dawn
auberge f inn; **auberge de jeunesse** youth hostel
aubergine f aubergine
aucun(e) none; no, not any
au-delà de beyond
au-dessous (de) under, below
au-dessus (de) above
augmentation f rise; raise; growth; increase
au gratin with cheese topping

aujourd'hui today; **aujourd'hui le chef vous propose ...** the chef's special today is ...
au revoir goodbye
aussi also; too; as well; **aussi grand que** as big as
autant so much; **autant que** as much/many as
autel m altar
auteur m author; writer
authentique genuine
autobus m bus; **service d'autobus** bus service
autocar m coach
autocollant m sticker
autocuiseur m pressure cooker
auto-école f driving school
automate m vending machine (*Switz*)
automatique automatic
automne m autumn
automobiliste m/f motorist
autoradio m car radio
autoriser to authorize
autoroute f motorway; **autoroute à péage** toll motorway; **autoroute de contournement** bypass
autos-tamponneuses fpl dodgems
auto-stop m hitchhiking
auto-stoppeur(euse) m/f hitchhiker
autour around; **autour de** around
autre other; **autres directions** other routes; **autre chose** something else
autrefois once
autrement otherwise
Autriche f Austria
autrichien(ne) Austrian
aux = à + les
aval: en aval downhill; downstream

avaler to swallow

avance: en avance early; **à l'avance** in advance

avancer to gain (*clock*); to advance

avant before; front; **avant que/de** before; **à l'avant** at the front; **en avant** forward(s)

avantage m advantage; benefit

avant-hier the day before yesterday

avant-première f preview

avec with

avenir m future

averse f shower (*rain*)

avertir to inform; to warn

avertisseur m horn; alarm

aveugle blind

avion m plane; **par avion** by air; by air mail

aviron m oar; rowing (*sport*)

avis m opinion; advice note; notice; **sans avis médical** without medical advice

avocat m avocado (*pear*); barrister; lawyer

avoine f oats

avoir to have

avouer to confess

avril m April

B

baba au rhum m rum baba

bagages mpl luggage; **bagages accompagnés** registered luggage; **bagages à main** hand-luggage

bagarre f fight

baguette f stick of (French) bread

baguettes fpl chopsticks

baignade f: **baignade interdite** no bathing; **baignade surveillée** supervised bathing

baigner: se baigner to bathe; to go swimming

baignoire f bath

bail m lease; **bail à céder** lease for sale

bain m bath

baisser to fall; to turn down; to reduce

bal m ball; dance

balade f walk; drive

balance f scales

balancer to swing

balançoire f swing

balcon m circle (*in theatre*); balcony

baleine f whale

balisé(e) signposted

balle f bullet; ball

ballon m balloon; ball; glass of wine (1 decilitre)

ballottine f: **ballottine de volaille/d'agneau** meat loaf made with poultry/lamb

ball-trap m clay pigeon shooting

balustrade f rail

banane f banana; **bananes flambées** bananas served in flaming brandy

banc m bench

bande f strip; tape; gang; **bande dessinée (B.D.)** comic strip

banlieue f suburbs; outskirts

banque f bank

banquette-lit f bed settee

baptême christening; baptism; **baptême de l'air** first flight

bar[1] m bar; **bar à café** (*in Switz*) unlicensed bar

bar[2] m bass (*fish*)

barbe f beard

barbue f brill

barquette f small tart

barrage m dam; **barrage routier** road block

barrer to block; to cross; to cross out

barrière f barrier; fence; **barrière automatique** automatic turnstile; automatic barrier

bas m bottom (*of page, list*); stocking; **en bas** below; downstairs

bas(se) low; **marée basse** low tide

base f basis; base; **de base** basic

basilic m basil

basquaise: poulet (à la) basquaise chicken in sauce of tomato, onion, pepper, garlic and parsley, served with rice

bassin m pond

bataille f battle

bâtard m type of Vienna loaf

batavia f Webb lettuce

bateau m boat; ship; **bateau de plaisance** pleasure boat; **bateau-mouche** river boat; pleasure steamer

bâtiment m building

bâtonnet glacé m ice lolly

batterie f battery

battre to beat; **se battre** to fight

bavarder to gossip

bavaroise f type of mousse

bavette f bib; **bavette (échalotes)** type of steak with shallots

bazar m general store

B.D. see **bande**

béarnaise see **sauce**

beau handsome, beautiful;

lovely; fine; **il fait beau** the weather's fine
beaucoup much; **beaucoup de** plenty of; many; much/a lot of
beau-fils *m* son-in-law; stepson
beau-frère *m* brother-in-law
beau-père *m* father-in-law; stepfather
beauté *f* beauty
beaux-parents *mpl* in-laws
bébé *m* baby
bécasse *f* woodcock
bécassine *f* snipe
béchamel *f* white sauce
beignet *m* fritter; doughnut
belge Belgian
Belgique *f* Belgium
belle beautiful; lovely; fine
belle-fille *f* daughter-in-law; stepdaughter
belle-mère *f* mother-in-law; stepmother
belle-sœur *f* sister-in-law
belon *m* Belon oyster
belvédère *m* panoramic viewpoint
Bénédictine *f* greenish-yellow liqueur
bénéfice *m* profit; benefit
béquille *f* crutch
berceau *m* cradle
Bercy *f* sauce made with white wine, shallots and butter
besoin *m* need; **avoir besoin de** to need
bétail *m* cattle
bête stupid
béton *m* concrete
bette *f* beet
betterave *f* beetroot
beurre *m* butter; **beurre d'anchois** anchovy paste; **beurre blanc** butter sauce made with white wine, shallots and

vinegar; **buerre de cacahuètes/de cacao** peanut/cocoa butter; **beurre maître d'hôtel** melted butter with parsley and lemon juice; **beurre noir** brown butter sauce
biberon *m* baby's bottle
bibliothèque *f* library
bicyclette *f* bicycle; **faire de la bicyclette** to cycle, go cycling
bidon *m* can
bien well; right; good; **bien sûr/entendu** of course
bien que although
bientôt soon; shortly
bienvenu(e) welcome
bière *f* beer; **bière blonde** lager; **bière brune** bitter; **bière à la pression** draught beer
bifteck *m* steak; **bifteck tartare** minced raw steak with raw egg, onion, tartar or Worcester sauce, capers
bigarade *f* orange sauce with sugar and vinegar
bigarreau *m* bigarreau cherry
bigorneau *m* winkle
bijou *m* jewel; **bijoux** jewellery; **bijoux (de) fantaisie** costume jewellery
bijouterie *f* jeweller's (shop); jewellery
bilan *m* results; consequences
billard *m* billiards
bille *f* marble
billet *m* ticket; note; **billet aller-retour** return ticket; **billet de banque** bank note; **billet de première/deuxième classe** first/second class ticket; **billet simple**

one-way ticket
biscotte *f* breakfast biscuit, rusk
biscuit *m* biscuit; **biscuit à la cuiller** sponge finger; **biscuit de Savoie** sponge cake
bisque *f*: **bisque de homard/d'écrevisses** lobster/crayfish soup
blanc white; blank; **blanc (de poulet)** breast of chicken; **chèque en blanc** blank cheque; **laissez en blanc** leave blank
blanche white; blank
blanchisserie *f* laundry
blanquette *f*: **blanquette de veau/d'agneau** stewed veal/lamb in white sauce
blé *m* wheat; **blé noir** buckwheat
blessé(e) injured
bleu(e) blue; very rare (*steak*); **bleu d'Auvergne** rich blue cheese, sharp and salty; **bleu de Bresse** mild, soft blue cheese; **bleu marine** navy blue
bloc *m* block; notepad; **bloc opératoire** operating theatre suite
blond(e) fair (*hair*); blond(e)
bloquer to block; **bloquer le passage** to be in the way
bock *m* glass of beer
bœuf *m* beef; **bœuf bourguignon** beef stew in red wine; **bœuf en daube** beef casserole; **bœuf à la ficelle** boiled beef served with mustard and pickles or vegetables or béarnaise sauce; **bœuf miroton** boiled beef in onion sauce; **bœuf à la**

mode beef braised in red wine with vegetables and herbs
boire to drink
bois *m* wood; **en bois** wooden
boisson *f* drink; **boissons chaudes/fraîches** hot/cold drinks
boîte *f* can; box; **en boîte** canned; **boîte d'allumettes** box of matches; matchbox; **boîte aux lettres** letter box; **boîte de nuit** night club; **boîte postale** PO Box; **boîte de vitesse** gearbox
bol *m* bowl; basin
bolée *f* bowl(ful)
bolet *m* boletus mushroom
bombe *f* bomb; aerosol; **bombe glacée** ice pudding
bon *m* token, voucher; **bon de commande** order form
bon(ne) good; right; **bon marché** cheap
bonbon *m* sweet; **bonbon à la menthe** mint
bonheur *m* happiness
bonhomme de neige *m* snowman
bonjour hullo; good morning/afternoon
bonne *see* **bon(ne)**
bonnet *m* cap; **bonnet de bain** bathing cap
bonsoir good evening
bord *m* border; edge; verge; **à bord** on board; **le bord de (la) mer** the seaside
bordeaux maroon
bordelaise: à la bordelaise in a red wine sauce with shallots, beef marrow and mushrooms

bordier *m*: **bordiers autorisés** local traffic only (*Switz*)
bordure *f* border
bosse *f* bump; dent; hump
botte *f* boot; bunch; **botte de caoutchouc** wellington boot
bottin *m* directory
bouche *f* mouth; **bouche d'égout** manhole; **bouche d'incendie** fire hydrant
bouchée *f* bite (*of food*); chocolate; **bouchée à la reine** chicken vol-au-vent
boucher[1] to block; to plug
boucher[2] *m* butcher
boucherie *f* butcher's shop; **boucherie chevaline** horsemeat butcher's
bouchon *m* stopper; cork; top; hold-up
boucle d'oreille *f* earring
boudin *m* black pudding; **boudin blanc** white pudding; **boudin aux pommes** black pudding with apple
boudoir *m* sponge finger
boue *f* mud
bouée de sauvetage *f* lifebelt
bouger to move
bougie *f* candle; spark plug
bouillabaisse *f* rich fish soup or stew
bouillir to boil
bouilloire *f* kettle
bouillon *m* stock
bouillotte *f* hot-water bottle
boulanger *m* baker
boulangerie *f* bakery
boule *f* ball; **boules** game similar to bowls played on rough ground with

metal bowls; **boule (de glace)** scoop of ice cream; **boule de neige** snowball
bouquet *m* bunch; bouquet
Bourgogne *f* Burgundy
Bourse *f* stock market, stock exchange; **bourse** grant
boussole *f* compass
bout *m* end; tip
bouteille *f* bottle; **bouteille thermos** vacuum flask
boutique *f* shop
bouton *m* button; switch; spot; knob
boxe *f* boxing
bracelet *m* bracelet; bangle
braderie *f* clearance sale
brasié(e) braised
branche *f* branch
brancher to plug in
brandade (de morue) *f* poached cod with garlic and parsley
bras *m* arm
brasserie *f* brewery; pub (serving meals)
break *m* estate (car)
bref brief
Bretagne *f* Brittany
bretelle *f* strap; **bretelles** braces; **bretelle d'accès** slip-road; **bretelle de raccordement** access road
breton(ne) from Brittany
brève brief
bricolage *m* do-it-yourself
brie *m* soft, mild cow's milk cheese
brillant(e) shiny; bright; brilliant
brioche *f* brioche (soft roll made with a very light dough)
briocherie *f* bakery/café

specialising in brioches, croissants etc

briquet m cigarette lighter

briser to smash; **brisez la glace** break the glass

britannique British

brocante f second-hand goods; flea market

broche f brooch; spit; **à la broche** spit-roasted

brochet m pike

brochette f skewer; kebab

brodé(e) embroidered; **brodé main** hand-embroidered

bronchite f bronchitis

bronzé(e) sun-tanned

brosse f brush; **brosse à cheveux** hairbrush; **brosse à dents** toothbrush; **brosse à ongles** nailbrush

brouillard m fog

bruit m noise

brûler to burn; **brûler un feu rouge** to go through a red light

brûlot m sugar flamed in brandy and added to coffee

brûlure f burn; **brûlures d'estomac** heartburn

brumeux(euse) misty

brun(e) brown; dark

brushing m blow-dry

brut(e) gross; raw; **(champagne) brut** dry champagne

Bruxelles Brussels

bruyant(e) noisy

bûche f log; **bûche de Noël** Yule log (cake)

buffet m buffet; sideboard

bulle f bubble

bulletin m bulletin; **bulletin météorologique** weather forecast

bureau m desk; office; study; **bureau de change** (foreign) exchange office; **bureau des objets trouvés** lost property office; **bureau de poste** post office; **bureau de réception** reception desk; **bureau de tabac** tobacconist's shop

but m goal; purpose; aim; **à but non lucratif** non-profit-making

butagaz ® m Calor gas ®

buvette f refreshment room; refreshment stall

C

ça that

cabane f hut; mountain hut

cabillaud m (fresh) cod

cabine f cabin; cubicle; **cabine d'essayage** changing room; **cabine téléphonique** telephone booth

cabinet m office; **cabinet médical/dentaire** doctor's/dentist's surgery; **cabinet de toilette** toilet

câble m cable

cacachuète f peanut

cacao m cocoa

cachemire m cashmere

cacher to hide

cadeau m gift

cadre m picture frame; surroundings; executive

café m coffee; café; **café crème** white coffee; **café décaféiné** decaffeinated coffee; **café express** espresso coffee; **café filtre** filter coffee; **café au lait** white coffee; **café lyophilisé** freeze-dried coffee; **café nature** black coffee; **café noir** black coffee; **café en poudre** instant coffee

cafetière f coffeepot

caille f quail

caisse f checkout; cashdesk; case; **caisse d'épargne** savings bank

caissier(ière) m/f cashier; teller

cake m fruit cake

calculatrice f calculator

calendrier m calendar

calisson (d'Aix) m small lozenge-shaped sweetmeat made of almond paste with icing on top

calmant m painkiller; tranquillizer

calmar m squid

calme calm

calvados m apple brandy

cambrioleur m burglar

camembert m soft creamy cheese from Normandy

camera f TV camera; cine-camera

camion m truck, lorry

camionnette f van

campagne f country; countryside; campaign

camper to camp

camping m camping; camp-site; **camping sauvage** camping on unofficial sites

camping-car m camper (van)

camping-gaz m camping stove

canapé m sofa; open sandwich

canapé-lit m bed settee

canard m duck; **canard à l'orange/aux olives** duck in orange sauce/with olives

caneton m duckling

canne f cane; walking stick; **canne à pêche** fishing rod

cannelle f cinnamon
canot m boat; **canot pneumatique** inflatable dinghy; **canot de sauvetage** lifeboat
cantal m hard strong cheese from Cantal in the Auvergne
cantine f canteen
canton m (in Switz) state
caoutchouc m rubber
capitaine m captain
capitale f capital (city)
capot m bonnet (of car)
câpres fpl capers
car[1] m coach
car[2] because
caractère m character
carburant m fuel
cardiologue m/f cardiologist
carnaval m carnival
carnet m notebook; diary; book; **carnet de chèques** cheque book
carnotzet m (in Switz) room in restaurant esp. for groups, serving mainly cheese dishes
carotte f carrot; **carottes Vichy** carrots cooked in butter and sugar
carpe f carp
carré m square; **carré d'agneau/de porc** loin of lamb/pork; **carré de l'Est** cow's-milk cheese similar to camembert but milder
carreau m tile; **à carreaux** check(er)ed
carrefour m intersection; crossroads
carrelet m plaice
carrière f career; quarry
carte f map; chart; card; menu; **carte d'abonnement** season ticket; **carte d'adhérent** membership card; **carte bleue** credit card; **carte**

de crédit credit card; **carte d'étudiant** student card; **carte grise** logbook; **carte d'identité** identity card; **carte orange** monthly or yearly season ticket; **carte postale** postcard; **carte routière** road map; **carte vermeille** senior citizen's rail pass; **carte verte** green card; **carte des vins** wine list; **carte de visite** visiting card; **carte de vœux** greetings card
carton m cardboard; carton; box
cartouche f cartridge (for gun); carton (of cigarettes)
cas m case; **en cas de** in case of
cascade f waterfall
case postale f (in Switz) PO Box
caserne f barracks; **caserne de pompiers** fire station
casier m rack; locker
casque m helmet; **casque protecteur** crash helmet
casse-croûte m snack
casser to break; **casser les prix** to slash prices
casserole f pot; saucepan
cassis m blackcurrant; blackcurrant liqueur
cassolette f individual fondue dish
cassonade f brown sugar crystals
cassoulet (toulousain) m stew made with beans, pork or mutton and sausages
cathédrale f cathedral
catholique catholic
cauchemar m nightmare
cause f cause; **à cause de** because of; **pour cause de** on account of

causer to cause
caution f security (for loan); deposit; **caution à verser** deposit required
cave f cellar
caveau m cellar
caverne f cave
caviar m caviar(e)
ce this; that
ceci this
céder to give in; **cédez la priorité/le passage** give way (to traffic)
cédratine f citron-based liqueur
C.E.E. f EEC
ceinture f belt; **ceinture de sécurité** safety belt, seat belt
célèbre famous
célébrer to celebrate
céleri m celeriac; celery; **céleri rémoulade** grated celariac in dressing
céleri-rave m celeriac
célibataire single
celle the one
celle-ci this one
celle-là that one
celles the ones
celles-ci these
celles-là those
celui the one
celui-ci this one
celui-là that one
cendre f ash; **sous la cendre** cooked in the embers
cendrier m ashtray
cent hundred
centaine f about a hundred
centenaire m centenary
centième hundredth
centre m centre; **centre commercial** shopping centre; **centre équestre** riding school; **centre hospitalier** hospital complex; **centre médical** clinic; **centre de secours**

first aid centre; **centre de sports et loisirs** leisure centre; **centre ville** city centre
cependant however
cèpes *mpl* boletus mushrooms
cercle *m* circle; ring
céréale *f* cereal
cérémonie *f* ceremony
cerf *m* deer
cerfeuil *m* chervil
cerf-volant *m* kite
cerise *f* cherry
certain(e) definite; sure; certain; **certains** some
certainement definitely; certainly
cervelle *f* brains (*as food*)
ces those; these
cesser to stop
c'est it/he/she is
cette this; that
ceux the ones
ceux-ci these
ceux-là those
C.F.F. *mpl* Swiss Railways
chacun(e) each; everyone
chaîne *f* chain; channel; (mountain) range; **chaîne hi-fi/haute fidélité** hi-fi; **chaînes obligatoires** snow chains compulsory
chair *f* flesh
chaise *f* chair; **chaise haute/de bébé** highchair; **chaise longue** deckchair
chalet *m*: **chalet-refuge** hut for skiers or hill walkers; **chalet-skieurs** hut for skiers
chaleur *f* heat
chambre *f* bedroom; room; lodgings; **chambre d'amis** guest room; **chambre à coucher** bedroom; **chambre d'enfants** nursery; **chambre individuelle** single room; **chambres**

communicantes communicating rooms
champ *m* field; **champ de courses** racecourse
champenoise: méthode champenoise champagne-style
champignon *m* mushroom; **champignon de Paris** button mushroom
championnat *m* championship
chance *f* luck
change *m* exchange
changement *m* change; **un changement de temps** a change in the weather
changer to alter; **changer de** to change; **changer de train à Marseille** to change trains at Marseilles
chanson *f* song; **chanson folklorique** folk song
chant *m* hymn; singing; **chant de Noël** carol
chanter to sing
chanterelle *f* chanterelle (*mushroom*)
chantier *m* building site; roadworks
Chantilly: crème Chantilly whipped cream
chapeau *m* hat
chapelle *f* chapel
chapelure *f* (dried) breadcrumbs
chaque each; every
charbon *m* coal
charcuterie *f* pork butcher's shop and delicatessen; cooked pork meats
charge *f* load; charge; responsibility; **à votre charge** payable by you; **charges comprises** inclusive of service charges

chariot *m* trolley; **chariot à bagages** luggage trolley
charmant(e) charming
charme *m* charm
charter *m* charter flight
chartreuse *f* yellow liqueur made from herbs and flowers
chasse *f* hunting; shooting; **chasse gardée** private hunting; private shooting
chasse-neige *m* snowplough
chasser to hunt
chasseur *see* **sauce**
chat *m* cat
châtaigne *f* chestnut
château *m* castle; mansion
chateaubriand *m* thick fillet steak, barded and lightly cooked in butter
chaud(e) warm; hot
chauffage *m* heating; **chauffage central** central heating
chauffe-biberon *m* bottle warmer
chauffe-eau *m* water heater
chauffer to heat; to overheat
chauffeur *m* chauffeur; driver
chaussée *f* carriageway; **chaussée déformée** uneven road surface; **chaussée rétrécie** road narrows
chaussette *f* sock
chausson *m*: **chausson aux pommes** apple turnover
chaussure *f* shoe; **chaussure de ski** ski boot
chauve-souris *f* bat
chef *m* chef; chief; head; leader; **chef d'orchestre**

conductor; **chef de train** guard

chef-d'œuvre *m* masterpiece

chef-lieu *m*: **chef-lieu de département** county town

chemin *m* path; lane; track; **chemin de fer** railway

cheminée *f* fireplace; mantelpiece; chimney

chemise *f* shirt; **chemise de nuit** nightdress

chemisier *m* blouse

chêne *m* oak

chèque *m* cheque; **chèque bancaire** cheque; **chèque postal** post office Girocheque; **chèque de voyage** traveller's cheque

chéquier *m* cheque book

chercher to look for; to search for; **aller chercher** to go and fetch

cher (chère) dear; expensive

chéri(e) *m/f* darling

cherry *m* cherry brandy

cheval *m* horse; **faire du cheval** to go horseriding; **cheval de course** racehorse

cheveux *mpl* hair

cheville *f* ankle

chèvre *f* goat; **fromage de chèvre** goat cheese

chevreau *m* kid (*leather*)

chevreuil *m* roe deer; venison

chez at the house of

chicorée *f* chicory (*for coffee*); endive; **chicorée braisée** braised endive

chien *m* dog

chiffre *m* figure; number

chimie *f* chemistry

chimique chemical

chinois(e) Chinese

chips *fpl* crisps

chirurgie *f* surgery; **chirurgie esthétique** cosmetic surgery

chirurgien *m* surgeon

choc *m* shock; bump

chocolat *m* chocolate; drinking chocolate; **chocolat à croquer** plain chocolate; **chocolat froid** iced drinking chocolate; **chocolat au lait** milk chocolate; **grand chocolat** large hot chocolate

chœur *m* choir

choisir to pick; to choose

choix *m* range; choice; **dessert au choix** choice of desserts

chômage *m* unemployment

chope *f* tankard

chose *f* thing

chou *m* cabbage; **chou à la crème** cream puff; **choux de Bruxelles** Brussels sprouts

choucroute *f* sauerkraut; **choucroute garnie** sauerkraut served with boiled potatoes and assorted pork meats

chou-fleur *m* cauliflower

chou-rave *m* kohlrabi

chrétien(ne) *m/f* Christian

C.H.U. *m* hospital

chute *f* fall; **risque de chute de pierres** danger: falling rocks; **chute d'eau** waterfall

ciboulette *f* chives

ci-dessous below

ci-dessus above

cidre *m* cider

ciel *m* sky; **à ciel ouvert** open-air

cil *m* eyelash

cime *f* peak

cimetière *m* cemetery;

graveyard

cinq five

cinquante fifty

cinquième fifth

cintre *m* coat hanger

cirage *m* shoe polish

circuit *m* (round) trip; circuit; **circuit touristique** excursion; scenic route

circulation *f* traffic

cirque *m* circus

ciseaux *mpl* scissors

cité *f* city; housing estate

citron *m* lemon; **citron pressé** fresh lemon drink; **citron vert** lime

citronnade *f* still lemonade

civet *m*: **civet de lapin/ de lièvre** rich rabbit/hare stew with red wine and onions

clafoutis *m* fruit, especially cherries, cooked in batter

clair(e) clear; light

claire *f* oyster bed; fattened oyster

classe *f* grade; class; **première classe** first class; **classe affaires** business class

classique classical

clé *f* key; spanner; **clé de contact** ignition key

clef *see* **clé**

client(e) *m/f* guest (*at hotel*); client; customer

clientèle *f* customers, clientèle; custom; practice (*of doctor, lawyer*)

clignotant *m* indicator

climat *m* climate

climatisation *f* air conditioning

climatisé(e) air-conditioned

clinique *f* nursing home, (private) clinic

cloison *f* partition;

cloison amovible removable partition

clou m stud; nail; **clou de girofle** clove

cocher to tick

cochon m pig; **cochon de lait** suckling pig

cochonnailles fpl selection of cold pork/ham etc

cocotte f casserole dish

cocotte-minute f pressure cooker

code m code; **se mettre en code(s)** to dip one's (head)lights; **code postal** postcode; **code de la route** Highway Code

cœur m heart; **cœurs de laitue/de palmiers** lettuce/palm hearts

coffre m boot (of car)

coffre-fort m strongbox; safe

coiffeur m hairdresser; barber; **coiffeur pour hommes/dames/unisexe** ladies'/gents'/unisex hairdresser

coiffeuse f hairdresser; dressing table

coiffure f hairstyle

coin m corner; **coin cuisine** kitchen area

cointreau m orange-based liqueur

col m collar; pass (in mountains); **col fermé en hiver** pass closed in winter

colère f anger

colin m hake

colique f colic; diarrhoea

colis m parcel; **colis postaux** postal parcels

collant m tights

colle f glue; paste

collège m secondary school

coller to stick; to glue

collier m necklace; dog collar

colline f hill

colonie (de vacances) f holiday camp (for children)

colorant m colouring

coloris m colour

combat m fight; **combat de boxe/catch** boxing/wrestling match

combien how much/many

combinaison f flying suit; wet suit; petticoat

combustible m fuel

comédie f comedy; **comédie musicale** musical

comique m comedian

comité m committee

commande f order; **sur commande** to order

commander to order

commandes fpl controls

comme like; **comme si** as if, as though

commencer to begin

comment how

commerçant(e) m/f trader

commerce m commerce; business; trade

commissariat de police m police station

commode[1] convenient

commode[2] f chest of drawers

commun(e) common

communication f: **obtenir la communication** to get through

communiquer to communicate

compagnie f firm; **compagnie aérienne** airline

comparer to compare

compartiment m compartment; **compartiment non-fumeur** non-smoker

complet(ète) full (up)

composer to compose; to dial

composter: pour valider votre billet compostez-le your ticket is not valid unless date-stamped/punched

compote f stewed fruit

comprenant including

comprendre to understand; to comprise

comprimé m tablet

compris(e) including; **service compris** inclusive of service; **tout compris** all inclusive; **... non compris** exclusive of ...

comptable m/f accountant

comptant m: **payer (au) comptant** to pay cash; **acheter au comptant** to buy for cash

compte m account; **compte en banque** bank account; **compte courant** current account; **compte de dépôt** deposit account

compter to count; **compter sur** to rely on

compteur m speedometer; meter; **compteur kilométrique** ≈ milometer; **couper le courant/l'eau au compteur** to turn the electricity/water off at the mains

comptoir m bar; counter; **au comptoir** at the bar; at the counter

comté m county; cheese similar to gruyère

concentré m: **concentré de tomate** tomato purée

concerner to concern; **en ce qui concerne** regarding

concessionnaire m

agent; distributor; **concessionnaire agréé** registered dealer

concierge *m/f* caretaker; janitor

concombre *m* cucumber

concours *m* contest; aid

concurrent(e) *m/f* competitor; contestant

condamner to condemn

condition *f* conditon; **à condition que ...** on condition that ...

conducteur(trice) *m/f* driver

conduire to steer; to drive

conduite *f* driving; steering; behaviour; **conduite à gauche** left-hand drive

confection *f* ready-to-wear clothes

confiance *f* confidence; **de confiance** reliable

confirmer to confirm

confiserie *f* confectioner's shop

confit(e): fruits confits crystallized fruits

confit *m*: **confit d'oie/de canard** conserve of goose/of duck

confiture *f* jam; **confiture d'oranges** marmalade

conflit *m* conflict

conformément à in accordance with

confort *m* comfort; **tout confort** all mod cons

confortable comfortable

congé *m* leave; holiday

congélateur *m* freezer

congelé(e) frozen

congre *m* conger eel

congrès *m* congress

connaître to know

conscient(e) conscious

conseil *m* advice; **conseil municipal/régional**

town/regional council

conseiller to advise

conservateur *m* preservative

conservation: longue conservation long-life (*milk etc*)

conserve *f* canned food; **en conserve** canned

conserver to keep; **conservez votre titre de transport jusqu'à la sortie** keep your ticket until you leave the station

consigne *f* deposit; left-luggage office; **consigne automatique** left-luggage lockers; **consignes de sécurité** safety instructions

consigné(e): bouteille consignée/non consignée returnable/non-returnable bottle

consommateur(trice) *m/f* consumer

consommation *f* consumption; drink

consommer: à consommer avant ... eat before ...

constat *m* report; **constat à l'amiable** jointly agreed statement for insurance purposes

construire to construct; to build

consulat *m* consulate

consultation *f*: **consultations sur rendez-vous** consultations by appointment

contact *m*: **se mettre en contact avec** to contact

contagieux(euse) infectious; contagious

contemporain(e) contemporary

contenir to hold; to

contain

content(e) content(ed); pleased

contenu *m* contents

contigu(ë) adjoining

continu(e) continuous

continuel(le) continual

continuer to continue

contraceptif *m* contraceptive

contractuel(le) *m/f* traffic warden

contraire *m* opposite; **au contraire** on the contrary

contrat *m* contract; **contrat de location** lease

contravention *f* fine; parking ticket

contre against; versus

contrebande *f* contraband; **passer en contrebande** to smuggle

contrebas: (en) contrebas (down) below

contre-filet *m* sirloin

contre-indiqué(e) contra-indicated

contre-ordre *m*: **sauf contre-ordre** unless otherwise directed

contribuer to contribute

contrôle *m* check; **contrôle radar fréquent** frequent radar checks

contrôler to check

contrôleur *m* ticket inspector

convenance *f*: **à votre convenance** when it suits you

convenir to be suitable

conventionné(e): médecin conventionné ≈ National Health Service doctor

convenu(e) agreed

convoi *m*: **convoi exceptionnel** wide (or dangerous) load

copie f copy

copieux(euse) hearty; generous

copropriété f: **en copropriété** jointly owned

coq m cock(erel); **coq de bruyère** grouse; **coq au vin** chicken in red wine with mushrooms, bacon and garlic

coque f shell; cockle; **à la coque** soft-boiled (egg)

coquelet m cockerel

coqueluche f whooping cough

coquillage m shell; **coquillages** shellfish

coquille f shell; **coquille Saint-Jacques** scallop; **coquilles de poisson** fish served in scallop shells

coquillettes fpl pasta shells

corbeille f basket

corde f rope; cord; string

cordonnerie f shoe repairer's shop; shoe repairing

coriandre f coriander

corne f horn

cornemuse f (bag)pipes

cornet m cornet; cone

corniche f coast road

cornichon m gherkin

corps m body

correspondance f connection; correspondence; **acheter quelque chose par correspondance** to buy something by mail order

correspondant(e) m/f person phoning (or being phoned)

Corse f Corsica

cosmétiques mpl cosmetics

costume m costume; suit; **costume national** national dress

côte f coast; hill; rib; **côte de bœuf** rib of beef; **côte de porc (charcutière)** pork chop (with tomato and mushroom sauce); **côte de veau/d'agneau** veal/lamb cutlet

côté m side; **à côté de** beside; **à côté** nearby; next door

Côte d'Azur f Riviera

côtelette f cutlet; **côtelette de porc/ d'agneau/de veau/de mouton** pork/lamb/veal/ mutton chop

cotisation f subscription

coton m cotton; **coton hydrophile** cotton wool

cou m neck

couche f nappy; layer

couche-culotte f disposable nappy and waterproof pants all in one

coucher to put to bed; **on peut coucher 3 personnes dans l'appartement** the apartment sleeps 3; **se coucher** to go to bed

couchette f couchette; bunk

coude m elbow; bend (in pipe, wire etc)

couette f continental quilt

couffin m Moses basket

couler to sink; to run (water)

couleur f colour

coulis m purée

couloir m corridor; **couloir d'autobus** bus lane

coulommiers m creamy white cow's-milk cheese, similar to camembert

coup m stroke; shot; hit; blow; **coup de soleil** sunburn

coupe f goblet; dish; cup (trophy); **coupe (de cheveux)** haircut (style); **coupe de fruits** fruit salad; **coupe glacée** ice cream and fruit

coupé(e) off (machine)

coupon m coupon; remnant; roll (of cloth)

coupon-réponse m reply coupon

coupure f cut; **coupure de courant** power cut

cour f court; courtyard

courageux(euse) brave

couramment fluently

courant m power; current; **être au courant (de)** to know (about); **pour couper le courant** in order to cut off the power; **courant d'air** draught; **courant dangereux** (in sea) dangerous current

courant(e) common; standard; current

courbature f ache

courge f marrow (vegetable)

courir to run

couronne f crown

courrier m mail; post

cours m lesson; course; rate; **cours intensif** crash course; **cours particuliers** private lessons; **en cours de réparation** under repair

course f race (sport); errand; **faire les courses** to go shopping; **course de taureaux** bullfight; **courses de chevaux** horseracing

court(e) short; **à court terme** short term

court-bouillon m stock for fish, made with root vegetables and white wine or vinegar

court de tennis *m* tennis court

courtier *m* broker

couscous *m* spicy Arab dish of steamed semolina with a meat stew

coussin *m* cushion

coût *m* cost; **coût de la vie** cost of living

couteau *m* knife

coûter to cost

coûteux(euse) expensive

coutume *f* custom

couture *f* seam; sewing

couvent *m* convent

couvercle *m* top; lid

couvert *m* cover charge; place setting

couvert(e) covered

couverts *mpl* cutlery

couverture *f* blanket; cover; wrapper; **couverture chauffante** electric blanket

couvrir to cover

crabe *m* crab

cracher to spit

craindre to be afraid of; to be easily damaged by

crampe *f* cramp

cravate *f* (neck)tie

crayon *m* pencil

crédit *m* credit; **à crédit** on credit; **la maison ne fait pas de crédit** no credit given here

créditer to credit

crème *f* cream; **un (café) crème** white coffee; **crème anglaise** custard; **crème de cacao** sweet liqueur with a chocolate flavour; **crème caramel** egg custard topped with caramel; **crème Chantilly** whipped cream; **crème fouettée** whipped cream; **crème glacée** ice cream; **crème hydratante** moisturising

cream; **crème pâtissière** confectioner's custard; **crème renversée** cream mould

crémerie *f* dairy

crémeux(euse) creamy

crêpe *f* pancake; **crêpe flambée** pancake served in flaming brandy; **crêpe fourrée** stuffed pancake; **crêpe Suzette** pancake with orange sauce, served in flaming brandy and often orange liqueur

crêperie *f* pancake shop/restaurant

cresson *m* watercress

crevaison *f* puncture

crevette *f* shrimp; **crevette rose** prawn

cri *m* cry; shout

cric *m* jack

crier to scream; to shout

crise *f* crisis; **crise cardiaque** heart attack

critique *f* criticism; review

crochet *m* hook

croire to believe

croisière *f* cruise

croissance *f* growth

croix *f* cross

croquant(e) crisp, crunchy

croque au sel *f:* **à la croque au sel** with a sprinkling of salt

croque-madame *m* toasted cheese sandwich with ham and fried egg

croque-monsieur *m* toasted ham and cheese sandwich

croquer to crunch; to munch

crottin de Chavignol *m* type of goat cheese

croustade *f* pastry shell with filling

croustillant(e) crisp

croûte *f* crust; **en croûte** in a pastry crust

C.R.S. *mpl* French riot police

cru(e) raw; **premier cru** first-class wine; **cru classé** classified wine; **un vin de grand cru** a vintage wine

cruche *f* fig

crudités *fpl* selection of salads and raw vegetables

crustacés *mpl* shellfish

cueillir to pick *(flowers)*

cuiller *f* spoon; **cuiller à café** teaspoon; **cuiller à dessert** dessertspoon; **cuiller à soupe** tablespoon; soup spoon

cuillère = cuiller

cuillerée *f* spoonful; **cuillerée à soupe** tablespoonful

cuir *m* leather

cuire to cook; **faire cuire à feu doux** cook gently

cuisine *f* cooking; cuisine; kitchen; **cuisine familiale** home cooking; **cuisine fine** high-class cuisine

cuisinier *m* cook

cuisinière *f* cook; cooker

cuisse *f* thigh; **cuisses de grenouille** frogs' legs; **cuisse de poulet** chicken leg

cuissot *m* haunch of venison/wild boar

cuit(e) done

cuivre *m* copper; **cuivre jaune** brass

culotte *f* panties

culture physique *f* physical training

culturisme *m* body-building

cure *f* course of treatment; **cure thermale** course of treatment at a spa

curieux(euse) curious; funny

cuvée f vintage

cuvette f bowl

cyclisme m cycling

cycliste m/f cyclist

cygne m swan

cylindrée f (cubic) capacity (of engine)

D

d'abord at first

d'accord okay (agreement)

daim m suede

dame f lady; queen (in cards); **dames** ladies' (toilets); draughts

dangereux(euse) dangerous

dans into; in; on

dansant(e): soirée dansante dinner-dance

danse f dance; dancing; **danse folklorique** folk dance

danser to dance

darne f thick fish steak

date f date (day)

datte f date (fruit)

daube f stew

dauphin m dolphin

daurade f sea bream

davantage more; longer

dé m dice; **en dés** diced

débarcadère m landing stage

débat m debate

débit m debit; **débit de boissons** drinking establishment

débiter to debit

déboucher to clear; to uncork

debout standing; upright; **être debout** to stand

début m beginning

débutant(e) m/f beginner

décaféiné(e) decaffeinated

décapotable convertible

décapsuleur m bottle opener

décembre m December

décès m death

décevoir to disappoint

décharge f electric shock; **décharge publique** rubbish dump

décharger to unload

déchirer to tear; to rip

déci m (in Switz) one decilitre of wine

décider to decide

déclaration f statement; **déclaration d'accident** notification of accident

déclarer to state; to declare; **rien à déclarer** nothing to declare

déclencher to release (mechanism); to set off (alarm)

décliner: décliner toute responsabilité to accept no responsibility

décollage m takeoff

décolleté m low neck; **décolleté en V** V-neck

décongeler to defrost

décontracté(e) relaxed

décorer to decorate

décortiqué(e) shelled

découper to cut out; to cut up; to carve (meat)

découvert m overdraft

découvrir to uncover; to discover; to find out

décret m decree

décrire to describe

déçu(e) disappointed

dédouaner to clear through customs

déduire to deduct

défaillance f (mechanical) failure

défaire to unpack; to unfasten; to undo; to untie

défaut m fault; defect

défectueux(euse) imperfect; faulty; defective

défendre to defend; to forbid

défense f: **défense d'entrer** no entry; **défense de fumer** no smoking

défilé m parade

dégager to clear

dégâts mpl damage

dégeler to thaw

dégivrer to defrost; to de-ice

degré m degree

dégriffé(e): vêtements dégriffés designer seconds

déguisement m disguise; fancy dress

dégustation f tasting; sampling

dehors outside; outdoors; **en dehors de** apart from

déjà already

déjeuner m lunch; breakfast (Switz only); **petit déjeuner** breakfast

délai m: **dans le délai fixé** within the time limit stipulated

délasser to relax; to entertain

délestage m: **itinéraire de délestage** alternative route avoiding heavy traffic

délice m delight

délit m offence; **tout délit sera passible d'amende** all offences will be punishable by a fine

délivré(e) issued (passport etc)

demain tomorrow

demande f request; application; demand (for

goods); **demandes d'emploi** situations wanted; **sur demande** on request; on application

demander to ask (for); to claim (lost property, baggage); **se demander si ... ** to wonder whether ...

démangeaison f itch

démaquillant m make-up remover

démarqué(e) reduced (goods)

démarreur m starter (in car)

démêler to untangle

déménagement m move (change of house); removal

déménager to move house

demi(e) half; **trois kilomètres et demi** three and a half kilometres; **un demi** (in France) approx. half pint of draught beer; (in Switz) half litre of wine

demi-douzaine f half dozen

demi-heure f half-hour

demi-pension f half board

demi-sec medium-dry

demi-sel slightly salted

demi-tarif m half-fare

demi-tour m U-turn

déneigé(e) cleared of snow

dénoyauté(e) stoned (fruit)

dent f tooth

dentelle f lace

dentier m denture

dentifrice m toothpaste

dentiste m/f dentist

dépannage m: **service de dépannage** breakdown service

dépareillé(e) incomplete

départ m departure; **au départ** at the start; at the place of departure; **au départ de** (leaving) from

département m department; (in France) regional divison

départementale: (route) départementale B-road

dépassement m: **dépassement interdit** no overtaking

dépasser to exceed; to overtake; **ne pas dépasser la dose prescrite** do not exceed the prescribed dose

dépêcher: se dépêcher to hurry; **dépêchez-vous!** hurry up!

dépendre to depend

dépenser to spend

dépenses fpl expenditure; outgoings

dépilatoire: crème dépilatoire depilatory cream

dépit: en dépit de in spite of

déplacer: se déplacer to travel

dépliant m brochure

déposé(e): marque déposée registered trademark

déposer to deposit; to lay down; **défense de déposer des ordures** dumping of rubbish prohibited

dépositaire m/f agent

dépôt m deposit; depot; **dépôt d'ordures** rubbish dump

déprimé(e) depressed

depuis since

dérangement m: **en dérangement** out of order

déranger to disturb

dérapage m skid

dériveur m sailing dinghy (with centreboard)

dermatologue m/f dermatologist

dernier(ère) last; **en dernier** last

derrière at the back; behind

des = de + les

dès from; since; **dès votre arrivée** as soon as you arrive

désaccord m disagreement

désagréable unpleasant

descendre to come/go down; to get/take down

déshabillé m négligée

déshydraté(e) dehydrated

désinfectant m disinfectant

désir m wish; desire

désistement m withdrawal

désodorisant m air freshener

désolé(e) sorry

désordre m mess; muddle

désormais from now on

désossé(e) boned (meat)

dessaler to soak (fish etc)

desséché(e) dried (up)

dessert m dessert

desserte f: **la desserte du village est assurée par autocar** there is a coach service to the village

dessin m design; drawing; **dessin animé** cartoon (animated); **dessin humoristique** cartoon (drawing)

dessous underneath; **en dessous (de)** underneath

dessus on top; **en dessus (de)** above

destinataire m/f

addressee; consignee
destination f destination; **à destination de** bound for
détachant m stain remover
détacher to remove; to untie; **détachez le coupon** tear off the coupon; **détachez suivant le pointillé** tear off along the dotted line
détail m detail; **en détail** in detail; **au détail** retail; **prix de détail** retail price
détaillant m retailer
détaxé(e): produits détaxés duty-free goods
détendre: se détendre to relax
détente f relaxation
déterminé(e) determined
détour m detour
détournement m hijacking
détruire to destroy
deux two; **les deux** both
deuxième second; **deuxième classe** second class
deux-pièces m two-piece (*suit, swimsuit*); two-roomed flat
devant in front (of)
développement m development
devenir to become
déviation f diversion
devis m quotation (*price*)
devises (étrangères) fpl foreign currency
dévisser to unscrew
devoir¹ m duty (*obligation*)
devoir² to owe; to have to; must; **il devrait gagner** he ought to win
diabète m diabetes
diabétique m/f diabetic
diabolo m lemonade and

fruit or mint cordial
diamant m diamond
diapositive f slide
diarrhée f diarrhoea
diététique dietary; health foods
dieu m god; **Dieu** God
difficile difficult
difficulté f difficulty
diffuseur m diffuser; distributor; air freshener
digue f dyke; jetty
diluer to dilute
dimanche m Sunday
diminuer to decrease
dinde f turkey; **dinde aux marrons** turkey with chestnut stuffing
dindonneau m young turkey
dîner m dinner; dinner party; lunch (*Switz*); **dîner aux chandelles** candlelit dinner; **dîner dansant** dinner-dance; **dîner spectacle** cabaret dinner
diplomate m diplomat; type of trifle
dire to say; to tell
direct(e) direct; **train direct** through train
directement directly
directeur m manager; director; headmaster; principal (*of school etc*)
direction f management; direction; **toutes directions** through traffic; all routes
directives fpl instructions
discours m speech
discret(ète) discreet
discrétion f: **discrétion assurée** discretion guaranteed; **vin à discrétion** unlimited wine
disparaître to disappear
disparu(e) missing
disponible available
disposition f: **à votre**

disposition at your service
disque m record; disc; **disque de stationnement** parking disc
dissolvant m: **dissolvant (gras)** nail varnish remover
dissoudre to dissolve
distinguer to distinguish
distractions fpl entertainment
distraire to distract
distribuer to distribute; to deliver (*mail*)
distributeur m distributor (*in car*); **distributeur automatique** vending machine
distribution f distribution; delivery (*of mail*)
divers(e) various
diviser to divide
dix ten
dix-huit eighteen
dixième tenth
dix-neuf nineteen
dix-sept seventeen
docteur m doctor
doigt m finger; **doigt de pied** toe
domicile m home; address
dommage m damage
donc so
donner to give; to give away; **donner sur** to open onto; to overlook; **donner droit à** to entitle to
donneur m donor
dont whose; of which
dorade see **daurade**
doré(e) golden
dorénavant from now on
dormir to sleep
dortoir m dormitory

dos m back
douane f customs;
  exempté de douane
  duty-free
douanier m customs
  officer
doubler to overtake; to
  double
douce gentle; soft; mild
doucement quietly;
  gently
douche f shower
douleur f pain
douloureux(euse) sore;
  painful
doute m doubt; **sans**
  doute no doubt
Douvres Dover
doux gentle; soft; mild
douzaine f dozen
douze twelve
douzième twelfth
dragée f sugared almond
drap m sheet; **drap de**
  bain bath sheet
drapeau m flag
drap-housse m fitted
  sheet
drogue f drug
droguerie f hardware
  shop
droit m right (*entitlement*);
  droits de douane
  customs duty
droit(e) right (*not left*);
  straight
droite f right-hand side; **à**
  droite on/to the right;
  tourner à droite to turn
  right
drôle funny
du = de + le
dû (due) due
duplex m split-level
  apartment
dur(e) tough; hard;
  hard-boiled
durant during
durer to last
duvet m sleeping bag

E

eau f water; **eau distillée**
  distilled water; **eau**
  gazeuse/plate fizzy/still
  water; **eau de Javel**
  bleach; **eau minérale**
  mineral water; **eau du**
  robinet tap-water; **eau**
  de toilette toilet water;
  eau-de-vie brandy
éblouir to dazzle
ébullition f: **porter à**
  ébullition to bring to
  the boil
écaille f scale (*of fish*);
  shell; tortoiseshell; flake
écart: à l'écart de away
  from
échalote f shallot
échanger to exchange
échangeur m interchange
échantillon m sample
écharpe f scarf; sling
échéant: le cas échéant
  if the case arises
échecs mpl chess
échelle f ladder; scale
éclairage m lighting
éclairer to light up
éclater to burst; to
  explode
écluse f lock (*in canal*)
école f school
économie f economy;
  economics; **économies**
  savings
écorce f peel (*of orange,
  lemon*); bark
écorchure f graze
Écossais(e) m/f Scot;
  écossais(e) Scottish
Écosse f Scotland
écouter to listen (to)
écouteur m receiver
écran m screen
écraser to crush; to run
  over; **s'écraser** to crash
  (*plane*)
écrevisse f crayfish
  (*freshwater*); **écrevisses à**
  la nage crayfish in white
  wine, vegetables and
  herbs
écrire to write
écrit: par écrit in writing
écrouler: s'écrouler to
  collapse
écureuil m squirrel
écurie f stable
Édimbourg Edinburgh
édredon m eiderdown;
  quilt
effet m effect
efficace effective; efficient
effondrer: s'effondrer to
  collapse
efforcer: s'efforcer de to
  try hard to
effrayer to frighten
égal(e) even; equal
également equally; too
églefin m haddock
église f church
égout m drain
égouttoir m draining-
  board; dishrack
égratignure f scratch
élargissement m
  widening
élection f election;
  élections législatives
  general election
électricité f electricity
électrique electric(al)
électro-ménager m
  household electrical
  appliances
élément m unit; element
élevage m breeding; farm
élève m/f pupil
élevé(e) high
élever to raise; to breed;
  s'élever à to amount to
éliminatoire f heat
  (*sports*)
éliminé(e) out (*team,
  player*)
élire to elect

elle she; her; it
elle-même herself
elles they; them
elles-mêmes themselves
éloigné(e) distant
élu(e) elected
emballage *m* packing
embarquement *m* boarding; **carte d'embarquement** boarding pass
embauche *f*: **pas d'embauche** no vacancies
embouteillage *m* traffic jam
embrasser to kiss
embrayage *m* clutch
émeraude *f* emerald
émeute *f* riot
émigrer to emigrate
émincé *m* thinly sliced meat in a sauce
émis(e) issued (*ticket*)
émission *f* programme; broadcast; issue (*of ticket*)
emmener to take
emmenthal *m* hard Swiss cheese, similar to gruyère
empêchement *m*: **en cas d'empêchement ...** in case of any problem ...
empêcher to prevent
emplacement *m*: **emplacement réservé aux taxis** parking area reserved for taxis
emploi *m* use; job; employment
employé(e) *m/f* employee
employer to use; to employ
employeur *m* employer
empoisonnement *m* poisoning
emporter to take away; **à emporter** take-away
emprunt *m* loan
emprunter to borrow;

empruntez l'itinéraire ... follow the route ...
en some; any; in; to; **en train/voiture** by train/car
en-cas *m* snack
enceinte pregnant
enchanté(e) delighted
encombrements *mpl* obstructions; hold-ups
encore still; yet; **encore une fois** once more; **encore de** more
encornet *m* squid
encre *f* ink
endives *fpl* chicory
endormi(e) asleep
endroit *m* place, spot
énergie *f* energy
énervé(e) annoyed; nervous
enfant *m* child
enfin at last
engager to engage; **s'engager à faire** to undertake to do
engelure *f* chilblain
enlever to remove; to take off; to take away
enneigement *m* snowfall; **bulletin d'enneigement** snow report
ennui *m* nuisance; trouble; **ennuis de moteur** engine trouble
ennuyer: s'ennuyer to be bored
énorme enormous
enregistrement *m*: **enregistrement des bagages** check-in (desk)
enrhumé(e): être enrhumé(e) to have a cold
enrobé(e): enrobé(e) de chocolat/caramel chocolate-/caramel-coated
enseignement *m* education
enseigner to teach
ensemble together
ensoleillé(e) sunny

ensoleillement *m* hours of sunshine
ensuite then
entendre to hear
enterrement *m* funeral
enthousiaste enthusiastic
entier(ère) whole
entorse *f* sprain
entourer to surround
entracte *m* interval
entrain *m*: **plein(e) d'entrain** lively
entraîner to pull along; **s'entraîner** to train
entre between
entrecôte *f* rib steak; **entrecôte Bercy** rib steak in butter, white wine and shallot sauce; **entrecôte chasseur** rib steak in sauce with shallots, white wine, tomato and mushrooms; **entrecôte grillée** grilled rib steak; **entrecôte marchand de vin** rib steak in red wine sauce with shallots; **entrecôte minute** minute steak
entrée *f* entry, entrance; admission; hall; starter (*food*); **prix d'entrée** admission fee; **entrée gratuite** admission free; **entrée interdite** no entry; **entrées froides/chaudes** cold/hot starters
entremets *m* cream dessert
entrepôt *m* warehouse
entrepreneur *m* contractor
entreprise *f* firm; company
entrer to come in; to enter; to go in
entretien *m* upkeep; maintenance
entrevue *f* interview
enveloppe *f* envelope;

enveloppe autocollante self-seal envelope; **enveloppe timbrée à votre adresse** stamped addressed envelope
envelopper to wrap
envers[1] toward
envers[2] *m*: **à l'envers** upside down; back to front; inside out
envie *f* envy; **avoir envie de** to want; to feel like
environ around; about
environs *mpl* surroundings
envisageable that can be considered
envoi *m* dispatching; remittance; consignment; **envoi express** express mail; **envoi recommandé** registered post
envoyer to send
épais(se) thick
épargne *f* saving
épaule *f* shoulder
éperlan *m* smelt (*fish*)
épi *m* ear (*of corn*); **épi de maïs** corn-on-the-cob
épice *f* spice
épicé(e) spicy
épicerie *f* grocer's shop; **épicerie fine** delicatessen
épidémie *f* epidemic
épilation *f*: **épilation à la cire** hair removal by waxing
épiler: crème à épiler hair-removing cream
épinards *mpl* spinach
épingle *f* pin; **épingle de nourrice/de sûreté** safety pin
éplucher to peel
éponge *f* sponge
époque *f* age; **d'époque** period (*furniture*)
épouser to marry
épreuve *f* proof; print (*photographic*)

épuisé(e) sold out; exhausted; out of stock
équilibre *m* balance
équipage *m* crew
équipe *f* team; shift
équipement *m* equipment; facilities; **équipement sportif** sports equipment
équitation *f* horse riding
erreur *f* mistake; error
escale *f* stopover; call; port of call
escalier *m* stairs; flight of steps; staircase; **escalier roulant/mécanique** escalator; **escalier de secours** fire escape
escalope *f* escalope; **escalope de veau** veal escalope; **escalope viennoise/milanaise** veal escalope in breadcrumbs/in breadcrumbs and tomato sauce
escargot *m* snail
escrime *f* fencing
espace *m* space
espadon *m* swordfish
Espagne *f* Spain
espagnol(e) Spanish
espèce *f* sort; **en espèces** in cash
espérer to hope; to hope for
espoir *m* hope
esprit *m* mind; spirit
essai *m* trial; test; essay
essayer to try; to test
essence *f* petrol; **essence ordinaire** ≈2-star petrol; **essence sans plomb** unleaded petrol
essorer to spin(-dry); to wring
essuie-glace *m* windscreen wiper
essuyer to wipe
est *m* east; **de l'est** eastern

est-ce que: est-ce que c'est cher? is it expensive?; **quand est-ce que vous partez?** when are you leaving?
esthéticienne *f* beautician
esthétique *f* beauty salon
estimer to estimate
estivants *mpl* (summer) holiday-makers
estomac *m* stomach
estouffade: à l'estouffade braised or steamed in very little cooking liquid
estragon *m* tarragon; **crème d'estragon** cream of tarragon (soup)
esturgeon *m* sturgeon
et and
établissement *m* establishment
étage *m* storey; **premier étage** 1st floor; **à l'étage** upstairs
étagère *f* shelf
étain *m* tin; pewter
étanche waterproof; watertight
étang *m* pond
étant donné given
étape *f* stage
état *m* state; **l'État** the state; **état des lieux** inventory of fixtures
États-Unis *mpl* United States
été *m* summer
éteindre to turn off; to switch off
étendre to spread (out)
éternuer to sneeze
étiquette *f* label; tag
étoile *f* star
étonnant(e) amazing
étouffée *f*: **à l'étouffée** braised
étrange strange
étranger(ère) *m/f* foreigner; **à l'étranger**

overseas; abroad
être to be
étroit(e) narrow; tight
étude f study; office;
practice (of lawyer)
étudiant(e) m/f student
étudier to study
étui m case, box
étuvée: à l'étuvée
braised
européen(ne) European
eux them
eux-mêmes themselves
évanoui(e) unconscious
événement m occasion;
event
évidemment obviously
évident(e) obvious
évier m sink
éviter to avoid
évoluer to develop; to
evolve
exact(e) exact; correct;
accurate
exactement exactly
examen m examination;
test
excédent de bagages m
excess baggage
excès m excess; **excès
de vitesse** speeding
exclure to exclude
exclusivité f exclusive
rights
excursion f trip; outing;
excursion
excuser to excuse;
s'excuser to apologize
excuses fpl apologies
exemplaire m copy (of
book etc)
exemple m example
exempt(e) d'impôts
tax-free
exigence f requirement
exiger to demand; to
insist on
exonéré(e) exempt
expédier to dispatch
expéditeur m sender
expérimenté(e)

experienced
expert-comptable m
chartered accountant
explication f explanation
expliquer to explain
explorer to explore
exploser to explode
exportateur m exporter
exportation f export
exporter to export
exposition f exhibition
exprès on purpose;
deliberately; **en/par
exprès** express (post)
express m espresso
coffee; express train
exprimer to express
extérieur(e) outside;
exterior; **à l'extérieur**
outside
externe external
extincteur m fire
extinguisher
extra top-quality; first-
rate
extra-fin(e) extra fine
**extra-fort(e): moutarde
extra-forte** extra-strong
mustard
extrait m extract
extra-sec very dry
Extrême-Orient m Far
East

F

fabricant m manufacturer
fabrication f
manufacturing; **de
fabrication artisanale**
craftsman-made
face: en face de facing;
opposite; **en face**
opposite
facile easy
façon f way; manner; **de
toute façon** anyway; **ne
pas utiliser de façon
prolongée** do not use

over a prolonged period
facteur m postman
facture f invoice; bill
faible weak; faint
faïence f earthenware
faim f hunger; **avoir faim**
to be hungry
faire to make; to do; **il
fait chaud** it is hot; **je le
ferai** I shall do it; **faites
le 4** dial 4
faisan m pheasant
fait m fact
fait(e) mature (cheese);
ripe; **fait main** handmade
falaise f cliff
falloir to be necessary; **il
faut faire** I/you etc must
do
fameux(euse) famous
famille f family
fantaisie fancy
farce f farce; dressing;
stuffing
farci(e) stuffed
fard m: **fard à paupières**
eye shadow
farine f flour; **farine
lactée** baby cereal
fart m ski wax
fatigué(e) tired
faubourg m suburb
fausse fake; false; wrong
faut see **falloir**
faute f fault; mistake
fauteuil m armchair; seat
(at front of theatre);
fauteuil roulant
wheelchair
faux fake; wrong; false;
**détecteur de faux
billets** forged banknote
detector
faux-filet m sirloin
favori(te) favourite
fée f fairy
félicitations fpl
congratulations
féminin(e) feminine
femme f woman; wife;
femme de chambre

chambermaid; **femme de ménage** cleaner (*of house*)

fenêtre *f* window

fenouil *m* fennel

fente *f* crack; slot

fer *m* iron (*material, golf club*); **fer à repasser** iron (*for clothes*)

féra *f* (*in Switz*) delicate freshwater fish

férié(e): jour férié public holiday

ferme[1] firm

ferme[2] *f* farmhouse; farm

fermé(e) shut

fermer to close; to shut; to turn off (*water*); **fermer à clé** to lock

fermeture *f* closing; *f* **fermeture éclair** zip

fermier *m* farmer

fermier(ère): poulet/ beurre fermier farm chicken/butter

ferroviaire railway, rail

fête *f* feast day; holiday; fête; **fêtes (de fin d'année)** Christmas and New Year holidays; **fête votive** village fête

fêter to celebrate

feu *m* fire; traffic lights; **feu d'artifice** fireworks; **feu de joie** bonfire; **feu rouge** red light

feuille *f* sheet (*of paper*); leaf; **feuille de maladie** form for reimbursement of medical charges

feuilleté *m*: **feuilleté aux escargots** pastry with snail filling

feutre *m* felt; felt-tip pen

feux *mpl* traffic lights; **feux de détresse** hazard lights; **feux de position** sidelights

fève *f* broad bean; charm in cake (*for Twelfth Night*)

février *m* February

fiançailles *fpl* engagement

ficelle *f* string

fiche *f* slip (*of paper*)

fiche-horaire *f* train timetable

fièvre *f* fever; **avoir de la fièvre** to have a temperature

figue *f* fig

figure *f* face; figure

fil *m* thread; lead (*electrical*); **fil à coudre** cotton (*thread*); **fil électrique** wire; **fil de fer** wire; **fil de fer barbelé** barbed wire

file *f* lane; row (*behind one another*); **stationner en double file** to double-park

filet *m* net; fillet (*of meat, fish*); **filets d'anchois** anchovy fillets; **filet à bagages** luggage rack; **filet mignon** small steak; **filet à provisions** string bag; **filet de sole aux amandes** fillet of sole with almonds

fille *f* daughter; **jeune fille** girl (*young woman*)

fillette *f* girl (*child*)

film *m* film; **film d'aventure** adventure film; **film d'épouvante** horror film; **film policier** detective film

fils *m* son

filtre *m* filter

fin *f* end

fin(e) thin (*material*); fine (*delicate*)

finale *f* finals (*sports*)

finalement finally; eventually

financier(ère) financial

fine *f* liqueur brandy

fines herbes *fpl* mixed herbs

finir to end; to finish

fisc *m* Inland Revenue

fixe fixed

fixer to arrange; to fix

flacon *m* bottle (*small*)

flamand(e) Flemish

flambé(e) flamed, usually with brandy

flamme *f* flame

flan *m* custard tart; **flan aux cerises** cherry tart; **flan au roquefort** savoury tart with Roquefort cheese

flâner to stroll

flèche *f* arrow

fléché(e): itinéraire fléché route signposted with arrows

fléchette *f* dart (*to throw*); **fléchettes** game of darts

flétan *m* halibut

fleur *f* flower

fleuriste *m/f* florist

fleuve *m* river

flipper *m* pinball

flocon *m* flake; **flocons d'avoine** rolled oats

flotter to float

flotteur *m* float (*for swimming, fishing*)

fluor *m* fluoride

flûte *f* flute; long, thin loaf

foi *f* belief; faith

foie *m* liver; **foie gras** goose liver; **foie de volaille** chicken liver

foire *f* fair

fois *f* time; **une fois** once

folle mad

foncé(e) dark (*colour*)

fonction: en fonction de according to

fonctionnaire *m/f* civil servant

fonctionnement *m*: **en cas de non fonctionnement** in the event of a malfunction

fonctionner to work; **fonctionne sur secteur et sur piles** mains and battery operated

fond m back (*of hall, room*); bottom; **fond d'artichaut** artichoke heart

fondre to melt; to thaw; **faire fondre** to melt

fonds m: **fonds de commerce** business

fondue f: **fondue bourguignonne/ savoyarde** meat/gruyère cheese fondue

fontaine f fountain

footing m jogging

force f strength; force

forestière: **à la forestière** garnished with sautéed mushrooms, potatoes and bacon

forêt f forest

forfait m fixed price; **forfait tout compris** all-inclusive price

forfaitaire: **prix/ indemnité forfaitaire** inclusive price/payment

formation f training (*for job*)

forme f figure (*of human*); form; shape; **en** (**bonne**) **forme** fit; **en bonne et due forme** duly

formel(le) positive (*definite*)

formidable great (*excellent*)

formulaire m form (*document*)

formule f formula; method, system; programme; **selon la formule choisie** depending on the method chosen

fort(e) strong; stout; loud; loudly

fou mad

foudre f lightning

fouet m whip; whisk

fouetter to whip (*cream, eggs*)

fougère f fern

fouiller to search

foulard m scarf

foule f crowd

foulure f sprain

four m oven; **four à micro-ondes** microwave oven; **au four** baked

fourchette f fork

fourgonnette f delivery van

fourmi f ant

fournir to provide; to supply

fournitures fpl supplies; **fournitures scolaires** school stationery

fourré(e) fur-lined (*coat, boots*); filled (*pancake etc*)

fourrière f pound (*for animals, cars*)

fourrure f fur

foyer m hostel; hearth; **foyer de jeunes** youth club

fraîche fresh; cool; wet (*paint*)

frais[1] fresh; cool

frais[2] mpl costs; expenses; **frais de banque** bank charges; **frais médicaux** medical expenses; **frais de réservation/ d'annulation** booking/ cancellation charges

fraise f strawberry; **fraises des bois** wild strawberries

fraisier m sponge cake filled with strawberries and lemon cream

framboise f raspberry

français(e) French

frangipane f almond paste

frappé(e) iced (*drink*)

frapper to hit; to strike; to knock

frein m brake; **freins à disque** disc brakes; **frein à main** handbrake; **freins à tambour** drum brakes

freiner to brake

frêne m ash (*tree*)

fréquemment frequently

frère m brother

fresque f fresco

friand m sausage roll; **friand au fromage** cheese pasty

friandises fpl sweets

fricandeau m: **fricandeau** (**de veau**) rolled, filled veal fillet

frigidaire m fridge

frisée f curly endive

frit(e) fried

frites fpl French fried potatoes; chips

friture f fried food; **friture de poissons** fried fish

froid(e) cold; **j'ai froid** I'm cold

froisser to crease; to strain (*muscle*)

fromage m cheese; **fromage blanc** (**aux herbes**) soft white cheese (with herbs); **fromage à tartiner** cheese spread; **fromage frais** cream cheese; **fromage de tête** pork brawn

fromagerie f cheese dairy

froment m wheat

front m forehead; **front de mer** sea front

frontière f border; frontier; boundary

frotter to rub

fruit m fruit; **fruits de mer** shellfish (*on menu*); seafood; **fruit givré** fruit sorbet (served in skin of the fruit); **fruit de la passion** passion fruit; **fruits confits** crystallized

fruits; **fruits fourrés** stuffed fruits; **fruits secs** dried fruit; **fruits au sirop** fruit in syrup
fruité(e) fruity
fuite f leak
fumé(e) smoked (*salmon etc*)
fumée f smoke
fumer to smoke
fumeur m smoker
funiculaire m funicular railway
furoncle m boil
fuseau m ski pants; **fuseau horaire** time zone
fusible m fuse
fusil m gun; rifle

G

gagnant(e) m/f winner
gagner to earn; to gain; to win
gai(e) merry; cheerful
galantine f boned poultry/game, stuffed, cooked in a gelatine broth and served cold
galerie f gallery; roof rack; art gallery (*commercial*); **galerie marchande/ commerciale** arcade
galette f flat cake; **galette des rois** cake eaten on Twelfth Night
gallois(e) Welsh
gambas fpl large prawns
gamme f range
gant m glove; **gants de caoutchouc** rubber gloves; **gant de toilette** facecloth
garantie f guarantee
garantir to guarantee
garçon m boy
garde m guard (*sentry*);

pharmacie/médecin de garde (la/le plus proche) (nearest) duty chemist/doctor on duty
gardé(e): gardé/non gardé attended/ unattended; with/without resident warden
garde-côte m coastguard
garder to keep; to guard; **garder les enfants** to baby-sit; **gardez votre ticket sur vous** keep your ticket; **gardez vos distances** keep your distance
garderie d'enfants f crèche
gardien(ne) m/f: **gardien d'immeuble** caretaker; **gardien de nuit** night porter
gare f railway station; **gare routière** bus terminal
garer to park
garni(e) served with vegetables; **hôtel garni** (*in Switz*) hotel serving breakfast only
garniture f accompanying vegetables
gas-oil m diesel fuel
gâteau m cake; gateau; **gâteau de riz** rice pudding; **gâteau sec** biscuit
gauche left; **à gauche** to/on the left
gaucher(ère) left-handed
gaufre f waffle
gaufrette f wafer
gaz m gas; **gaz d'échappement** exhaust (*fumes*)
gazeux(euse) fizzy
gaz-oil m diesel fuel
gazole see **gaz-oil**
gazon m grass
géant m giant
gel m frost

gelée f jelly; **poulet en gelée** chicken in aspic
geler to freeze
gélule f capsule
gencive f gum (*of teeth*)
gendarme m policeman
gendarmerie f police station
gêner to bother; **ne pas gêner la fermeture des portes** do not obstruct the doors
général: en général in general
généraliste m/f general practitioner
généreux(euse) generous
Genève Geneva
genièvre m juniper
génoise f sponge cake
genou m knee
genre m kind; gender
gens mpl people
gentil(le) kind; nice
gérant(e) m/f manager/ manageress
gercé(e): lèvres gercées chapped lips
gestion f management
gibelotte de lapin f rabbit stew with wine
gibier m game (*hunting*)
gigot (d'agneau) m leg of lamb
gilet m waistcoat; cardigan; **gilet de sauvetage** life jacket
gingembre m ginger
giratoire see **sens**
girofle see **clou**
girolle f chanterelle mushroom
gîte m self-catering house/flat; **gîte rural** self-catering house/flat in the country; **gîte d'étape** dormitory accommodation
givré(e): mandarine/ orange givrée

mandarin/orange sorbet served in its skin

glace f ice; ice cream; mirror; **glace napolitaine** layers of different-flavoured ice cream; **glace plombière** tutti-frutti ice cream; **glace à la vanille** vanilla ice cream

glacé(e) chilled; iced; glacé

glaçon m ice cube; **avec des glaçons** on the rocks

glissant(e) slippery; **chaussée glissante** slippery road surface

glisser to glide; to slide; to slip

gonflable inflatable

gorge f throat

goujon m gudgeon

goulache f goulash

gourde f flask

gourmand(e) greedy

gousse d'ail f clove of garlic

goût m flavour, taste

goûter¹ to taste

goûter² m afternoon tea

goutte f drip; drop

gouvernail m rudder

gouvernement m government

grâce à thanks to

gracieusement free of charge

gradins mpl terracing (at stadium)

grain m: **café en grains** coffee beans; **poivre en grains** whole peppercorns

graine f seed; **graines de soja** soya beans

graisse f fat; grease

grand(e) great; high (speed, number); big

Grande-Bretagne f Great Britain

grande surface f hypermarket

grandeur f size

grandir to grow

grand marnier m orange liqueur

grand-mère f grandmother

grand-père m grandfather

granité m water ice; **granité aux pommes** apple cake

gras(se) fat; greasy

gras-double m tripe

gratin m cheese-topped dish; **au gratin** with cheese topping; **gratin dauphinois** thinly-sliced potatoes baked with milk and cream and grated gruyère cheese

gratiné(e) with cheese topping; **gratinée au fromage** onion soup with grated cheese

gratis free

gratuit(e) free of charge

grave serious

gravillon m grit

gravure f print (picture)

grec Greek

Grèce f Greece

grecque Greek; **à la grecque** in olive oil and herbs

grêle f hail

grenade f pomegranate

grenadin m thick slice of veal fillet

grenadine f grenadine syrup

grenier m loft; attic

grenouille f frog; **cuisses de grenouille** frogs' legs

grève f strike (industrial); **en grève** on strike

grièvement: grièvement blessé seriously injured

gril m grill pan

grill m grillroom

grillade f grilled meat; **grillade au feu de bois** charcoal-grilled meat

grillé grilled

grille-pain m toaster

griller to grill

grimper to climb

griotte f Morello cherry

grippe f flu

gris(e) grey

grive f thrush (bird)

gros(se) fat (person); big (sum of money); large; **en gros** in bulk; wholesale; **gros sel** cooking salt

groseille f redcurrant; **groseille à maquereau** gooseberry

grossiste m/f wholesaler

grotte f cave

groupe m group; **groupe sanguin** blood group

gruyère m hard Swiss cheese with delicate flavour

gué m ford

guêpe f wasp

guérir to cure

guerre f war

gui m mistletoe

guichet m ticket office; **guichet automatique** automatic cash dispenser

guide¹ m guidebook

guide² m/f guide

guimauve f marshmallow

guitare f guitar

gymnase m gym(nasium); secondary school (Switz only)

gynécologue m/f gynaecologist

H

habiller to dress

habit m outfit; tails

habitant(e) m/f inhabitant; **loger chez**

l'habitant to stay with the locals

habiter to live (to reside); to live in

habitude f habit; **d'habitude** usually

habituel(le) usual; regular

haché(e): steak haché hamburger

hachis m minced beef; **hachis Parmentier** cottage pie

haleine f breath

halles fpl central food market

halte f: **faire halte à ...** to stop at ...

hamac m hammock

hareng m herring; **hareng salé/fumé** salt/smoked herring; **hareng saur** smoked herring

haricot m: **haricot de mouton** lamb or mutton stew

haricots mpl beans; **haricots blancs** haricot beans; **haricots rouges** kidney beans; **haricots verts** green beans

hasard m chance; **par hasard** by chance; **à tout hasard** just in case

hausse f rise

haut m top (of ladder); **en haut** high up; upstairs; **vers le haut** upwards

haut(e) high; tall; **à haute voix** aloud; **plus haut(e)** higher

hauteur f height

hebdomadaire weekly

hébergement m lodging

hémorroïdes fpl haemorrhoids

herbe f grass; **fines herbes** herbs

herboristerie f herbalist's shop

heure f hour; **à l'heure**

on time; punctual; on schedule; **de bonne heure** early; **toutes les heures** hourly; **heures d'affluence** rush hour; **heures creuses** slack periods; off-peak periods; **heures d'ouverture/de fermeture** opening/closing times; **heures de pointe** peak hours

heureusement fortunately

heureux(euse) happy; fortunate

hier yesterday

hippique: club hippique riding club

hippodrome m racecourse

histoire f history; story

hiver m winter

hollandais(e) Dutch

Hollande f Holland

homard m lobster; **homard à l'armoricaine** lobster cooked in oil, with tomatoes, shallots, white wine and sometimes brandy; **homard à la nage** lobster cooked in stock made with vegetables and white wine or vinegar; **homard Thermidor** lobster in white wine, with mushrooms, spices, mustard, flamed with brandy

homme m man

honnête honest

honoraires mpl fee

hôpital m hospital

horaire m timetable (for trains etc); schedule; **horaire des départs** departure board

horloge f clock

hors: hors de out of; **hors d'usage** out of service

hors-bord m speedboat with outboard motor

hors d'œuvre m hors d'oeuvre

hors-saison off-season

hors-taxe duty-free

hôte m host; guest; **hôte payant** paying guest

hôtel m hotel; **hôtel particulier** (private) mansion

hôtel de ville m town hall

hôtesse f hostess; **hôtesse de l'air** air hostess

houx m holly

huile f oil (edible, for car); **huile d'amandes douces** sweet almond oil; **huile d'arachide** groundnut oil; **huile de foie de morue** cod liver oil; **huile d'olive** olive oil; **huile solaire** suntan oil; **huile de tournesol** sunflower oil

huit eight

huitante eighty (Switz)

huitième eighth

huître f oyster

humain(e) human

humeur f: **de bonne humeur** in a good mood; **de mauvaise humeur** in a bad mood

humide damp; wet

hygiaphone m: **parlez devant l'hygiaphone** please speak through the hygienic grill

hygiénique hygienic

hypermarché m superstore; hypermarket

hypoallergique hypoallergenic

I

ici here

idée *f* idea

ignorer to ignore; not to know

il he; it; **il y a** there is/are

île *f* island; **île flottante** caramelized beaten egg white poached in milk, with almonds and vanilla custard

illustré *m* illustrated magazine; comic

ils they

image *f* picture; image

imiter to imitate

immédiat(e) immediate; instant

immédiatement immediately

immeuble *m* block of flats

immobile still

immobilier *m* real estate

impair(e) odd (*number*)

impasse *f* dead end

imperméable waterproof

imper(méable) *m* raincoat

importation *f* import

importer to import; to matter

impôts *mpl* taxation; (income) tax

imprenable: vue imprenable sur ... open outlook over ...

impressionnant(e) impressive

impressionner to impress

imprimerie *f* printing works; printing

imprimeur *m* printer

incapable unable; incapable

incassable unbreakable

incendie *m* fire

incertain(e) uncertain

inchangé(e) unchanged

incliner to tilt

inclure to include; **du 6 au 12 inclus** from 6th to 12th inclusive

inconnu(e) unknown; strange

incroyable incredible

indemniser to indemnify; to compensate

indépendant(e) independent; self-contained

indexé(e) index-linked

indicateur *m* guide; timetable

indicatif *m*: **indicatif de département** dialling code

indicatif(ive): à titre indicatif for (your) information

indications *fpl* instructions; directions (*to a place*)

indiquer to point out; to show; to specify

individuel(le) individual

industrie *f* industry

industriel(le) industrial

inférieur(e) inferior; lower

infirme disabled

infirmerie *f* infirmary

infirmière *f* nurse; **infirmière diplômée** registered nurse

information *f* piece of information

informations *fpl* news; information

informatique *f* data processing; computer science

infraction *f* offence

infrarouge infrared

infusion *f* herbal tea

ingénieur *m* engineer

initiales *fpl* initials

injuste unfair

inoffensif(ive) harmless

inondation *f* flood

inox *m* stainless steel

inoxydable rustproof; stainless

inquiet(ète) worried

inquiéter to worry

inscription *f* enrolment

inscrire to write (down); to enrol; **s'inscrire (à)** to enrol (in); to join

insecte *m* insect

insister to insist; to keep trying

insolation *f* sunstroke

insonorisé(e) soundproof

inspecter to inspect

inspecteur *m* inspector

installer to install; to put in; **s'installer** to settle in

instant *m* instant; moment

instantané(e) instant

institut *m* institute; **institut de beauté** beauty salon

instituteur(trice) *m/f* teacher (*primary school*)

intégralement in full

intendant *m* steward (*at club*)

intention *f*: **avoir l'intention de faire** to mean to do; to intend to do

interdiction *f*: **interdiction de fumer** no smoking

interdit(e) forbidden; **interdit au public** authorized personnel only

intéressant(e) interesting

intéresser to interest

intérêt *m* interest

intérieur(e) interior; inside; inner; **à**

l'intérieur inside; indoors

intérimaire temporary

interne¹ internal

interne² *m* houseman

interprète *m/f* interpreter

interrompre to interrupt

intersection *f* junction (*on road*)

intoxication alimentaire *f* food poisoning

introduire to introduce; to insert; **introduisez votre monnaie** insert money

inutile useless; unnecessary

invalide *m/f* disabled person

inventaire *m* inventory; stocktaking

invité(e) *m/f* guest

inviter to invite

iode *m* iodine

irlandais(e) Irish

Irlande *f* Ireland

issue *f*: **issue de secours** emergency exit; **rue/voie sans issue** dead end; no through road

Italie *f* Italy

italien(ne) Italian

itinéraire *m* route; **itinéraire bison fûté/ flèches vertes** alternative route avoiding heavy traffic; **itinéraire touristique** scenic route

ivoire *m* ivory

J

j' I

jamais never; ever

jambe *f* leg

jambon *m* ham; **jambon de Bayonne** smoked Bayonne ham; **jambon blanc** boiled ham; **jambon cru** smoked (raw) ham; **jambon cuit** cooked ham; **jambon à l'os** baked ham

jambonneau *m* knuckle of ham

janvier *m* January

jardin *m* garden; **jardin d'acclimatation** zoological garden(s); **jardin botanique** botanical garden; **jardin privatif** private garden(s)

jardinier *m* gardener

jardinière *f*: **jardinière (de légumes)** mixed vegetables

jarret *m* knuckle, shin (of veal, beef etc)

jauge *f* gauge; **jauge de niveau d'huile** dipstick

jaune yellow

je, j' I

jean *m* jeans

jet *m* spray; **jet d'eau** fountain

jetable disposable

jetée *f* pier

jeter to throw; to throw away; **à jeter** disposable

jeton *m* chip (*in gambling*); counter; token (*for machine*)

jeu *m* set (*collection*); pack (*of cards*); gambling; game; **jeu de cartes** card game; **jeu de dames** draughts

jeudi *m* Thursday

jeune young

joie *f* joy

joindre to join; to enclose

joli(e) pretty

jonquille *f* daffodil

joue *f* cheek

jouer to gamble; to play

jouet *m* toy

joueur *m* gambler; player (in sport)

jour *m* day; **tous les jours** every day; **le jour de l'An** New Year's Day; **le jour de Noël** Christmas Day; **jour de fermeture ...** closed on ...

journal *m* newspaper; news bulletin; diary

journée *f* day (*length of time*); **toute la journée** all day long

juge *m* judge

juger to try (*in law*); to judge

juif Jewish

juillet *m* July

juin *m* June

juive Jewish

julienne *f* vegetable consommé; vegetables cut into fine strips

jumeaux *mpl* twins

jumelé(e): (ville) **jumelée avec ...** (town) twinned with ...

jumelles *fpl* twins; binoculars

jupe *f* skirt

jus *m* juice; **au jus** in its own juice; **jus de citron** lemon juice; **jus de fruits** fruit juice; **jus d'orange** orange juice; **jus de pamplemousse** grapefruit juice; **jus de viande** gravy

jusqu'à until; till; **jusqu'à maintenant** up till now

juste fair; right; tight; just (only)

K

kart *m* go-cart

kascher kosher

kermesse *f* fair; charity fête

kilométrage m ≈ mileage; **kilométrage illimité** unlimited mileage

kinésithérapeute m/f physiotherapist

kiosque m kiosk; **kiosque à journaux** newsstand

kir m white wine with blackcurrant liqueur

klaxon m horn (of car)

klaxonner to sound one's horn

kouglof, kugelhof m cake containing raisins, speciality of Alsace

L

l' see le, la

la, l' the; her; it

là there; **là-bas** over there; **là-haut** up there

laboratoire m laboratory

lac m lake

laine f wool; **de/en laine** woollen; **laine d'agneau** lambswool; **laine peignée** worsted wool; combed wool

laisse f leash; **tenez votre chien en laisse** keep your dog on a leash

laisser to leave; to let (allow); **laisser un message** to leave a message

laissez-passer m pass (permit)

lait m milk; **lait aromatisé** flavoured milk; **lait caillé** junket; **lait concentré** condensed milk; **lait condensé (non sucré)** (unsweetened) evaporated milk; **lait démaquillant** cleansing milk; **lait demi-écrémé** semi-skimmed milk; **lait**

écrémé skim(med) milk; **lait entier** full-cream milk; **lait maternisé** baby milk; **lait en poudre** dried milk; **lait de poule** eggflip

laitages mpl milk products

laiterie f dairy

laitier: produit laitier dairy produce

laitue f lettuce

lame f blade; **lame de rasoir** razor blade

lampadaire m standard lamp

lampe f light; lamp; **lampe de poche** torch

lancer to throw; to launch

landau m pram

langouste f crayfish (saltwater)

langoustine f Dublin Bay prawn

langue f tongue; language

lapereau m young rabbit

lapin m rabbit

laque f hair spray

laquelle which, which one

lard m fat; (streaky) bacon; **lard fumé** smoked bacon; **lard maigre** lean bacon

lardon m lardon, strip of fat

large wide; broad

largeur f width

larme f tear

laurier m bay leaves

lavable: lavable à la/en machine machine-washable

lavabo m washbasin; **lavabos** toilets

lavage m washing

lavande f lavender

lave-linge m washing machine

laver to wash; to bathe

(wound etc); **se laver** to wash oneself

laverie automatique f launderette

lave-vaisselle m dishwasher

le, l' the; him; it; **le jeudi** on Thursdays

leçon f lesson; **leçons particulières** private lessons

lecture f reading

léger(ère) light (not heavy); weak (tea)

légumes mpl vegetables

lendemain m: **le lendemain** the next day

lent(e) slow

lentement slowly

lentille f lens (of glasses)

lentilles fpl lentils; contact lenses

lequel which, which one

les the; them

lesquel(le)s which, which ones

lessive f soap powder; washing (clothes); **faire la lessive** to do the washing

lettre f letter; **lettre par avion** air letter; **lettre explicative** covering letter; **lettre exprès** express letter; **lettre recommandée** registered letter

leur(s) them; their; **le/la leur** theirs; **les leurs** theirs (plural)

levain m: **pain sans levain** unleavened bread

levée f collection (of mail)

lever to raise; **se lever** to get up; to rise

lever du soleil m sunrise

levier m lever; **levier de vitesse** gear lever

lèvre f lip

levure f yeast

liaison f: liaison

hélicoptère/ferroviaire helicopter/rail link
libeller: libeller (un chèque) à l'ordre de ... to make out (a cheque) to the order of ...
libérer: la chambre devra être libérée le ... the room must be vacated on ...
librairie f bookshop
librairie-tabac-presse f bookseller's, tobacconist's and newsagent's shop
libre free; vacant
libre-service self-service
liège m cork
liégeois(e): café/chocolat liégeois coffee/chocolate ice cream with whipped cream
lier to tie up
lieu[1] m place; **au lieu de** instead of; **avoir lieu to** take place
lieu[2] m hake
lièvre m hare
ligne f line; service; route (transport); **grandes lignes** main lines (trains)
limande-sole f lemon sole
lime f file (tool); **lime à ongles** nailfile
limitation de vitesse f speed limit
limite f limit; boundary
limiter to limit; to restrict
limonade f lemonade
lin m linen (cloth)
linge m linen (for bed, table); underwear; laundry (clothes); **linge de literie et de toilette** bed linen and towels; **linge de maison** household linen
liquide m liquid; **liquide de freins** brake fluid
lire to read

lis m lily
lisse smooth
liste f list; **liste d'adresses** mailing list; **liste d'attente** waiting list; **liste des prix** price list
lit m bed; **au lit** in bed; **grand lit** double bed; **lit d'appoint** spare bed; **lit de camp** camp bed; **lit d'enfant** cot; **lit pliant** folding bed; **lit simple** single bed; **lits gigognes** stowaway beds; **lits jumeaux** twin beds; **lits superposés** bunk beds
literie f bedding
litre m litre
livarot m pungent and spicy cow's-millk cheese from Normandy
living m living room
livraison f delivery (of goods); **livraison des bagages** baggage claim; **livraison à domicile** deliveries carried out
livre[1] f pound; **livre sterling** sterling
livre[2] m book; **livre de poche** paperback
livrer to deliver
local m premises
locataire m/f tenant; lodger
location f rental; hiring (out); letting; **bureau de location** box office; (advance) booking office; **location à la journée/la semaine** daily/weekly hire (cars etc); **location à la semaine/au mois/à l'année** weekly/monthly/annual lets (property); **location de matériel de ski** ski equipment hire; **location de voitures** car hire
location-vente f hire

purchase
locaux mpl premises
logement m accommodation; housing
loger to accommodate; **loger chez des amis** to stay with friends
loi f law
loin far
loisir m leisure
Londres London
long long; **le long de** along
longe f: **longe de veau** loin of veal
longtemps (for) a long time
longue long
longueur f length
loquet m latch
loqueteau m: **maintenez le loqueteau levé** hold the handle up
lorsque when
lot m prize; lot (at auction)
loterie f lottery
lotion f lotion; **lotion après-rasage** aftershave (lotion)
loto m lottery
lotte f turbot; angler fish; **lotte à l'armoricaine/l'américaine** turbot/angler fish in sauce containing tomatoes, butter, cognac and white wine; **lotte au poivre vert** turbot/angler fish with green peppercorns
louer to let; to hire; to rent; **à louer** to let (house etc)
loukoum m Turkish delight
loup m wolf
lourd(e) heavy; close (stuffy)
loyer m rent
lubrifiant m lubricant
luge f sledge, toboggan
lui him; he; her; it

lui-même himself
lumière f light
lundi m Monday
lune f moon; **lune de miel** honeymoon
lunettes fpl glasses; **lunettes de protection** goggles; **lunettes de soleil** sunglasses
lutte f wrestling; struggle
luxe m luxury; **de luxe** de luxe, luxury; **appartement grand luxe** luxury apartment
luxueux(euse) luxurious
lycée m secondary school
lyonnaise: (à la) lyonnaise sautéed with onions

M

M sign for the Paris metro
m' me, myself
ma my
macaron m macaroon
macédoine f: **macédoine de fruits** fruit salad; **macédoine de légumes** mixed vegetables
mâcher to chew
machine f machine; **machine à coudre** sewing machine; **machine à écrire** typewriter; **machine à laver** washing machine
Madame f Mrs; Ms; Madam; Dear Madam
madeleine f small sponge cake
Mademoiselle f Miss
madère m Madeira (wine)
magasin m shop; **faire les magasins** to go round the shops; **grand magasin** department

store; **magasin de chaussures** shoe shop
magnétophone m tape recorder
magnétoscope m videocassette recorder
magnifique magnificent
magret (de canard) m breast fillet of fattened duck
mai m May
maigre thin (person); lean (meat)
maigrir to slim
maillot de bain m swimsuit
maillot jaune m leader in the Tour de France
main f hand; **fait(e) à la main** handmade; **à la main** by hand
maintenant now
maintenir to maintain; to support
maire m mayor
mairie f town hall
mais but
maïs m maize; **maïs doux** sweet corn
maison f house; home; firm; **à la maison** at home; **aux frais de la maison** on the house; **un gâteau maison** a home-made cake; **maison de campagne** house in the country; **maison (des jeunes et) de la culture** youth club and community centre; **maison de retraite** old people's home
maître m master
maître d'hôtel m head waiter; **entrecôte maître d'hôtel** rib steak fried in butter with parsley and lemon juice
maître nageur sauveteur m swimming and life-saving instructor

maîtriser to control
maïzena f cornflour
majuscule f: **en majuscules** in capitals
mal badly; **faire mal** to hurt; **avoir mal aux dents** to have toothache; **avoir le mal de mer** to be seasick; **avoir mal à l'oreille** to have earache; **avoir mal à la tête** to have a headache
malade m/f sick person; invalid; patient
maladie f sickness; disease; illness
malgré despite
malheureusement unfortunately
malle f trunk (for clothes etc)
maman f mum(my)
Manche (la) the Channel
manche[1] f sleeve
manche[2] m handle (of knife)
manchot m penguin
mandarine f tangerine
mandat m money order; **mandat international** international postal order; **mandat postal** postal order
manège m merry-go-round
manger to eat
mange-tout: haricots mange-tout runner beans; **pois mange-tout** mangetout peas
mangue f mango
maniable easy to handle
manière f manner
manifestation f demonstration (political)
manquant(e) missing
manque m shortage; lack; **par manque de ...** through lack of ...
manquer to miss; **manquer de** to lack

mansardé(e): chambre mansardée attic room
manteau *m* coat
manucure *m/f* manicurist
manuel *m* manual; handbook; textbook
maquereau *m* mackerel
maquette *f* model; sketch
maquillage *m* make-up
marais *m* swamp; **marais salant** salt pan
marbre *m* marble (*material*)
marc *m* spirit distilled from residue of grapes
marcassin *m* young wild boar
marchand *m* dealer; merchant; **marchand de journaux** newsagent; **marchand de légumes** greengrocer; **marchand de vin** wine merchant; red wine sauce with shallots
marchandises *fpl* goods
marche *f* step; stair; march; **attention à la marche** mind the step; **en marche** on (*machine*); moving (*vehicle*); **ne pas ouvrir en marche** do not open while the vehicle is in motion; **marche arrière** reverse (*gear*); **marche à pied** walking
marché *m* market; **marché aux puces** flea market; **bon marché** inexpensive; **meilleur marché** cheaper
marcher to walk; to go (*clock, mechanism*); to run (*machine, engine*); to work (*mechanism, clock*); **faire marcher** to operate (*machine*)
mardi *m* Tuesday; **mardi gras** Shrove Tuesday

mare *f* pond; pool
marécage *m* marsh, swamp
marée *f* tide; **marée basse** low tide; **marée haute** high tide
marengo: poulet/veau marengo chicken/veal cooked in white wine with tomatoes, garlic and mushrooms
mari *m* husband
mariage *m* wedding; marriage
marié *m* bridegroom
marié(e) married
Marie-Brizard ® *m* aniseed-flavoured aperitif
mariée *f* bride
marier: se marier to get married
marin *m* sailor
marinade *f*: **marinade de veau** marinaded veal
marine *f* navy
mariné(e) marinaded
marionnettes *fpl* puppets
marjolaine *f* marjoram
Maroc *m* Morocco
maroquinerie *f* fine leather goods
marque *f* make; brand; brand name; mark; **marque déposée** registered trademark; **cognac de marque** quality brandy
marquer to mark; to score
marrant(e) funny
marron *m* chestnut; **crème/purée de marrons** chestnut purée; **marrons glacés** chestnuts cooked in syrup and glazed
mars *m* March
marteau *m* hammer
mas *m* house or farm in the South of France

massepain *m* marzipan
masser to massage
matelas *m* mattress; **matelas pneumatique** air bed
matelote *f*: **matelote d'anguilles** stewed eels in red wine with onions
matériaux *mpl*: **matériaux de construction** building materials
matériel *m* equipment; kit
maternité *f* maternity hospital
matière *f* subject; material; **matière grasse** fat content
matin *m* morning
mauvais(e) bad; wrong
maux *mpl*: **maux de dents** toothache; **maux d'oreille** earache; **maux de tête** headaches; **maux de ventre** stomach pains
maximum: au maximum at the most; as much as possible
mayen *m* (*in Switz*) higher pasture where cattle graze in summer
mazot *m* (*in Switz*) small chalet
mazout *m* oil (*for heating*)
me, m' me, myself
mécanicien *m* mechanic
méchant(e) naughty; wicked
mèches *fpl* streaks, highlights (*in hair*)
méchoui *m* barbecue (of whole roast sheep)
médaillon *m* thin, round slice of meat
médecin *m* doctor; **médecin généraliste** general practitioner, GP
médicament *m* medicine; drug

Méditerranée f
Mediterranean (Sea)
méduse f jellyfish
méfier: se méfier de to
distrust; to be careful
about
meilleur(e) best; better
mélange m mixture;
blend
mélasse f molasses;
treacle; **mélasse raffinée**
(golden) syrup
membre m member
même same; even; **tout
de même** all the same
mémoire f memory
menacer to threaten
ménage m housework;
femme de ménage
cleaner
mener to lead
mensuel(le) monthly
menthe f mint; **menthe
à l'eau** peppermint
cordial; **thé à la menthe**
mint tea
mentholé(e)
mentholated
mentir to lie
menton m chin
menu m (set) menu;
menu à prix fixe set
price menu; **menu
gastronomique** gourmet
menu; **menu touristique**
tourist/low price menu
mer f sea; **mer du Nord**
North Sea; **en haute/
pleine mer** on the open
sea
mercerie f haberdashery
merci thank you
mercredi m Wednesday
mère f mother
merguez f spicy sausage
**meringué(e): tarte au
citron meringuée** lemon
meringue pie
mériter to deserve
merlan m whiting
mérou m grouper

merveilleux(euse)
wonderful, marvellous
mes my
messe f mass (church)
messieurs mpl men;
gentlemen('s toilets)
mesure f measurement;
fait(e) sur mesure
made-to-measure; **par
mesure d'hygiène** in the
interests of hygiene
mesurer to measure
météo f weather forecast
métier m trade;
occupation; craft
métrage m: **court/
moyen/long métrage**
short/medium-length/full-
length film
mètre m metre
métro m underground
railway
mets m dish (food)
metteur en scène m
producer (of play)
mettre to put; to put
on; to set (alarm);
mettre en marche to
switch on (engine); **ne
vous mettez pas en
situation irrégulière** do
not contravene the
regulations
meuble m piece of
furniture
meublé(e) furnished
meubles mpl furniture;
**meubles rustiques/de
style** rustic/period
furniture
**meunière: sole/limande
meunière** sole/lemon
sole coated in flour and
fried in butter with
lemon juice and parsley
meurtre m murder
**meurtrier(ière):
accident meurtrier** fatal
accident
mi-bas mpl knee socks
mi-chemin: à mi-

chemin half-way
micro m microphone
microbe m germ
midi m midday; noon; **le
Midi** the south of France
miel m honey
mien: le mien mine; **la
mienne** mine; **les miens**
mine (plural); **les
miennes** mine (plural)
mieux better; best; **le
mieux serait ...** the best
thing would be ...
mignon(ne) sweet, cute
mijoter to simmer
milieu m middle;
environment; **en plein
milieu** right in the
middle; **au milieu de la
nuit** in the middle of the
night
militaire military
mille thousand
millefeuille m cream/
vanilla slice
milliard m billion
millième thousandth
millier m thousand
million m million
mince slim; thin
mine f expression; mine
(for coal etc); **avoir bonne
mine** to look well
mineur(e) under age;
**interdit aux mineurs
non accompagnés d'un
adulte** no admission to
children not accompanied
by an adult
minimum: au minimum
at the very least
ministre m minister (in
government); **premier
ministre** prime minister
Minitel ® m view-data
system
minorité f minority
minuit m midnight
minute f minute
mirabelle f plum; plum
brandy

miroir m mirror

mise en plis f set (*for hair*)

mise en scène f production (*of play*)

mistral m strong northerly wind, in Provence

mi-temps f half-time

mitonner to cook with loving care

mixte mixed

mobilier m furniture

mode f fashion; **à la mode** fashionable

mode d'emploi m directions for use

modèle m model; **modèle réduit** small-scale model

moderniser to modernize

modifier to modify

modique modest

moelle f marrow (*beef etc*)

moelleux(euse) creamy, smooth; mellow

moi me

moi-même myself

moindre least

moine m monk

moins minus; less; **moins de** less than; **moins que** less than; **moins cinq** five to one; **le moins cher** the least expensive; **les enfants de moins de 10 ans** children under 10; **au moins** at least; **à moins que** unless

mois m month

moisson f harvest (*of grain*)

moitié f half; **à moitié** half; **à moitié prix** half-price

moka m coffee cream cake; mocha coffee; **crème moka** coffee

cream

molle soft

molletonné(e) fleecy-lined

moment m while; moment; point (*in time*); **en ce moment** at the moment; **pour le moment** for the time being

momentané(e) momentary; brief

mon my

monastère m monastery

monde m world; people

moniteur m instructor; coach

monitrice f instructress; coach

monnaie f currency; change (*money*); **faire de la monnaie** to get/give change; **rend/ne rend pas la monnaie** change/no change given

monnayeur m automatic change machine

Monsieur m Mr; Dear Sir (*on letter*); **monsieur** gentleman

monstre enormous

montagne f mountain

montant m amount (*total*); **montant à payer** amount payable

mont-blanc m: **mont-blanc à la Chantilly** chestnut cream dessert with whipped cream

monter to take up; to assemble (*parts of machine*); to go up; to rise; **monter à cheval** to ride a horse

montre f watch

montrer to show

monture f frames (*of glasses*)

moquette f wall-to-wall carpet(ing)

morceau m piece; bit;

cut (*of meat*); scrap

mordre to bite

morilles fpl morel mushrooms

Mornay see **sauce**

morsure f bite (*by animal*)

mort f death

mort(e) dead

mortadelle f mortadella

mortel(le) fatal

morue f salt cod

mosquée f mosque

mot m note (*letter*); word; **mots croisés** crossword

moteur m motor; engine

moto f motorbike

motocycliste m/f motorcyclist

motoneige f snowbike

mou soft

mouche f fly

mouchoir m handkerchief; **mouchoir en papier** paper hanky

mouillé(e) wet

moule f mussel; **moules marinières** mussels cooked in their shells with white wine, shallots and parsley

moulin m mill; **moulin à vent** windmill

moulu(e) ground

mourir to die

mousse f foam; moss; mousse; **mousse de foie de volaille** chicken liver mousse; **mousse à raser** shaving foam

mousseux(euse) sparkling

moustiquaire f mosquito net

moustique m mosquito

moutarde f mustard

mouton m sheep; lamb or mutton

mouvement m motion; movement

moyen: au moyen de by means of

moyens *mpl* means

moyen(ne) average; medium

moyennant: moyennant supplément in return for a supplement

Moyen-Orient *m* Middle East

muet(te) dumb

muguet *m* lily of the valley

multiplier to multiply

municipalité *f* borough

muni(e): muni(e) de supplied with; in possession of

munster *m* strong cheese from Alsace

mur *m* wall

mûr(e) mature; ripe

mûre *f* blackberry

muscade *f* nutmeg

muscadet *m* dry white wine from the Loire

muscat *m* muscatel: a sweet dessert wine

musée *m* museum; art gallery

musique *f* music

musulman(e) Muslim

mutuelle *f* mutual benefit insurance company

myope short-sighted

myrtille *f* bilberry, whortleberry

mystère *m* mystery

N

n' see ne

nacre *f* mother-of-pearl

nager to swim

naissance *f* birth

nappé(e) coated (*with chocolate etc*)

narine *f* nostril

natation *f* swimming

nature plain, without seasoning or sweetening; black, without sugar (*tea, coffee*)

naturel(le) natural; **au naturel** plain, without seasoning or sweetening

naturellement naturally (*of course*)

nausée *f* sickness; nausea

nautique: club nautique sailing club; **sports nautiques** water sports

navarin (de mouton) *m* mutton stew

navet *m* turnip

navette *f* shuttle (service)

navigation *f* sailing; **navigation de plaisance** yachting

navire *m* ship

ne, n': il ne vient jamais he never comes; **il n'y en a que 4** there are only 4

né(e) born

nécessaire[1] necessary

nécessaire[2] *m* bag; kit; **nécessaire à chaussures** shoe kit; **nécessaire à ongles** manicure set

nef *f* nave

négatif *m* negative (*of photo*)

négociant *m* merchant

neige *f* snow; **(à la) neige** with beaten egg whites

neiger to snow

nerf *m* nerve

n'est-ce pas don't I?/isn't it? etc

net(te) clear; neat; net (*income, price*)

nettoyage *m* cleaning; **nettoyage à sec** dry-cleaning

nettoyer to clean

neuf[1] new

neuf[2] nine

neutre neutral

neuve new

neuvième ninth

neveu *m* nephew

névralgie *f* headache; neuralgia

nez *m* nose

ni ... ni neither ... nor; **ni l'un ni l'autre** neither

niçois(e): salade niçoise lettuce with tomatoes, hard-boiled eggs, anchovies, black olives, green peppers; **à la niçoise** with garlic, olives, anchovies, onions and tomatoes

nid *m* nest

nièce *f* niece

nier to deny

n'importe any ...

niveau *m* level; standard; **niveau de vie** standard of living

noce *f* wedding

nocturne *m* late opening; **match en nocturne** floodlit fixture

Noël *m* Christmas

nœud *m* knot; bow (*ribbon*); **nœud papillon** bow tie

noir(e) black; **un café noir** a black coffee

noisette *f* hazelnut; **noisette d'agneau** small boneless slice of lamb

noix *f* walnut; **noix de cajou** cashew nut; **noix de coco** coconut; **noix de muscade** nutmeg; **noix de veau** type of veal steak

nom *m* name; **nom de famille** surname; **nom de jeune fille** maiden name

nombre *m* number

nombreux(euse) numerous; large (*crowd*)

non no; not

non-alcoolisé(e) nonalcoholic

nonante ninety (*Switz and Belgium*)
non-fumeur m non-smoker
non-prioritaire minor (*road*)
nord m north; **du nord** northern
normal(e) normal; standard (*size*); regular; **(essence) normale** ≈ 2-star petrol (*Switz*)
normalement normally
normande: à la normande usually cooked with mushrooms and cream
norme f: **conforme aux normes de fabrication/ de sécurité** conforms to manufacturing/safety regulations
nos our
notaire m solicitor
note f note; bill; memo
notre our
nôtre: le/la nôtre ours; **les nôtres** ours (*plural*)
nouilles fpl noodles
nourrir to feed
nourriture f food
nous we; us
nous-mêmes ourselves
nouveau new; **de nouveau** again
nouveautés fpl fashions
Nouvel-An m New Year
nouvelle new
nouvelles fpl news
novembre m November
noyau m stone (*in fruit*)
noyer[1]: **se noyer** to drown
noyer[2] m walnut
nu(e) naked; bare
nuage m cloud
nuit f night; **bonne nuit!** good night!
nul(le) void (*contract*); **nulle part** nowhere; anywhere; **match nul**

draw
numéro m number; act (*at circus etc*); issue (*of magazine*); **numéro d'appel** number being called; **numéro d'immatriculation/ minéralogique** registration number (*on car*); **numéro postal** postcode (*Switz*)
numéroté(e): place numérotée numbered seat

O

objectif m objective; target (*sales etc*); lens (*of camera*); **objectif grand-angulaire** wide-angle lens
objet m object; **objets de valeur** valuable items; **objets trouvés** lost property
obligatoire obligatory, compulsory
obliger to oblige
oblitérer to cancel (*stamp*); to stamp (*card, ticket*)
obsèques fpl funeral
obtenir to obtain; to get
obtention f: **pour l'obtention de ...** in order to obtain ...
occasion f occasion; bargain; opportunity; **d'occasion** used; second-hand
Occident m the West
occidental(e) western
occupé(e) engaged; taken; busy; hired (*taxi*)
occuper: s'occuper de to look after
octante eighty (*Belgium*)
octobre m October
œil m eye

œillet m carnation
œuf m egg; **œuf à la coque** boiled egg; **œuf dur** hard-boiled egg; **œuf mollet** soft-boiled egg; **œuf de Pâques** Easter egg; **œuf sur le/au plat** fried egg; **œuf poché** poached egg; **œufs brouillés** scrambled eggs; **œufs en gelée** lightly poached eggs served in gelatine; **œufs mayonnaise** eggs mayonnaise; **œufs mimosa** stuffed eggs; **œufs à la neige** floating islands
office m: **office du tourisme** tourist office
offre f offer; **offres d'emploi** situations vacant; **offre spéciale** special offer
offrir to offer; to give
oie f goose
oignon m onion
oiseau m bird
olive f olive
olivier m olive (*tree*); olive (*wood*)
ombre f shade; **ombre à paupières** eye shadow
omelette f omelette; **omelette baveuse** runny omelette; **omelette de la mère Poularde** omelette with potatoes; **omelette norvégienne** baked Alaska
on one
oncle m uncle
ondes fpl: **ondes courtes** short wave; **ondes moyennes** medium wave; **grandes ondes** long wave
ongle m nail (*on finger, toe*)
onze eleven
onzième eleventh

opposé(e) opposite
opticien m optician
option: en option optional
or m gold; **en or** gold(en)
orage m thunderstorm
orageux(euse) stormy
orange f orange; **orange pressée** fresh orange drink
orchestre m orchestra; band; stalls (*in theatre*)
orchidée f orchid
ordinaire ordinary; **(essence) ordinaire** ≈ 2-star petrol
ordinateur m computer
ordonnance f prescription
ordre m order; **à l'ordre de** payable to
ordures fpl rubbish
oreille f ear
oreiller m pillow
oreillons mpl mumps
orgeat m: **sirop d'orgeat** barley water
orgue m organ (*instrument*)
Orient m the East
orienté(e): orienté(e) à l'est/au sud facing east/ south
O.R.L. m ear, nose and throat specialist
orteil m toe
ortie f nettle; **ortie blanche** white deadnettle
os m bone
oseille f sorrel
otage m hostage
otite f ear infection
ou or; **ou ... ou** either ... or
où where; **le jour où ...** the day when ...
ouate f cotton wool
oublier to forget
ouest m west
oui yes
ouragan m hurricane

ours m bear
oursin m sea urchin
outil m tool
outre-mer overseas
ouvert(e) open; on (*water, gas etc*)
ouverture f overture; opening; **ouverture prochaine** opening soon; **l'ouverture se fera automatiquement** it will open automatically
ouvrable working (*day*)
ouvre-boîte m can-opener
ouvre-bouteilles m bottle-opener
ouvreuse f usherette
ouvrier m workman; worker
ouvrir to open; to turn on; to unlock

P

pagaie f paddle
paiement m payment; **paiement à la livraison** cash on delivery
paille f straw
pain m bread; loaf of bread; **petit pain** roll; **pain azyme** unleavened bread; **pain bis** brown bread; **pain de campagne** farmhouse bread; **pain au chocolat** croissant pastry with chocolate filling; **pain complet** wholemeal bread; **pain d'épices** gingerbread; **pain grillé** toast; **pain au levain** leavened bread; **pain de mie** sandwich loaf; **pain noir** black bread; **pain de poisson** fish loaf; **pain aux raisins** currant bun; **pain de seigle** rye bread;

pain de son bran bread
pair(e) even
paire f pair
paisible peaceful
paix f peace
palais m palace
pâle pale
palier m landing
palmes fpl flippers
palmier m palm tree
palourde f clam
pamplemousse m grapefruit
panaché m shandy
panais m parsnip
pancarte f notice
pané(e) in breadcrumbs
panier m basket; hamper; **panier-repas** packed lunch
panne f breakdown; **tomber en panne** to break down; **en panne** on tow; out of order
panneau m sign; **panneau d'affichage** notice board; **panneau indicateur** signpost
panoramique: vue panoramique panoramic view
pansement m bandage; (sticking) plaster
pantalon m trousers
papa m dad(dy)
pape m pope
papeterie f stationer's shop
papier m paper; **papiers** (identity) papers; (driving) licence; **papier d'aluminium** foil (*for food*); **papier carbone** carbon paper; **papier d'emballage** wrapping paper; **papier hygiénique** toilet paper; **papier à lettres** writing paper
papillon m butterfly
papillote: en papillote

wrapped in buttered paper and baked

paquebot *m* liner

Pâques Easter

paquet *m* package; pack; packet; bundle

par by; through; per; **passer par Londres** to go via London; **par an** per annum; **par ici** about here; this way; **par jour** per day; **deux fois par jour** twice a day; **40F par semaine** 40 francs a week; **par personne** per person

paraître to appear; **vient de paraître** just out

paralysé(e) paralysed

parapluie *m* umbrella

parasol *m* parasol; beach umbrella

parc *m* park; **parc d'attractions** amusement park; **parc pour bébé** playpen; **parc gardé** attended car park; **parc de stationnement** car park

parce que because

parcmètre *m* parking meter

parcourir to cover (*distance*)

parcours *m* distance; journey; route

pardessus *m* overcoat (*man's*)

pardon sorry; pardon?

pardonner to forgive

pare-brise *m* windscreen

pare-chocs *m* bumper

pareil(le) the same; similar

parent(e) *m/f* relation, relative

paresseux(euse) lazy

parfait *m* ice cream dessert with fruit

parfait(e) perfect

parfois sometimes

parfum *m* perfume; flavour

parfumerie *f* perfume shop; perfumes

pari *m* bet

parisien(ne) Parisian

parking *m* car park; **parking couvert/ découvert/souterrain** covered/open-air/ underground car park; **parking surveillé/gardé** attended car park

parlement *m* parliament

parler to speak; to talk; **parlez-vous anglais?** do you speak English?

Parmentier *see* hachis

parmi among(st)

paroisse *f* parish

parole *f* word; speech

part *f* share (*part*); **autre part** somewhere else

partager to share

partance: en partance pour bound for

partenaire *m/f* partner

parti *m* party (*political*)

participer to participate

particulier(ière) private; particular; **leçon particulière** private lesson; **en particulier** in particular; **vente de particulier à particulier** private sale

partie *f* part; round (*in competition*); **partie de tennis** game of tennis; **en partie** partly

partir to leave; to go; to come out (*stain*); to set off; **à partir de** from

partout everywhere

pas¹ not; **il ne l'a pas fait** he didn't do it; **pas du tout** not at all; **pas de voitures** no cars

pas² *m* step; pace

passage *m* passage; **de passage** passing through;

passage clouté pedestrian crossing; **passage interdit** no through way; **passage à niveau** level crossing; **passage protégé** priority over secondary roads; **passage souterrain** underpass (*for pedestrians*)

passager(ère) *m/f* passenger

passé(e) past

passe(-partout) *m* master key

passeport *m* passport

passer to pass; to spend (*time*); to show (*movie*); **passer la nuit** to stay the night; **passer devant** to pass (*place*); **quand passe le film?** when is the film on?; **se passer** to happen

passerelle *f* gangway (*bridge*)

passe-temps *m* pastime

passible: passible d'amende/de prison liable to a fine/ imprisonment

passionnant(e) exciting

pastèque *f* watermelon

pasteur *m* minister (*of religion*)

pasteurisé(e) pasteurized

pastille *f* pastille; **pastille de menthe** peppermint; **pastilles pour la toux** cough drops

pastis *m* aniseed- flavoured aperitif

patate douce *f* sweet potato

pataugeoire *f* paddling pool

pâte *f* pastry; dough; paste; batter; **pâte d'amandes** almond paste; **pâte à beignets** fritter batter; **pâte à crêpes** pancake batter;

pâte feuilletée puff pastry; **pâte à frire** batter (for frying); **pâtes de fruits** crystallized fruit; **pâte à modeler** Plasticine ®; **pâte sablée** shortbread dough

pâté m pâté; **pâté de campagne** coarse-textured pâté usually made with pork; **pâté en croûte** pâté in a pastry crust

pâtes fpl pasta

patin m skate; **patins à glace** ice skates; **patins à roulettes** roller skates

patiner to skate

patinoire f skating rink

pâtisserie f cake shop; pastry (cake)

patron m boss

patronne f boss

patte f leg (of animal); paw; foot

paupière f eyelid

paupiettes de veau fpl veal olives

pause-café f coffee break

pauvre poor

pavé m: **pavé (de viande)** thick piece of steak

pavillon m detached house

payant(e) who may pay(s); which must be paid for

payé(e) paid; **payé(e) d'avance** prepaid

payer to pay; to pay for; **faire payer quelque chose** to make a charge for something

pays m land; country; **du pays** local

paysage m scenery

Pays-Bas mpl Netherlands

pays de Galles m Wales

P.C.V.: téléphoner en P.C.V. to make a

reverse charge call

P.D.G. see **président**

péage m toll (on road etc)

peau f hide (leather); skin; **peau de mouton** sheepskin

pêche f peach; fishing; **pêche sous-marine/en mer** underwater/sea fishing

pêcheur m angler

pectoral(e): sirop pectoral/pâtes pectorales cough syrup/ pastilles

pédale f pedal

pédiatre m/f paediatrician

pédicure m/f chiropodist

peigne m comb

peignoir m dressing gown; bathrobe

peindre to paint; to decorate

peine f sorrow; bother (effort); **ce n'est pas le peine** it's not worth it; **à peine** scarcely; **défense d'entrer sous peine d'amende/de poursuites** trespassers will be fined/ prosecuted

peintre m painter

peinture f paint

peler to peel

pelle f spade; shovel; dustpan

pellicule f film (for camera); **pellicules** dandruff

pelote f ball (of string, wool); **pelote basque** pelota (ball game for 2 players hitting a ball against a specially marked wall)

pelouse f lawn

peluche f: **jouets en peluche** soft toys

pencher to lean; **se pencher** to lean over

pendant during; **pendant**

que while

penderie f wardrobe

pendule f clock

péniche f barge

pensée f thought

penser to think; **penser à** to think of; to think about

pension f: **demi-pension** half board; **pension complète** full board; **pension de famille** guest-house; boarding house

pente f slope; **en pente** sloping; on a slope

Pentecôte f Whitsun

pépinière f garden centre; nursery

percer to pierce

perche f perch

perdre to lose; **se perdre** to lose one's way; **perdre son temps** to waste one's time

perdreau m young partridge

perdrix f partridge

père m father; **père Noël** Santa Claus

périmé(e) out of date

période f period (of time); **période des vacances** holiday season

périphérique m ring road

perle f bead; pearl

permanent(e): de façon permanente permanently

permanente f perm

permettre to permit (something); **permettre à quelqu'un de** to allow someone to

permis m permit; **permis de conduire** driving licence; **permis de séjour** residence permit

Pernod ® m aniseed-based aperitif

perroquet *m* parrot

persil *m* parsley

persillade *f* oil, vinegar and parsley seasoning

personne *f* person; nobody; anybody

personnel *m* staff; personnel

perspective *f* view; prospect

perte *f* loss; **à perte de vue** as far as the eye can see

peser to weigh

pétanque *f* type of bowls played in the South of France

pet-de-nonne *m* fritter made with choux pastry

pétillant(e) fizzy

petit(e) little; small; slight; short (*person*); **petit déjeuner** breakfast; **petit pot** (jar of) baby food; **petit salé** salt pork; **petits pois** (garden) peas

petit-beurre *m* butter biscuit

petite-fille *f* granddaughter

petite friture *f* whitebait

petit-fils *m* grandson

petit-suisse *m* fresh unsalted double-cream cheese, eaten with sugar or fruit

pétrole *m* oil; paraffin

peu little; **peu de** few; little **un peu (de)** a little

peuplier *m* poplar

peur *f* fear; **avoir peur de** to be afraid of

peut-être perhaps; possibly

phare *m* headlight; lighthouse; **phare antibrouillard** fog lamp

pharmacie *f* chemist's (shop), pharmacy

phoque *m* seal; sealskin

photo *f* photo; **photo d'identité** passport photo

photocopie *f* photocopy

photocopier to photocopy

photographe *m/f* photographer

photographie *f* photography; photograph

photographier to photograph

physique physical

piano *m* piano; **piano à queue** grand piano

pichet *m* jug

pièce *f* room (*in house*); coin; play (*theatrical*); component (*for car etc*); **pièce d'identité** (means of) identification; identity paper; **pièce montée** tiered cake; wedding cake; **pièce de rechange** spare part; **pièces détachées** spare parts

pied *m* foot; **à pied** on foot; **pieds de porc** pigs' trotters

piège *m* trap

pierre *f* stone; **pierre à briquet** flint (*in lighter*)

piéton *m* pedestrian

piétonnier(ère) pedestrianized

pigeonneau *m* young pigeon

pignon *m* pine kernel

pilaf *m* spicy rice cooked in stock to which mutton, chicken or fish is added

pile *f* pile; battery (*for radio etc*)

pilé(e) crushed; ground (*almonds*)

pilote *m* pilot

pilule *f* pill

piment *m* chili

pin *m* pine

pince *f* pliers; dart (*in clothes*); **pince à cheveux** hair clip; **pince à épiler** tweezers

pinceau *m* brush

pincée *f* pinch (*of salt etc*)

pincer to pinch

pinces *fpl* pliers

pinède *f* pinewood

pingouin *m* penguin

ping-pong *m* table tennis

pintade *f* guinea fowl

pipérade *f* lightly scrambled eggs with tomato and peppers

piquante see **sauce**

pique-nique *m* picnic

piqûre *f* bite (*by insect*); injection; sting

pire (que) worse (than); **le/la pire** the worst

piscine *f* swimming pool; **piscine chauffée (de plein air)** (open-air) heated pool

pissaladière *f* onion tart with black olives, anchovies and sometimes tomatoes

pissenlit *m* dandelion; **salade de pissenlit au lard** dandelion salad with bacon

pistache *f* pistachio (nut)

piste *f*; **piste d'atterrissage** landing strip; runway; **piste cyclable** cycle track; **piste de danse** dance floor; **piste de luge** toboggan run; **piste de ski** ski run

pistolet *m* pistol, gun

pittoresque quaint

placard *m* cupboard

place *f* square (*in town*); seat; space (*room*); place; **place du marché** marketplace; **place forte** fortified town; **sur place** on the spot; **places debout/assisses** standing

room/seats
placer to place
plafond *m* ceiling
plage *f* beach
plaindre: se plaindre to complain
plaine *f* plain
plain-pied: de plain-pied on the same level; at street level
plaire to please
plaisanterie *f* joke
plaisir *m* enjoyment; pleasure
plan *m* map (*of town*); plan; **plan d'eau** lake
planche *f* board; plank; **planche à roulettes** skateboard; **planche de surf** surf board; **planche à voile** (*board*) windsurfer; (*sport*) windsurfing; **faire de la planche à voile** to go windsurfing
plancher *m* floor
planeur *m* glider
planter to plant
plaque *f* plate (*of glass, metal*); **plaque chauffante/de cuisson** hotplate; **plaque d'immatriculation/ minéralogique** number plate
plaqué(e) or/argent gold-/silver-plated
plat *m* dish; course (*of meal*); **plat du jour** dish of the day; **plat de résistance** main course; **plats à emporter** take-away meals; **plats préparés/cuisinés** ready-made meals/meals cooked on the premises
plat(e) level (*surface*); flat; **à plat** flat (*battery, tyre*)
platane *m* plane (*tree*)
plateau *m* tray; **plateau de fromages** assorted

cheeses; **plateau de fruits de mer** seafood platter
plâtre *m* plaster
plein(e) full; solid (*not hollow*); **plein(e) de** full of; **en/de plein air** open-air; **plein sud** facing south; **à plein temps** full-time; **faites le plein** fill it up
pleurer to cry
pleuvoir to rain; **il pleut** it's raining
pliant *m* folding chair
pliant(e) collapsible; folding
plier to bend; to fold
plissé(e) pleated
plomb *m* lead
plombier *m* plumber
plombières *f* tutti-frutti ice cream with whipped cream
plongée *f:* **plongée sous-marine** (skin) diving
plongeoir *m* diving board
plonger to dive
pluie *f* rain
plume *f* feather
plupart *f* majority; most
plus plus; more; most; **ne ... plus** no longer (*in time*); **nous n'avons plus de lait** we've no more milk; **plus ou moins** more or less; **en plus** extra
plusieurs several
plutôt rather
pluvieux(euse) rainy, wet
P.M.U. *m* system of forecast betting
pneu *m* tyre; **pneu à carcasse radiale** radial tyre
poche[1] *f* pocket
poche[2] *m* paperback
poché(e) poached
poêle *m* stove

poêle (à frire) *f* frying pan
poêlé(e) fried
poids *m* weight; **poids lourd** heavy goods vehicle
poignée *f* handle
poignet *m* wrist
poil *m* hair; coat (*of animal*); bristle
poinçonner to punch (*ticket etc*)
poing *m* fist
point *m* stitch; dot; point; **à point** medium (*steak*); **point de rassemblement** assembly point; **point de rencontre** meeting point; **point de vente** sales outlet; **point de vue** viewpoint
pointe *f* point (*tip*); **pointes d'asperges** asparagus tips; **heures de pointe** rush hour
pointillé: suivant le pointillé along the dotted line
pointure *f* size (*of shoes*)
poire *f* pear; pear brandy; **poire belle Hélène** poached pear served with vanilla ice cream and hot chocolate sauce
poireau *m* leek
pois *m* spot (*dot*); **petits pois** peas; **pois cassés** split peas; **pois chiches** chick peas
poisson *m* fish; **poisson rouge** goldfish
poissonnerie *f* fishmonger's shop
poitrine *f* breast; bust; chest
poivrade: à la poivrade in vinaigrette sauce with pepper; in white wine sauce with pepper
poivre *m* pepper

poivré(e) peppery
poivron *m* pepper (*capsicum*); **poivron vert/rouge** green/red pepper
poli(e) polite
police *f* policy (*insurance*); police; **police d'assurance** insurance policy; **police secours** emergency services
policier *m* policeman; **film/roman policier** detective film/novel
politique[1] political
politique[2] *f* politics, policy
Pologne *f* Poland
polonais(e) Polish
pommade *f* ointment; cream
pomme *f* apple; **pomme (de terre)** potato; **pommes chips** potato crisps; **pommes dauphine** potatoes mashed with butter, egg yolks and flour, deep fried as croquettes; **pommes duchesse** potatoes mashed with butter and egg yolks; **pommes/pommes de terre au four** baked apples/potatoes; **pommes frites** chips; **gratin de pommes de terre** potatoes with cheese topping baked in the oven; **pommes de terre au lard** potatoes with bacon; **pommes mousseline** mashed potatoes; **pommes noisette** deep-fried potato balls; **pommes de terre nouvelles** new potatoes; **pommes paille** potatoes sliced like straws and fried; **pommes de terre en robe des champs** jacket potatoes; **pommes de terre sautées** sauté potatoes; **pommes vapeur** boiled patotoes
pommier *m* apple tree
pompe *f* pump; **pompe à essence** petrol pump
pompes funèbres *fpl* undertaker's
pompier *m* fireman
poney *m* pony
pont *m* bridge; ramp (*in garage*); deck (*of ship*); extended weekend; **pont à péage** toll bridge
pont-l'évêque *m* softish, mature, square-shaped cheese
populaire popular
porc *m* pork; pig
porcelaine *f* porcelain; china
porche *m* porch
port *m* harbour; port; **port de plaisance** yachting harbour; **port du casque obligatoire** crash helmets must be worn
portatif(ive) portable
porte *f* door; gate
porte-bagages *m* luggage rack (*in train*)
porte-bébé *m* carrycot
porte-clés *m* key ring
portée *f*: **à votre portée** within your means
portefeuille *m* wallet
porte-monnaie *m* purse
porter to carry; to wear
porteur *m* porter
portier *m* doorman
portière *f* door (*of car*)
portillon *m*: **portillon automatique** automatic barrier
portion *f* helping; portion
porto *m* port (*wine*)
port-salut *m* mild, firm cow's-milk cheese
portuaire port, harbour

portugais(e) Portuguese
poser to put; to lay down; **poser une question** to ask a question
positif(ive) positive
posologie *f* dosage
posséder to own
possibilité *f* possibility
possible possible; **faire tout son possible** to do all one possibly can
poste[1] *m* (radio/TV) set; extension (*phone*); **poste de contrôle** checkpoint; **poste de secours** first-aid post
poste[2] *f* post; **mettre à la poste** to post
pot *m* pot (*for jam, for plant*); carton (*of yoghurt etc*); potty; **pot d'échappement** exhaust pipe
potable: **eau potable** drinking water
potage *m* soup; **potage du jour** soup of the day
potager *m* kitchen/vegetable garden
pot-au-feu *m* beef stew
poteau *m* post (*pole*); **poteau indicateur** signpost
potée *f* hotpot (of pork or beef with vegetables)
poterie *f* pottery
potiron *m* pumpkin
poubelle *f* dustbin
pouce *m* thumb
poudre *f* powder; **en poudre** powdered
poudreuse *f* powder snow
poularde *f* fattened chicken
poule *f* hen; **poule en daube** chicken casserole; **poule au pot** stewed chicken with vegetables; **poule au riz** chicken

with rice
poulet *m* chicken; **poulet chasseur** chicken in sauce of wine, mushrooms, tomatoes and herbs; **poulet frites** chicken with chips; **poulet rôti** roast chicken
poumon *m* lung
poupée *f* doll
pour for; **20 pour cent** 20 per cent; **pour faire** in order to do
pourboire *m* tip
pourcentage *m* percentage
pourquoi why
poursuivre to chase; **poursuivre en justice** to sue
pourtant however
pourvu que provided, providing; as long as
pousse-café *m* (after-dinner) liqueur
pousser to push; to grow
pousses de soja *fpl* beansprouts
poussette *f* pushchair
poussière *f* dust
poutre *f* beam (*of wood*)
pouvoir[1] *m* power
pouvoir[2] to be able; **pouvoir faire quelque chose** to be able to do something
praire *f* clam
prairie *f* meadow
praline *f* sugared almond
praliné(e) almond-flavoured
pratique handy; practical; **pas pratique** inconvenient
préalablement beforehand
précédent(e) previous
précieux(euse) precious
précipiter: se précipiter to rush

précis(e) precise; exact; specific
préciser to specify
préfecture de police *f* police headquarters
préférer to prefer
premier(ère) first; **de premier ordre** high-class; **en première** in first (gear); **voyager en première** to travel first-class; **de première classe** first-class (*work etc*); **premiers secours** first aid
prendre to take; to get; to have (*meal, shower, drink*); **prendre froid** to catch cold
prénom *m* first name; forename; Christian name
préparer to prepare; to fix; **se préparer** to get ready
près near; **près de** near; **près de la maison** near the house; **tout près** close by; **à peu près** roughly
pré-salé *m* salt meadow lamb
présélection *f*: **respecter la présélection** (*in Switz*) keep in lane
présent(e) present; **à présent** at present; now
présenter to present (*give*); to introduce (*person*); **se présenter à l'enregistrement** to check in (*at airport*); **présenter une pièce d'identité** to show some identification; **veuillez présenter tous les articles à la caissière** please show all items to the assistant at the cash desk
préservatif *m* condom

président *m* chairman; president; **président-directeur général (P.D.G.)** president (*of company*)
presque almost; nearly
presqu'île *f* peninsula
pressé(e) in a hurry; **orange/citron pressé(e)** fresh orange/lemon drink
presse-citron *m* lemon-squeezer
presser to press; to squeeze (*lemon*); **se presser** to hurry
pressing *m* dry-cleaner's
pression *f* pressure; **(bière à la) pression** draught beer; **faites vérifier la pression de vos pneus** have your tyre pressure checked
prestations *fpl* service (*in hotel etc*)
prêt *m* loan
prêt(e) ready; **prêt à cuire** ready to cook
prêt-à-porter *m* ready-to-wear
prêter to lend
prêtre *m* priest
preuve *f* evidence; proof
prévision *f* forecast
prier to pray
prière *f* prayer; **prière de ...** please ...
primaire primary
primeurs *fpl* early fruit and vegetables
principalement mainly
printemps *m* spring
prioritaire with right of way
priorité *f* right of way; **cédez la priorité** give way; **réservé en/par priorité à** strictly reserved for; **priorité à droite** give way to traffic coming from the right
prise *f*: **prise (de**

courant) plug; socket; **prise en charge** pick-up charge (*taxi*); hire charge (*rented car*); **prise multiple** adaptor; **prise de sang** blood test
privatif(ive) private
privé(e) private
prix *m* price; prize; **à prix réduit** cut-price; **acheter quelque chose au prix coûtant** to buy something at cost; **prix du billet** fare; **prix cassés** prices slashed; **prix choc** drastic reductions; **prix de la course/du parcours** fare (*in taxi*); **prix coûtant** cost price; **prix d'entrée** entrance fee; **prix fixe** fixed price; **prix imbattables** unbeatable prices; **prix sacrifiés** giveaway prices
probable probable; likely; **peu probable** unlikely
procédé *m* process
procès *m* trial (*in law*)
processus *m* process
procès-verbal *m* minutes; statement; parking ticket
prochain(e) next
proche close (*near*)
procurer: se procurer to get, obtain
producteur *m* producer
produire to produce
produit *m* product; commodity
produits *mpl* produce; products; **produits de beauté** beauty products; **produits d'entretien** cleaning products; **produits fermiers** farm produce; **produits laitiers** dairy produce
professeur *m* professor; teacher (*secondary school*)

professionnel(le) professional
profiter de to take advantage of
profiteroles *fpl* small cases of choux pastry with a sweet filling
profond(e) deep; **peu profond(e)** shallow
profondeur *f* depth
programme *m* programme; syllabus; schedule
programmer to programme
progrès *m* progress; **faire des progrès** to make progress
progressif(ive) gradual
projet *m* project; plan; scheme
prolonger to prolong; to extend
promenade *f* walk; promenade; ride (*in vehicle*); **faire une promenade** to go for a walk
promener: se promener to walk
promesse *f* promise
promettre to promise
promoteur (immobilier) *m* property developer
promotion *f*: **promotion sur ...** special offer on ...
promotionnel(le): menu promotionnel special low-price menu
prononcer to pronounce
pronostic *m* forecast
propos *mpl* talk; **à propos de** about
proposer to propose (suggest); **proposer de faire quelque chose** to offer to do something
propre clean; own
propreté *f* cleanliness; tidiness; **en parfait état**

de propreté perfectly clean (and tidy)
propriétaire *m/f* owner
propriété *f* property
protecteur(trice) protective
protéger to protect
protéine *f* protein
protestant(e) Protestant
protester to protest
prouver to prove
provenance: en provenance de from
provençal(e): (à la) provençale cooked in olive oil, with tomatoes, garlic and parsley
province *f* province (*region*)
provision *f* supply, stock; funds; **chèque sans provision** dud cheque
provisions *fpl* groceries
provisoirement for the time being
proximité: à proximité nearby; **à proximité de** near (to)
prudence *f*: **prudence!** drive carefully!; **par mesure de prudence** as a precaution
prudent(e) careful; wise; prudent
prune *f* plum; plum brandy
pruneau *m* prune; damson (*Switz only*); **pruneau sec** prune (*Switz only*)
prunelle *f* sloe; sloe gin
psychiatre *m/f* psychiatrist
psychologue *m/f* psychologist
P.T.T. *fpl* Post Office
public public
publicité *f* advertising; advertisement; publicity
publique public
puce *f* flea; **(marché**

aux) puces flea market
puis then
puisque since
puissance f power
puissant(e) powerful
puits m well (*for water*)
pull m sweater
punir to punish
pur(e) pure; **pure laine vierge** pure new wool
purée f purée; **purée de pommes de terre** mashed potatoes
puzzle m jigsaw (puzzle)
P.V. m parking ticket
pyjama m pyjamas

Q

quai m platform (*in station*); wharf; quay
qualifié(e) qualified; skilled
qualifier: se qualifier pour to qualify for (*in sports*)
qualité f quality; **articles de qualité** quality goods
quand when
quand même even so
quant à as for
quantité f quantity
quarantaine f about forty; quarantine
quarante forty
quart m quarter; **un quart d'heure** a quarter of an hour; **4 heures moins le quart** (a) quarter to 4; **4 heures et quart** (a) quarter past 4
quartier m neighbourhood; district
quatorze fourteen
quatre four
quatre-vingt-dix ninety
quatre-vingts eighty
quatrième fourth

que that; than; whom; what; **mieux que** better than; **ce que** what
quel(le) which; what
quelconque: pour une raison quelconque for some reason
quelque some
quelque chose something
quelquefois sometimes
quelque part somewhere
quelques a few
quelques-uns(unes) some, a few
quelqu'un somebody; someone; anybody; anyone; **quelqu'un d'autre** someone else
quenelle f light fish, poultry or meat dumpling
question f question; issue
quetsche f damson; damson brandy
queue f queue; tail; **faire la queue** to stand in line; to queue; **queues de langouste** lobster tails
qui who; which; **à qui** whose; **avec qui** with whom; **ce qui** what
quincaillerie f hardware
quinzaine f about fifteen; a fortnight
quinze fifteen
quitter to quit; to leave (*room, club, school*)
quoi what
quotidien(ne) daily

R

rabais m reduction; **au rabais** at a discount; **3% de rabais** 3% off
rabbin m rabbi
râble m: **râble de lapin/ lièvre** saddle of rabbit/

hare
raccourcir to shorten
raccrocher to hang up (*phone*)
raclette f hot, melted cheese served with boiled potatoes and pickles
raconter to tell
rade f (natural) harbour
radiateur m heater; radiator
radio f radio; X-ray (*photo*); **à la radio** on the radio
radiographier to X-ray
radiologue m/f radiologist
radis m radish
raffiné(e) refined
rafle f raid (*by police*)
rafraîchi(e): fruits rafraîchis fruit salad
rafraîchissements mpl refreshments
rage f rabies
ragoût m stew; casserole
raide steep
raie f skate (*fish*); stripe; streak; **raie au beurre noir** skate in brown butter sauce
raifort m horseradish
raisin m grape; **raisin sec** sultana; raisin; currant; **raisins de mars** redcurrants (*Switz only*)
raison f reason; **avoir raison** to be right; **à raison de** at the rate of; **pour raison de santé** for health reasons
raisonnable sensible; reasonable
ralentir to slow down
rallonge f (extra) table leaf; extension cable
rallye m rally (*sporting*)
ramasser to pick up (*object*)
rame f oar; train

ramener to bring back; to take back

ramequin *m* ramekin, individual soufflé dish

rampe *f* handrail (*on stairs*); ramp (*slope*)

randonnée *f* hike; **faire une randonnée** to go for a hike; **chemins de grande randonnée** hiking routes; **randonnée pédestre** walk, ramble

rang *m* row; rank

rangée *f* row

rangement *m* cupboard space; storage space

ranimer to receive

rapatriement *m* repatriation

râpé(e) grated

rapide¹ quick; fast

rapide² *m* express train

rappel *m* reminder

rappeler to remind; to ring back; **se rappeler** to remember

rapport *m* report; record (*register*); relationship; **qui a rapport à** relevant to

rapporter to bring back

raquette *f* racket (*tennis*); bat (*table tennis etc*); snowshoe

rare rare; scarce; unusual

rarement seldom

rascasse *f* scorpion fish

raser: se raser to shave

rasoir *m* razor; **rasoir électrique** shaver

rassembler to assemble

ratatouille (niçoise) *f* aubergines, peppers, courgettes, tomatoes cooked in olive oil

R.A.T.P. Paris transport authority

ravelé(e) restored (*building*)

ravi(e) delighted

rayé(e) striped; scratched

rayon *m* shelf; department (*in store*); ray; beam (*of light*); **rayon hommes** menswear (*department*)

rayure *f*: **à rayures** striped

R. de C. see **rez-de-chaussée**

réabonnement *m* renewal of subscription

réagir to react

réalisteur *m* director (*of film*)

réalité *f* reality

réanimation *f*: **(service de) réanimation** intensive care unit

reboucher: reboucher le flacon après usage recork the bottle after use

récemment lately; recently

récent(e) recent

récépissé *m* receipt

récepteur *m* receiver (*phone*)

réception *f* reception

recette *f* recipe

recevoir to receive; to get; to entertain (*give hospitality*)

rechapé *m*: **(pneu) rechapé** retread

recharge *f* refill

rechargeable refillable (*lighter, pen*)

réchaud *m* (portable) stove

réchauffer to warm

recherche *f* research

rechercher to look for; to retrieve (*data*)

récipient *m* container

réclamation *f* complaint

réclame *f* advertisement; **en réclame** on offer

récolte *f* crop

recommandé(e): **(envoi) en recommandé** registered mail

recommander to recommend; to register

récompense *f* reward

reconduire to take back

reconnaissant(e) grateful

reconnaître to recognize

reçu *m* receipt

recueil *m* collection

récupérer to get back

récurer: poudre/tampon à récurer scouring powder/pad

redevance *f* licence fee (*radio, TV*); rental charge (*telephone*)

réduction *f* reduction; **carte de réduction** card entitling holder to a discount

réduire to reduce; **réduit de moitié** reduced by half

réfection: travaux de réfection repair work

réfléchir to reflect; to think over

refléter to reflect

réfrigéré(e) refrigerated

refroidir to cool (down); to get cold

refuge *m* mountain hut

refus *m* refusal

refuser to reject; to refuse

régaler: se régaler to have a delicious meal

regard *m* look

regarder to look; to watch; to look at; to concern

régate *f* regatta

régime *m* diet (*slimming*); **suivre un régime** to be on a diet

région *f* region; area

registre *m* register

réglable adjustable; payable

règle *f* rule; ruler (*for measuring*); **en règle** in order

règlement *m* regulation; payment; **règlement par chèque** payment by cheque; **règlement en espèces/au comptant** payment in cash

régler to tune (*engine*); to adjust; to settle; **à régler sur place** to be paid at time of purchase/booking etc

règles *fpl* period (*menstruation*)

réglisse *f* liquorice

regretter to regret; to miss

régulier(ère) regular; steady

rein *m* kidney (*of person*); **mal de reins** backache

reine *f* queen

reine-claude *f* greengage

rejoindre to (re)join

réjouir: se réjouir de to be delighted about

relais routier *m* transport café (good, inexpensive food)

relatif(ive) relative

relier to connect

religieuse *f* nun; cream bun (made with choux pastry)

remarque *f* comment; remark

remarquer to notice

rembourser to pay back; to refund

remède *m* remedy

remercier to thank

remettre to put back; to replace; to return; to postpone

remise *f* shed; discount; **remise en état** repair; restoration

remontée mécanique *f* ski lift

remonte-pente *m* ski lift

remorque *f* trailer;

towrope

remorquer to tow

remplaçant(e) *m/f* substitute

remplacement *m* replacement

remplacer to replace

remplir to fill; to fill in/out/up; **remplir une fiche d'hôtel** to check in (*at hotel*)

remporter to win (*prize*)

remuer to toss (*salad*); to stir

renard *m* fox

rencontrer to meet

rendez-vous *m* date; appointment

rendre to give back; to return; to make; **se rendre compte de** to realize; **se rendre à** to go to; **cet appareil rend/ne rend pas la monnaie** change given/no change given at this machine

renforcer to strengthen

renommé(e) famous

renoncer: renoncer à to give up

renouveler to renew

renouvellement *m* renewal; replenishment

rénové(e): entièrement rénové completely modernized

renseignement *m* piece of information

renseignements *mpl* information; directory enquiries; **bureau de renseignements** information desk/office; **renseignements téléphoniques** telephone enquiries

rentable profitable

rentrée *f* return to work after the summer break; **rentrée (des classes)**

start of the new school year

rentrer to go/come back in; to go/come back; **rentrer à la maison** to go home

renverser to spill; to knock down/over

renvoyer to return (*send back*); to dismiss (*employee*)

réparations *fpl* repairs

réparer to repair; to mend

repas *m* meal

repassage *m* ironing

repasser to iron

répertoire *m* list; **répertoire des rues** street index

répéter to repeat

répétition *f* rehearsal; repetition

répondeur automatique *m* answering machine

répondre to reply; to answer; **répondre au téléphone** to answer the phone

réponse *f* answer; reply

reportage *m* report (*in press*)

repos *m* rest; **maison de repos** nursing home

reposer: se reposer to rest

reprendre: reprenez votre ticket remove your ticket

représentation *f* performance (*of play*)

reprise *f* trade-in; repeat (*film*)

réputé(e) renowned

requin *m* shark

R.E.R. *m* Greater Paris high-speed commuter train

réseau *m* network; **réseau ferroviaire** rail

network

réservation f reservation; booking; **réservation de groupe** block booking

réserve f: **réserve de chasse/pêche** hunting/fishing preserve; **réserve naturelle** nature reserve; **sous réserve de** subject to

réserver to reserve; to book

réservoir m tank

résidence f residence; **résidence universitaire** hall of residence; **résidence secondaire** second home

résidentiel(le) residential

respirer to breathe

responsabilité f responsibility

responsable responsible

ressembler à to resemble; to look like

ressort m spring (of metal etc)

ressortir to stand out

ressortissant(e) m/f national

restaurant m restaurant

restauration f catering; **travaux de restauration** restoration work

restauré(e) restored

restaurer: se restaurer to have something to eat

restauroute see **restoroute**

reste m rest

rester to remain; to stay; **il reste de la crème** there's some cream left

restoroute m roadside or motorway restaurant

résultat m result

rétablir: se rétablir to recover (from illness)

retard m delay; **en retard** late; **le train a**

pris du retard the train has been delayed; **avoir du retard** to be behind schedule

retarder to lose (clock, watch); to delay

retenir to reserve (seat etc)

retirer to withdraw; to collect (tickets)

retouche f alteration

retour m return (going/coming back); **par retour (du courrier)** by return (of post)

retourner to return; to go back; to turn over

retrait m withdrawal; collection; **en cas de non-retrait** in the event of failure to collect (tickets); **retrait d'espèces** cash withdrawal

retraite f retirement; pension; **prendre sa retraite** to retire

retraité(e) m/f old-age-pensioner

rétrécir to shrink

retrouver to find; to meet

rétroviseur m rear-view mirror

réunion f meeting

réussir to succeed; to pass

rêve m dream

réveil m alarm clock

réveiller to wake; **se réveiller** to wake up

réveillon m: **réveillon (de Noël/de la Saint-Sylvestre)** Christmas/New Year's Eve (party)

revendre to resell

revenir to return; to go back; to come back

revenu m revenue; income

rêver to dream

réviser to service (car)

revoir to see again; to revise; **au revoir** goodbye

revue f revue; review

rez-de-chaussée m ground floor

Rhône m Rhône

rhum m rum

rhumatisme m rheumatism

rhumatologue m/f rheumatologist

rhume m cold (illness); **rhume des foins** hay fever

rhumerie f bar specializing in rum-based drinks

riche wealthy; rich

richesses fpl wealth

ride f wrinkle

rideau m curtain

rien nothing; anything

rillettes fpl potted meat made from pork or goose

rinçage m rinse

rincer to rinse

rire[1] to laugh

rire[2] m laugh; laughter

ris de veau m calf sweetbread

risque m risk

risquer to risk

rissolé(e): pommes (de terre) rissolées fried potatoes

rivage m seashore

rive f shore

riverains: sauf riverains no entry except for access; residents only; **stationnement réservé aux riverains** parking for residents only

rivière f river

riz m rice; **riz au lait** rice pudding; **riz pilaf** pilau rice

R.N. see **route**

robe f gown; dress; **robe de chambre** dressing gown; **robe de grossesse** maternity dress; **robe de mariée** wedding dress; **robe de soirée** evening dress (*woman's*)

robinet m tap; **eau du robinet** tap water

roche f rock (*substance*)

rocher m rock (*boulder*)

rodage m: **en rodage** running in

rœsti mpl (*in Switz*) potato slivers fried with onion and bacon

rognon m kidney (*to eat*)

roi m king; **les rois/la fête des rois** Twelfth Night

romaine f cos lettuce

roman m novel; **roman à suspense** thriller; **roman policier** detective novel

Romandie f French-speaking Switzerland

romarin m rosemary

romsteak m rump steak

rond m ring (*circle*)

rond(e) round

rond-point m roundabout

roquefort m rich, pungent blue-veined cheese made from ewe's milk

rosbif m roast beef; roasting beef

rose pink

rôti m roast meat; joint; **rôti de bœuf/porc/veau** roast beef/pork/veal

rôtir to roast

rôtisserie f steakhouse; roast meat counter

roue f wheel; **roue de secours** spare wheel

rouge red; **rouge à lèvres** lipstick

rougeole f measles

rouget m mullet

rouille f rust

roulade f rolled meat or fish with stuffing

roulé m Swiss roll

rouler to roll; to go (*car*); **roulez lentement** drive slowly

route f road; route; **en route** on the way; **route de délestage** relief road; **route départementale** B-road; **route nationale (R.N.)** trunk road; **route à quatre voies** dual carriageway

routier m lorry driver; **(relais) routier** transport café (good, inexpensive food)

Royaume-Uni m United Kingdom

ruban m tape; ribbon

rubéole f German measles

rubrique f column (*in newspaper*); heading

rue f street; **rue à sens unique** one-way street; **grand-rue** high street

ruelle f lane (*in town*); alley

ruines fpl ruins

ruisseau m stream; gutter

rumsteck m rump steak

rutabaga m swede

S

s' oneself; himself; herself; itself; themselves

S.A. Ltd; plc

sa his; her; its

sabayon m dessert of egg yolks, sugar and white wine, served warm

sable m sand; **de sable** sandy (*beach*); **sables mouvants** quicksand

sablé m shortbread

sac m bag; sack; **sac de couchage** sleeping bag; **sac à dos** rucksack; **sac à main** handbag; **sac en plastique** plastic bag; **sac de voyage** travelling bag

sachet m sachet; **sachet de thé** tea bag

sacoche f bag

safran m saffron

sage good (*well-behaved*); wise

saignant(e) rare (*steak*)

saignement de nez m nosebleed

saindoux m lard

saint(e)[1] holy

saint(e)[2] m/f saint

saint-honoré m gateau decorated with whipped cream and choux pastry balls

saint-nectaire m firm, fruity-flavoured cow's-milk cheese from the Auvergne

saint-paulin m mild cow's-milk cheese

Saint-Sylvestre f New Year's Eve

saisir to snatch; to grab; to seize

saison f season; **pleine saison** high season; **haute/basse saison** high/low season

salade f lettuce; salad; **en salade** in vinaigrette; **salade campagnarde** green salad with chicken and diced cheese; **salade composée** salad dish; **salade de fruits** fruit salad; **salade lyonnaise** potato salad with sausage and gherkins; **salade de pommes de terre** cold boiled potatoes in vinaigrette; **salade russe**

Russian salad; **salade verte** green salad
salaire m wage; wages; salary; **salaire brut/net** gross/net wage or salary
salaisons fpl salt meats
sale dirty
salé m salt pork
salé(e) salty; savoury
salle f: **salle d'attente** waiting room; **salle de bains** bathroom; **salle de départ** departure lounge; **salle d'eau** shower room; **salle d'exposition** showroom; **salle de jeux** games room; **salle à manger** dining room; **salle de séjour** living room
salmis m ragout of game stewed in rich sauce of wine and vegetables
salon m sitting room; lounge; **salon de l'automobile** motor show; **salon de beauté** beauty salon; **salon de coiffure** hairdressing salon; **salon de thé** tea-shop
salopette f dungarees
salsifis m salsify
samedi m Saturday
S.A.M.U. m emergency medical service
sandwich m: **sandwich au jambon** ham sandwich; **sandwichs divers/variés** assorted sandwiches
sang m blood
sanglier m wild boar
sanguine f blood orange
sanitaire: appareils/ installations sanitaires bathroom appliances/ plumbing
sans without
santé f health; **à votre santé!** cheers!; **en bonne**

santé healthy
sapeurs-pompiers mpl fire brigade
sapin m fir (tree); **sapin de Noël** Christmas tree
sarcelle f teal; small freshwater duck
sardine f sardine
S.A.R.L. f limited company
sarrasin m buckwheat
sarriette f savory
satisfaire to satisfy
sauce f sauce; **sauce béarnaise** thick sauce made with butter, egg yolks, shallots, vinegar and herbs; **sauce beurre noir** brown butter sauce; **sauce blanche** white sauce; **sauce bordelaise** brown sauce with mushrooms, red wine and shallots; **sauce bourguignonne** sauce with red wine, onions, herbs and spices; **sauce chasseur** sauce with white wine, shallots, tomatoes and mushrooms; **sauce diable** hot, spicy sauce with cayenne pepper, white wine, herbs and vinegar; **sauce gribiche** sauce made with hard-boiled egg yolks, oil and vinegar; **sauce hollandaise** sauce made with butter, egg yolks and lemon juice; **sauce madère** sauce with Madeira wine; **sauce Mornay** cheese sauce; **sauce moutarde** mustard sauce; **sauce normande** sauce with white wine and cream; **sauce piquante** sauce with white wine, vinegar, shallots, pickles and

herbs; **sauce poivrade** sauce for game made with meat juices, pepper and vinegar; **sauce poulette** sauce made with white stock, wine, lemon juice, parsley and sometimes mushrooms; **sauce raifort** horseradish sauce; **sauce rémoulade** mayonnaise with onions, capers, gherkins and herbs; **sauce de soja** soy(a) sauce; **sauce suprême** sauce made with white stock, wine and cream; **sauce tartare** tartar sauce; **sauce vinaigrette** salad dressing made with oil, wine vinegar and seasoning
saucisse f sausage; **saucisse de Francfort** Frankfurter
saucisson m slicing sausage; **saucisson à l'ail** garlic sausage; **saucisson sec** (dry) pork and beef sausage
sauf except (for)
sauge f sage (herb)
saumon m salmon
sauté m: **sauté de poulet/mouton/veau** chicken/mutton/veal lightly browned in hot butter, oil or fat
sauter to jump; to blow (fuse)
sauvage wild
sauvetage m rescue
savarin m ring-shaped cake, soaked in syrup and a liqueur or spirit
savoir to know; **pour en savoir plus** to find out more
savon m soap
savonnette f bar of soap
scarole f endive

scène f scene; stage (in theatre)

Schweppes ® m tonic water

scolaire school

Scotch ® m Sellotape ®; whisky

se oneself; himself; herself; itself; themselves

séance f meeting; performance

seau m bucket; pail

sec (sèche) dried (fruit, beans); dry

sèche-cheveux m hair dryer

sèche-linge m drying cabinet

sécher to dry

sécheresse f drought

séchoir m dryer; **séchoir à linge** clotheshorse

second(e) second; **de seconde main** second-hand

secondaire secondary

seconde f second (time); second class

secouer to shake

secourisme m first aid

secours m help; **au secours!** help!

secret secret

secrétaire m/f secretary

secrétariat m office

secrète secret

sécurité f security; safety; **en sécurité** safe; **pour votre sécurité** for your safety; **sécurité routière** road safety; **sécurité sociale** social security

sédatif m sedative

seigle m rye

sein m breast

seize sixteen

seizième sixteenth

séjour m stay; visit

séjourner to stay (reside)

sel m salt; **sans sel** unsalted; **sels de bain**

bath salts; **sel de cuisine** cooking salt; **sel fin/de table** table salt

sélectionné(e) selected

self m self-service restaurant

selle f saddle; **selle d'agneau** saddle of lamb

selon according to

semaine f week; **en semaine** during the week; **semaine commerciale** trade week

semblable like; similar; alike

sembler to seem; to look

semelle f sole (of shoe)

semestriel(le) half-yearly, six-monthly

semoule f semolina

sens m sense; meaning; direction; **sens giratoire** roundabout; **sens de l'humour** sense of humour; **sens interdit** no entry; **sens unique** one-way street

sensation f sensation; feeling

sensible sensitive

sentier m footpath; **sentier de grande randonnée** ramblers' path

sentir to smell; to taste; to feel

séparé(e) separate

séparément separately

séparer to separate

sept seven

septante seventy (Switz and Belgium)

septembre m September

septième seventh

série f series; set; **série noire** crime thrillers

sérieux(euse) serious; reliable

serpent m snake

serre f greenhouse

serré(e) tight

serrer to grip; to squeeze; **véhicules lents serrez à droite** slow-moving vehicles keep to the right-hand lane

serre-tête m headband

serrure f lock

serveur m waiter; barman

serveuse f waitress; barmaid

servez-vous help yourself

service m service; service charge; favour; **service après-vente** after-sales service; **service compris/non compris (s.n.c.)** service included/not included; **service de réanimation** intensive care unit

serviette f towel; serviette; briefcase; **serviette hygiénique** sanitary towel; **serviette éponge** terry towel; **serviette de toilette** hand towel

servir to dish up; to serve; **cela ne sert à rien** it's no use; **se servir de** to use

ses his; her; its

seul(e) alone; lonely; **un seul** only one

seulement only

shampooing m shampoo

short m shorts

si if; whether; yes (to negative question)

Sicile f Sicily

sida m AIDS

siècle m century

siège m seat; head office; **siège social** registered office

sien: le sien his; hers; **la sienne** his; hers; **les**

siens his; hers; **les siennes** his; hers
sieste f siesta
sifflet m whistle (object)
signal m signal; **signal d'alarme** alarm (on train); **le signal sonore annonce la fermeture des portes** the acoustic signal warns that the doors are about to close; **dès que le signal sonore fonctionne** when you hear the signal
signaler to report
signalisation f: **panneau de signalisation** road sign; **feux de signalisation** traffic lights; **signalisation automatique** automatic signalling
signe m sign
signer to sign
signifier to mean
silencieux(euse) silent; quiet
s'il vous plaît please
simple simple; single
singe m monkey; ape
sinistre m accident
sinon otherwise; if not
sirène f siren
sirop m syrup; **sirop pour la toux** cough mixture
site m site (of building); **site classé** classified site; **site naturel** natural site; **site touristique** tourist spot
situation f situation; position (job)
situé(e) located; **bien situé(e) pour les magasins** convenient for shops
six six
sixième sixth
skaï ® m leatherette
ski m ski; skiing; **ski alpin**

Alpine skiing; **ski de fond** langlauf; **ski hors piste** off-piste skiing; **ski nautique** water-skiing; **ski de randonnée** cross-country skiing
skieur(euse) m/f skier
slip m underpants; panties; **slip de bain** swimming trunks
S.M.I.C. m index-linked minimum statutory wage
smoking m dinner jacket
snack m snack bar
s.n.c. see **service**
S.N.C.F. f French railways
société f company; society
soda m fizzy drink; **soda à l'orange** orangeade
sœur f sister
soie f silk; **soie sauvage** wild silk
soif f thirst; **avoir soif** to be thirsty
soigner to treat
soi-même oneself
soin m care; **aux bons soins de** care of, c/o; **soins du visage** face care; facials
soir m evening; **le soir** in the evening; **ce soir** tonight
soirée f evening; party; **soirée dansante** dinner-dance
soit: soit ... soit either ... or
soixante sixty
soixante-dix seventy
soja m soya; soya beans; **germes de soja** beansprouts
sol m ground; soil
solaire solar; sun
soldat m soldier
solde m balance (remainder owed)
soldes mpl sales (cheap

prices); **les soldes ne sont ni repris ni échangés** no exchange or refund on sale goods; **soldes de fins de série** oddments sale; **soldes de grands couturiers** sale of designer clothes; **soldes permanents** sale prices all year round
sole f sole (fish); **sole meunière** sole cooked in butter and served with lemon; **sole normande** sole in a sauce of white wine and cream
soleil m sun; sunshine; **prendre un bain de soleil** to sunbathe
solide solid; tough; strong; durable
sombre dark
somme f sum (total amount)
sommeil m sleep; **avoir sommeil** to be sleepy
sommelier m wine waiter
sommet m summit, top
somnifère m sleeping pill
son¹ his; her; its
son² m sound
sonner to ring; to strike
sonnette f bell (on door); **sonnette d'alarme** alarm bell
sorbet m water ice
sorte f sort, kind; **de sorte que** so that
sorti(e) out (not at home)
sortie f exit; **sortie de bain** bathrobe; **sortie interdite** no exit; **sortie de secours** emergency exit; **sortie de véhicules** exit for vehicles; **sortie le 6 mai** (film) opens on 6th May
sortir to take out; to release (book, film); to come out; to go out

S.O.S. médecins m emergency doctor service

souci m concern; worry

soudain suddenly

soudain(e) sudden

souffler to blow

souffrir to suffer

souhaiter to wish; to wish for

soulager relieve

soulever to lift

soulier m shoe

souligner to underline; to emphasize

soupe f soup; **soupe à l'oignon (gratinée)** (French) onion soup; **soupe au pistou** thick soup from Provence, with beans, potatoes, courgettes, garlic and basil

souper m supper; dinner (Switz)

source f source; spring (of water)

sourcil m eyebrow

sourd(e) deaf

sourire[1] to smile

sourire[2] m smile

souris f mouse

sous underneath; under

sous-préfecture f sub-prefecture

sous-sol m basement; **en sous-sol** underground

sous-titré(e): film en version originale sous-titrée film in the original version with subtitles

sous-vêtements mpl underwear; underclothes

souterrain(e) underground

soutien-gorge m bra

souvenir m souvenir; memory; **se souvenir de** to remember

souvent often

sparadrap m sticking-plaster

spécialiser: se spécialiser to specialize

spécialité f: **spécialités régionales** regional specialities

spectacle m scene (sight); show (in theatre); entertainment; **spectacle de variétés** variety show; **spectacle de cabaret** cabaret; **spectacle son et lumière** son et lumière display

spiritueux mpl spirits

sport m: **sports d'hiver** winter sports

sportif(ive) sports; athletic

stade m stadium

stage m training period; training course

stagiaire m/f trainee

standard m switchboard

standardiste m/f switchboard operator

starter m choke (of car)

station f station; **station balnéaire** seaside resort; **station d'essence** filling station; **station de métro** underground station; **station de sports d'hiver** winter sports resort; **station de taxis** taxi rank; **station thermale** spa

stationnement m parking; **stationnement alterné** parking on alternate sides depending on date; **stationnement en double file** double-parking; **stationnement gênant** you are requested not to park here; **stationnement interdit/réglementé** no/restricted parking

station-service f service station

steak m: **steak frites** steak and chips; **steak au poivre** steak with peppercorns; **steak tartare** minced raw steak mixed with raw egg, onion, tartar sauce, parsley and capers

stérilet m coil, I.U.D.

store m blind (at window)

strictement strictly

studio m studio; one-room flat

stylo m pen; **stylo à bille** ballpoint pen; **stylo (à) plume** fountain pen

substantiel(le) filling (food)

subtil(e) subtle

subventionner to subsidize

succès m success

succursale f branch (of store, bank etc)

sucer to suck

sucette f lollipop

sucre m sugar; **sucre de canne** cane sugar; **sucre cristallisé/raffiné** coarse-grained/refined sugar; **sucre glace** icing sugar; **sucre en morceaux** lump sugar; **sucre roux** brown sugar; **sucre semoule** granulated sugar; **sucre vanillé** vanilla sugar

sucré(e) sweet

sud m south; **du sud** southern

suffire to be enough

suggérer to suggest

suisse Swiss

Suisse f Switzerland; **Suisse romande** French-speaking Switzerland; **Suisse allemande/alémanique** German-speaking Switzerland

suite f series;

continuation; **toute suite** at once
suivant according to
suivant(e) following
suivre to follow; **faire suivre** to forward (*letter*)
sujet *m* topic; subject
super(carburant) *m* four-star petrol
supérette *f* mini-market
superficie *f* area (*of surface*)
supérieur(e) upper; higher; superior (*quality*)
supermarché *m* supermarket
supplément *m* supplement; **vin en supplément** wine extra; **sans supplément (de prix)** no extra charge
supplémentaire extra
supporter to support; to bear
supposer to suppose; to assume
suppositoire *m* suppository
suprême: suprême de volaille chicken breast in creamy sauce
sur on; onto; on top of; upon; **2 sur 10** 2 out of 10; **3 mètre sur 5** 3 metres by 5
sûr(e) sure
sûreté *f*: **pour plus de sûreté** as an extra precaution
surf *m* surfing
surgelés *mpl* frozen foods
surprendre to surprise
surpris(e) surprised
surtout especially
surveillant(e) *m/f* supervisor; **surveillant de plage** lifeguard
surveiller to watch; to supervise
survêtement *m* track-suit

survivre to survive
sus: en sus in addition
Suze ® *f* gentian-based liqueur
s.v.p. please
sympathique nice; pleasant
syndicat *m* trade union; syndicate
syndicat d'initiative *m* tourist office

T

t' you (*familiar form*)
ta your (*familiar form*)
tabac *m* tobacco; tobacconist's (*shop*); **tabac-journaux** tobacconist and newsagent
tabbouleé *m* steamed semolina served cold with tomato, cucumber, olive oil, lemon juice
table *f* table; **table de chevet** bedside table; **table d'hôte** fixed-price menu; **table des matières** contents (*table in book*); **table pliante** folding table
tableau *m* painting; picture; chart; **tableau de bord** dash(board); **tableau des départs/ arrivées** departures/ arrivals board; **tableau des horaires** timetable
tablette de chocolat *f* bar of chocolate
tabouret *m* stool
tache *f* spot; stain
taie d'oreiller *f* pillowcase
taille *f* height (*of person*); size (*of clothes*); waist; **taille unique** one size
tailleur *m* tailor; suit

(*women's*)
taire: se taire to be silent
talc *m* talc(um powder)
talon *m* heel; stub (*counterfoil*)
tamisé(e): lumière tamisée subdued lighting
tampon *m* pad; plug; tampon; **tampon abrasif/à récurer** scourer; **tampon (hygiénique)** tampon
tant so many/much; **tant de** such a lot of, so much/many
tante *f* aunt(ie)
taper to slam; to knock; **taper à la machine** to type
tapis *m* carpet; **tapis de sol** groundsheet
tard late; **plus tard** later; **au plus tard** at the latest
tarif *m* rate; tariff; **tarif des consommations** drinks tariff; **tarif dégressif** gradually decreasing tariff; **tarif douanier** customs tax; **tarif préférentiel** preferential rate; **tarif réduit** reduced rate
tarte *f* flan; tart; **tarte au citron meringuée** lemon meringue pie; **tarte au fromage** cheese flan; **tarte Tatin** upside-down tart of caramelized apples, served hot
tartelette *f* (small) tart
tartine *f* slice of bread and butter (or jam); **tartine beurrée** slice of bread and butter
tartiner: à tartiner for spreading
tas *m* heap
tasse *f* cup; mug
taureau *m* bull

taux m rate; **taux de change** exchange rate; **taux de l'inflation** rate of inflation; **taux fixe** flat rate; **taux d'intérêt** interest rate

taxe f duty; tax (on goods); **toutes taxes comprises (t.t.c.)** inclusive of tax; **taxe d'aéroport** airport tax; **taxe de séjour** tourist tax; **taxe à la valeur ajoutée (T.V.A.)** value-added tax

taxer to tax (goods)

taxi m taxi

T.C.F. m Touring Club de France (similar to the AA)

te, t' you (familiar form)

teint m complexion; **grand teint** fast colour

teinture f dye

teinturerie f dry-cleaner's

tel(le) such

télé f TV

télébenne f gondola lift

télécabine f gondola lift

télécarte f phonecard

télécommande f remote control

télécopie f fax

téléobjectif m telephoto lens

téléphérique m cableway; cable car

téléphone m telephone; **par téléphone** by telephone

téléphoner to telephone; **téléphoner en P.C.V.** to reverse the charges

télésiège m chair lift

téléski m ski tow; **téléski à perche** button lift; **téléski à archet** T-bar lift

téléviseur m television (set)

télévision f television; **télévision en couleur** colour TV; **à la télévision** on television

telle such

tellement so (much)

témoin m witness

tempête f storm; **tempête de neige** snowstorm

temple m church; temple

temporaire temporary

temps m weather; time; **peu de temps** a short time; **de temps en temps** occasionally; from time to time; **à temps in time**; **à temps partiel/à mi-temps** part-time

tendance f tendency; trend

tendre¹ tender

tendre² to stretch

tendron de veau m breast of veal

tendu(e) tense

tenir m to hold; to keep

tennis m tennis; **tennis sur gazon** lawn tennis; **les tennis** gym shoes; sneakers

tension f blood pressure; voltage

tentative f attempt

tente f tent

tenter to attempt; to tempt

tenue f clothes, dress; **tenue de soirée** evening dress

tergal ® m Terylene ®

terme m: **à long/court terme** long-/short-term

terminer to end

terrain m ground; land; field (for football etc); course (for golf); **terrain à bâtir/constructible** building land for sale; **terrain de camping** camping site; **terrain de sport** playing field

terrasse f terrace

terre f land (opposed to sea); earth; ground; **à terre** ashore

terrine f terrrine; pâté

tes your (familiar form)

tête f head; **tête de veau** calf's head

tétine f dummy; teat (for bottle)

T.G.V. see **train**

thé m tea; **thé au citron** lemon tea; **thé au lait** tea with milk; **thé nature** tea without milk

théâtre m theatre

thermomètre m thermometer

thon m tuna(-fish)

thym m thyme

ticket m ticket (for bus, metro); **ticket de caisse** receipt; **ticket de quai** platform ticket; **ticket repas** meal voucher; **ticket restaurant** luncheon voucher

tiède lukewarm

tiédir: faire tiédir to warm

tien: le tien/la tienne yours (familiar form); **les tien(ne)s** yours

tiercé m system of forecast betting

tiers m third party; **assurance au tiers** third party insurance; **pharmacie pratiquant le tiers payant** chemist belonging to the French social security scheme

tigre m tiger

tilleul m lime (tree); lime tea

timbrage m: **dispensé de timbrage** postage paid

timbre(-poste) m (postage) stamp

timide shy

tir m: **stand de tir** shooting range; **tir à l'arc** archery; **tir au fusil** rifle shooting; **tir au pigeon** clay pigeon shooting

tire-bouchon m corkscrew

tirer to pull; to shoot

tiroir m drawer

tisane f herbal tea

tissé(e) woven

tissu m material; fabric

tissu-éponge m terry towelling

titre m title; **titres** qualifications; **à titre indicatif** for information only; **à titre provisoire** provisionally; **titre de transport** ticket

titulaire m/f: **être titulaire de** to be the holder of (*card etc*)

toboggan m flyover (*road*); slide (*chute*)

toi you (*familiar form*)

toile f canvas

toilette f washing; getting ready; **faire sa toilette** to wash oneself

toilettes fpl toilet; powder room

toi-même yourself (*familiar form*)

toit m roof; **toit ouvrant** sunroof

tomate f tomato; pastis with grenadine cordial

tomber to fall (over/ down); to drop; **faire tomber** to knock over; **laisser tomber** to drop (*let fall*)

tomme (de Savoie) f mild soft cheese

ton your (*familiar form*)

tonalité f dial(ling) tone; **tonalité occupée** engaged signal

tonique m tonic (*medicine*)

tonne f tonne, metric ton

tonneau m barrel

tonnerre m thunder

topinambour m Jerusalem artichoke

tordre to twist

tort m fault; **avoir tort** to be wrong

torticolis m stiff neck

tortue f tortoise

tôt early; **plus tôt** earlier; **trop tôt** too soon

totalité f: **en totalité** entirely

toucher to feel; to touch

toujours always; still

tour[1] f tower; **tour de contrôle** control tower

tour[2] m trip; walk; ride; trick; **à tour de rôle** in turn; **tour (de piste)** lap (*of track*); **tour de poitrine** bust measurements

tourisme m tourism; tourist trade; sightseeing

touriste m/f tourist; **classe touriste** tourist class

touristique tourist; **guide touristique** tourist guide; **menu touristique** tourist/low-price menu; **prix touristiques** special prices for tourists

tournant m turn, bend

tournedos m thick slice of beef fillet; **tournedos Rossini** beef fillet with foie gras and truffles, in Madeira wine sauce

tournée f: **faire la tournée de** to go round; to visit

tourner to turn; to spin

tournesol m sunflower

tournevis m screwdriver

tournoi m tournament

tourte f pie

tous all (*plural*): **tous les deux jours** every other day

Toussaint f: **la Toussaint** All Saints' Day

tousser to cough

tout(e) all; everything; **tout ce qu'il vous faut** all you need; **tout de même** all the same (*nevertheless*); **pas du tout** not at all; **tout droit** straight ahead; **tout terrain** all-purpose (*vehicle*); **tout à fait** quite, completely; **tout de suite** straight away; **toute la journée** all day

toutefois however

toutes all (*plural*)

tout le monde everybody, everyone

toux f cough

traduction f translation

traduire to translate

train m train; **par le train** by train; **train autos-couchettes** car-sleeper train; **train à grande vitesse (T.G.V.)** high-speed train

traîneau m sleigh, sledge

trait m line

traitement m treatment; course of treatment

traiter to treat; to process

traiteur m caterer

trajet m journey

tramway m tram(car)

tranche f slice

tranquille quiet

tranquillisant m tranquillizer

transférer to transfer

transit: en transit in transit

transpiration f perspiration

transport m transport; **transports en commun**

public transport
transporter to carry; to transport; to ship (*goods*)
travail *m* work; **travail temporaire** temporary work
travailler to work
travaux *mpl* road works
travers: à travers through
travers de porc *m* pork spare rib
traversée *f* crossing (*voyage*)
traverser to cross
treize thirteen
treizième thirteenth
tremper to dip (*into liquid*); **faire tremper** to soak
tremplin *m* diving board; ski jump
trente thirty
trentième thirtieth
très very; much
trésor *m* treasure
tricot *m* knitting; sweater; **tricots** knitwear
trimestre *m* term
trimestriel(le) quarterly; three-monthly
tripes *fpl* tripe; **tripes à la mode de Caen** tripe cooked in cider and Calvados, with pig's trotters, vegetables and herbs
triste sad
trois three
troisième third; **troisième âge** senior citizens; years of retirement
tromper to deceive
trompette *f* trumpet
tronçon *m* section of road
trop too; too much; **trop de** too much; too many
trottoir *m* pavement; **trottoir roulant** moving walkway

trou *m* gap; pit; hole
troubles *mpl* trouble
troupe *f* troop
troupeau *m* flock
trousse *f* case; kit; **trousse de pharmacie** first-aid kit; **trousse de toilette** toilet bag
trouver to find; **se trouver** to be (situated)
truc *m* trick; tip
truffe *f* truffle; **truffes au chocolat** chocolate truffles
truffé(e) with truffles
truite *f* trout; **truite aux amandes** trout cooked in butter and chopped almonds; **truite au bleu** boiled fresh trout
tsigane: orchestre tsigane gypsy band
T.S.V.P. PTO
t.t.c. see taxe
tu *pron* (*familiar form*)
tuba *m* snorkel
tube *m* tube; hit record
tuer to kill
tuile *f* tile (*on roof*)
tulipe *f* tulip
turbot *m* turbot
tuteur(trice) *m/f* guardian
tuyau *m* pipe; hose; **tuyau d'échappement** exhaust
T.V.A. *f* VAT
type *m* type; fellow
typique typical

U

ulcère *m* ulcer
ultérieur(e) later (*date etc*)
ultra-rapide high-speed
un(e) one; a; an; **l'un (l'une) de vous deux**

either of you; **l'un (l'une) l'autre** one another
uni(e) plain (*not patterned*)
uniquement only
unir to unite
unisexe unisex
unitaire unit (*price*)
unité *f* unit
univers *m* universe
université *f* university
urgence *f* urgency; emergency; **d'urgence** urgently; **(service des) urgences** emergency unit
urticaire *f* nettle rash
usage *m* use; **en usage** in use; **à usage interne/ externe** for internal/ external use
usager *m* user
usé(e) worn
user to wear out; to use
usine *f* factory
utile useful
utiliser to use

V

vacances *fpl* holiday(s); **en vacances** on holiday; **grandes vacances** summer holidays; **vacances scolaires** school holidays
vacancier *m* holiday-maker
vaccin: vaccin anti-grippe flu vaccine
vacciner to vaccinate
vache *f* cow
vacherin *m* mild cow's-milk cheese; ice-cream in a meringue shell
vachette *f* calfskin
vague *f* wave (*in sea*)
vain: en vain in vain
vaincre to defeat
vaisselle *f* crockery; **faire**

la vaisselle to wash up

valable valid

valeur f value

valider: validez votre ticket stamp/punch your ticket

validité f: **durée de validité** (period of) validity; **validité illimitée** valid indefinitely

valise f suitcase

vallée f valley

vallonné(e) hilly

valoir to be worth; **valoir la peine** to be worth it; **il vaut mieux** it's better

vanille f vanilla

vannerie f wickerwork, basketwork

vapeur f steam; **cuire à la vapeur** to steam (*food*)

vaporisateur m spray (*container*)

varicelle f chicken pox

varié(e) varied; various; variegated

varier to vary

variété f variety

variole f smallpox

V.D.Q.S. see **vin**

veau m calf; veal

vedette f star (*celebrity*); launch (*boat*)

végétal(e) vegetable

végétarien(ne) vegetarian

véhicule m vehicle; **véhicule de tourisme/ utilitaire** private/ commerical vehicle

veille f: **la veille** the day before; **la veille de Noël** Christmas Eve

veillée f evening; evening gathering

veiller: veiller à ce que to make sure that

veine f vein

vélo m bike

véloski m skibob

velours m velvet; **velours côtelé** corduroy

velouté m: **velouté de tomates** cream of tomato soup

vendange(s) f grape harvest

vendeur m sales assistant

vendeuse f sales assistant

vendre to sell; **à vendre** for sale

vendredi m Friday; **le Vendredi Saint** Good Friday

vénéneux(euse) poisonous (*substance*)

venimeux(euse) poisonous (*snake*)

venir to come

vent m wind

vente f sale; **en vente** on sale; **date limite de vente** sell-by date; **vente à crédit** hire purchase; **vente au détail** retail; **vente directe au public** we sell direct to the public; **vente aux enchères** auction; **vente en gros** wholesale

ventilateur m fan (*electric*); ventilator

ventre m stomach

verdure f greenery

verger m orchard

verglacé(e): chaussée verglacée icy road surface

verglas m black ice; **risque de verglas** risk of (black) ice

vérification f check(ing)

vérifier to audit; to check; **vérifiez la pression de vos pneus** check your tyre pressure; **vérifiez votre ticket de caisse** check your receipt; **vérifiez votre monnaie** check your change

vérité f truth

vermicelle m vermicelli

vernis m varnish; **vernis à ongles** nail polish, nail varnish

verre m glass; **verre à vin** wineglass; **verres de contact** contact lenses

verrou m bolt; **verrou de sûreté** security lock

verrue f wart

vers toward(s); about; **vers le haut** upward(s)

versant m side; slope

versement m payment; instalment

verser to pour; to pay; **verser des arrhes/un acompte** to pay a deposit/make a down payment

version f: **version originale (v.o.)** original version (*film*)

vert(e) green

vertige m dizzy spell

verveine f verbena; verbena tea

veste f jacket

vestiaire m cloakroom

vêtement mpl clothes; **vêtements de sport** casual clothes, casual wear; sportswear

vétérinaire m/f vet

veuillez: veuillez consulter l'annuaire please consult the directory

viande f meat; **viande froide/hachée** cold/ minced meat; **viande séchée** (*in Switz*) thin slices of cured beef, usually eaten with pickles and rye bread

viandox ® m ≈ Bovril ®

vice-président m vice-chairman; vice president

vichyssoise f cream of leek and potato soup

vidange f emptying; oil change (car); waste outlet

vide empty

vide-ordures m rubbish chute

vider to empty; to drain (sump, pool)

vie f life; **à vie** for life

vieille old

vietnamien(ne) Vietnamese

vieux old

vigne f vine; vineyard

vignette f road tax disc

vignoble m vineyard

vigueur f: **en vigueur** in force; current

village m village

ville f town

villégiature f holiday; holiday resort

vin m wine; **vin du cru** locally grown wine; **vin cuit** liqueur wine; **vin délimité de qualité supérieure (V.D.Q.S.)** classification for a quality wine, guaranteeing it comes from a particular area; **vin de pays** good but not top-class wine; **vin en pichet/bouteille** wine by the carafe/ bottled wine

vinaigre m vinegar

vinaigrette f vinaigrette sauce; salad dressing

vingt twenty

vingtaine f: **une vingtaine de** around twenty

vingtième twentieth

vinicole wine-growing; wine-making

violet(te) purple

violon m violin

violoncelle m cello

vipère f adder

virage m bend (in road); curve; corner; **virage dangereux** dangerous

bend; **virage sans visibilité** blind corner

virement m transfer; **ordre de virement bancaire** banker's order; **virement postal** ≈ post office Giro transfer

vis f screw

visa m visa; **visa de transit** transit visa

visage m face

viser to stamp (visa)

visite f visit; consultation (of doctor); **visite guidée** guided tour; **visites à domicile** house calls

visiter to visit (place); to tour (town)

visiteur m visitor

vison m mink

visser to screw; **visser à fond** to screw home

vitamine f vitamin

vitaminé(e) with added vitamins

vite quickly; fast

vitesse f gear (of car); speed; **vitesse limitée à ... speed limit ...**

viticole wine-growing

vitrail m stained-glass window

vitre f pane; window (in car, train)

vitrine f shop window

vivant(e) lively; alive

vivre to live

v.o. see **version**

vœu m wish; **meilleurs vœux** best wishes

voici here is/here are

voie f lane (of road); line; track (for trains); **par voie buccale/orale** orally; **voie de droite** inside lane; **voie express** expressway; **voie ferrée** railway; **voie de gauche** outside lane

voilà there is/are

voile f sail; sailing

voilier m yacht; sailing boat

voir to see; **se voir** to show (be visible)

voisin(e) m/f neighbour

voiture f car; coach (of train); **voiture automatique** automatic (car); **voiture d'enfant** pram; **voiture de location** hire car; **voiture de pompiers** fire engine; **voiture de sport** sports car

voix f voice; vote

vol m flight; theft; **vol régulier** scheduled flight; **vol plané** gliding (sport); **vol à voile** hang-gliding

volaille f poultry

volant m steering wheel

volcan m volcano

voler to fly; to steal

volet m shutter; section

voleur m thief

volonté f will; **à volonté** as much as you like (wine etc); **des circonstances indépendantes de notre volonté** circumstances beyond our control

vomir to be sick; to vomit

vomissement m vomiting; vomit

vos your (polite, plural form)

voter to vote

votre your (polite, plural form)

vôtre: le/la vôtre yours; **les vôtres** yours

vouloir to want

vous you; to you (polite, plural form)

vous-même yourself (polite form)

vous-mêmes yourselves

voûte f arch

voyage m trip; journey; **voyage d'affaires**